PAt Gill

Illicit Sex

EDITED BY

THOMAS DiPIERO

& PAT GILL

Illicit Sex

IDENTITY POLITICS

IN EARLY MODERN

CULTURE

The University of Georgia Press

Athens & London

©1997 by the

University of Georgia Press

Athens, Georgia 30602

All rights reserved

Designed by Richard Hendel

Set in Bell

by Books International, Inc.

Printed and bound by Braun-Brumfield, Inc.

The paper in this book meets the guidelines for

permanence and durability of the Committee on

Production Guidelines for Book Longevity of the

Council on Library Resources.

Printed in the United States of America

01   00   99   98   97   C   5   4   3   2   1

01   00   99   98   97   P   5   4   3   2   1

Library of Congress Cataloging in Publication Data

Illicit sex : identity politics in early modern culture / edited by

Thomas DiPiero and Pat Gill.

p.   cm.

Includes bibliographical references.

ISBN 0–8203–1838–8 (alk. paper)—ISBN 0–8203–1884–1 (pbk.: alk. paper)

1. Popular culture—Europe—History.   2. Sexuality in popular

culture—Europe—History.   3. Sex in literature—Europe—History.

4. Identity (Psychology)—Europe—History.   I. DiPiero, Thomas,

1956–   .   II. Gill, Pat, 1950–   .

HM104.I45   1997

305.3'094—dc20   95-46620

British Library Cataloging in Publication Data available

Contents

Illicit Sex

Introduction
Illicit Determinations

Thomas DiPiero & Pat Gill

These essays on European culture of the seventeenth to the early nineteenth centuries consider the constitution of the modern subject as it was formed through the regulation of desire, sexuality, gender, and racial coding. The contributors appraise the manner in which the often conflicting discourses of gender, race, sexuality, and class intersect in seventeenth- and eighteenth-century Europe to provide specific, more or less authorized attributes with which people might identify. Each looks as well at how particular desires or modes of being were marginalized or prohibited. In general, the writers in this collection argue that some valorized characteristics pertain only to a restricted, privileged portion of the general population; other, more debased characteristics are forcefully assigned to more marginal members. The rigid control of access to these culturally valued features—and to the power, wealth, and social prestige that accompany them—determines what we call a politics of identity.

In this book we presume that the choices available to people concerning what they can be depend on a complex network of social production and interaction. This means that a given culture offers a limited, albeit tremendously large, number of social behaviors or modes with which people might identify. These modes, which determine what a given individual is said to "be," may appear natural or essential, but they are nevertheless determinate products of specific political, economic, and historic factors. The modes of social definition that we choose to assume or that are imposed on us range from such things as occupation or marital status to national identity or sexuality, and we are not always aware of what specific categories of subjectivity our culture subtly makes available to us. Furthermore, it is important to understand that even the concept of a social mode—whether a form of sexual desire, a gender identity, or a familial relationship—is itself the product of specific forms of social activity that in turn produce knowledge. In other words, there is nothing particularly natural about being, say, a straight white male. Our discursive apprehension of the world, however, creates categories both for the relatively benign purposes of taxonomy and for the more suspect aims of domination. The contributors to this volume recognize that the categories they deploy in the analysis of subjective identity are heuristic devices that aid in an understanding of social interaction; however, they also understand that these classifications have very real social effects, regardless of how abstract or constructed they may be. These social effects accrue political meanings—the privileging of white masculinity, for example, or the marginalization of same-sex desire—that constitute the politics of identity.

Analysis of identity politics in early modern culture depends on jettisoning many traditional assumptions about cultural artifacts. Traditionally, scholars of history and literature have analyzed the text or event in order to increase or revise knowledge in their fields. The critical approaches themselves, however, were rarely if ever put into question. The essays in this volume do not eschew the valuable insights gained by these literary and historical analyses, but do not settle for them, either. Rather, each study interrogates received paradigms of knowledge by suggesting different methods for understanding the relationship between texts and the human subjects they implicate. Some forge new models with which to explore the cultural manifestations of gender, national identity, and sexuality; others bring overlooked contextual considerations to bear on older critical assessments. In the process, they offer a vivid picture of a culture at the crossroads, a culture deciding on or stumbling into the sexual, gendered, juridical definitions of what will come to be known as modern cultural identity.

Early modern Europe, especially in the eighteenth century, offers a particularly fruitful terrain for the analysis of the politics of identity for two complementary reasons. First, virtually all modern Western notions of equality, as well as the language used to define it, originate in the seventeenth and eighteenth centuries. The principles of natural justice and civil egalitarianism to which politicians and political philosophers continue to refer derive not only from documents as politically monumental as the American Declaration of Independence and the Bill of Rights or the French *Déclaration des droits de l'homme et du citoyen*, but also from such philosophical and political writings as Montesquieu's *De l'Esprit des Lois*, Hume's *Moral and Political Philosophy*, Rousseau's *Contrat social* and *Discours sur l'origine de l'inégalité*, and Locke's *Of Civil Government* and *Treatises of Government*. The majority of political thinkers in early modern Europe, rejecting existing conceptions of the individual subjected to the state, proposed instead paradigms of mutual determination between the subject and the society to which it belonged.

Second, many of our modern conceptions of the *individual*—both as political subject and as psycho-social being—emerged in some form during the seventeenth and eighteenth centuries. Mistrustful of received paradigms of truth, the most influential political and moral philosophers of the century regarded religion, despotism, and tradition as mystifying institutions that held people in thrall by depriving them of their critical capacities. They advocated rationalism and empiricism as means of liberation from these subjugating institutions.[1] More crucially, however, they demonstrated that the ideas of equality and freedom from tyranny that they prized could be developed independently of traditional received truths and could originate instead with the reasoning capabilities of the newly conceived rational individual.

It is generally the late eighteenth century to which critics and social analysts point when discussing identifiably bourgeois modern individuals, armed with Enlightenment notions of autonomy and truth, confident in their rational philosophy of an ordered universe, and comfortable in their teleological conception of natural progress. Of course, any such description is necessarily both reductive and exaggerated, and the great Enlightenment thinkers and writers of the age—Samuel Johnson, Edmund Burke, Voltaire, Samuel Richardson, and Mary Wollstonecraft, in addition to those mentioned earlier—offer ample testimony to the social contradictions, religious doubts, political pessimisms, and moral confusions of the time. Nevertheless, a definable set of beliefs and behaviors that informed and regulated conceptions of private and social selves, of pleasure and desire, of society, literature, and law, emerged at the end of that century under the aegis of Enlightenment Humanism and has been acknowledged, applied, elaborated, or contended with ever since.[2]

Trends implicit in Reformation tenets and under way since the time of Elizabeth I were fully realized and explicit in the politics of the Restoration and the eighteenth century. Dissenting religions that had taken root accommodated the developing bourgeois ethos of the moral authorization of personal acquisition, private judgment, and subjective self-assessment[3] and prepared for the secularization of authority and power, as well as an increasingly rigid public morality.[4] Competing constitutional theories and highly vocal opposition parties altered the conception of the monarchy and the authority of Parliament.[5] Concerns about social and political transformations were expressed tacitly and overtly both in court literature and in popular writings. Increased social mobility and political turmoil threatened traditional definitions and social hierarchies. In the attempts by various groups either to maintain or determine the status quo—that powerful realm of the usual, the norm—the proper use of persuasive discourse became a contested issue.[6] The Restoration and eighteenth century witnessed heated, determined battles waged against duplicity in language and the abuse of eloquence, battles whose contested weapons were rhetorical tropes and whose ultimate prize was interpretive authority.

Interpretive authority and the control of cultural meaning dictate to a very large extent the sorts of subjective models available for identification and emulation. The eighteenth-century insistence on the individual as the origin not only of thought and knowledge but also of action revolutionized people's relationship to power and therefore to received notions of truth. Now everyone could accede to an understanding of the natural world so long as he or she possessed the powers of reason and judgment required to decode its system. Yet, since the natural world—along with the human institutions that formed part of it—seemed to follow a perceptible universal order, the faculties of reason and observation necessary to apprehend it were universalized along with it. Once the venerated concepts of nature, reason, observation, and knowledge were idealized and consequently banished from the domain of empiricism, they could be readily politicized. Truth as a lofty, abstract ideal could easily—and cynically—justify inequitable social relations. Herbert Marcuse points out, for example, that since Enlightenment values allowed all to aspire to the heights of reason, "the freedom of the soul was used to excuse the poverty, martyrdom, and bondage of the body" (109). And, during the process in which the ostensibly natural and universal phenomena just elaborated became ideological tools placed in the service of (hegemonic) class, gender, and racial interests, only subjects who conformed to specific identity characteristics could fully deploy the tools of reason and participate completely in their culture.

It is a commonplace among literary and cultural theorists writing in the late twentieth century that the bourgeois subject is a social construct. Particularly when dealing with issues pertaining to gender, race, or sexuality, recent critics endeavor to prove the cultural determinacy, and not the ontological inherence, of specific aspects of identity. Indeed, the suggestion that individual and group characteristics exist in predictable or causal relation can cast suspicion on even the most deft analysis. As a consequence, theorists frequently demonstrate considerable rhetorical dexterity in order to escape charges of essentialism. The historical specificity of the notion of a constructed subject, however, has only recently been interrogated. In the seventeenth and eighteenth centuries, European critics and philosophers insistently sought to uncover precisely what their modern counterparts reject: the essential kernel of humanity, that part that remains unchanged when social trappings are stripped away. Whether contemplating the fundamental features of human freedom or the uncultivated human being ideally able to exercise that freedom, early modern European writers seeking a universal human essence articulated a range of antagonisms in contemporary social life and thought. Those antagonisms, centered in contemporary political, philosophical, and aesthetic discourse, implicitly set the parameters establishing the acceptable limits of human identity.

Antagonisms arise when individuals or groups compete for scarce materials; those materials can be social and cultural as well as physical. Debates concerning the true essence of the "natural" human being and political disputes over the freedoms that could be extended to different groups of people produced some of the most salient philosophical conflicts operating in early modern European culture. These polemics contested a singular and enormously important social composition: the constitution of the self. That the definition of the self was the subject of much philosophical debate made its determination a matter of some urgency and consequence. It is not surprising, then, that the prerogative to establish the proper definition became a valuable and contested commodity during this period. By legislating or otherwise stipulating the boundaries of acceptable subjectivity, hegemonic groups maintained or achieved ascendancy, becoming apparently as a matter of course the apotheosis or standard of "normal" or prized personal characteristics. In other words, a dominant group helped to sustain its control by reproducing in the people subjected to it not only a reverence for specific personal traits and values but also the desire to imitate or possess them. In short, the personal became concurrently a philosophical and political concern.

Early modern European thinkers in search of the "uncultivated" human being posited specific cultural traits as desirable, consequently opening a political dimension to the supposedly natural phenomenon of human subjectivity. What often concerned these thinkers was the alienating effect civilization had on an individual's ostensibly natural state. The act of representation became a destructive process of conversion. Jean-Jacques Rousseau, for example, began his literary career considering how the sciences and arts—the crowning achievements of civilization—have contributed to weakening and debasing human beings, lamenting in the *Discours sur les sciences et les arts* that "people no longer dare to appear what they are" (40). Rousseau fantasized a time before culture and history, a time when being was unencumbered by representation and the composition of the individual self bore no trace of cultural determinacy. Diderot toyed with a similar idea in his *Supplément au voyage de Bougainville*, positing that "there existed a natural man: into the interior of that man was introduced an artificial man; and there arose inside a continuous war that lasts a lifetime" (183). Enlightenment philosophers in general hypothesized a chasm separating civilized people from their ostensibly natural ancestors. Although they tended to conceptualize that chasm in temporal terms, the human degradation they described charts the historical and concomitantly political aspects of representation.

Of course neither Rousseau nor Diderot was the first to theorize the corruption of humankind's pure and natural goodness, nor were all early modern philosophers in agreement concerning the superiority of the aboriginal state. In the seventeenth century Thomas Hobbes famously argued that life before state government was "solitary, poor, nasty, brutish, and short." Unlike Diderot and Rousseau, Hobbes contended that the idea of human freedom, so cherished and vaunted in Western culture, is not an *individual* freedom but a collective one: "The Libertie, whereof there is so frequent, and honourable mention, in the Histories, and Philosophy of the Ancient Greeks, and Romans, and in the writings, and discourse of those that from them have received all their learning in the Politiques, is not the Libertie of Particular men; but the Libertie of the Common-wealth" (266). Although he begins with a vastly different premise, Hobbes's conclusions anticipate those of Rousseau and Diderot. Even as these three philosophers in some way acknowledge the social constructedness of civilized people, they at the same time impose their own internalized set of political attitudes onto social vice and virtue. Explicitly linking human freedom to a generalized or socialized form of desire, Hobbes reveals that even the most intimate and fundamental aspects of the individual self have a historical—and thus necessarily politicized—dimension. As they historicize the processes of contemporary civilization, then, these critics set culturally determinate terms for what is to be considered natural and desirable.

The regulation of desire in early modern European philosophical and political discourse had perhaps the most profound influence on delineating the ways in which individuals could perceive themselves and thus determine what a self could be. John Locke wondered how individual liberties helped fashion a sense of self and whether, in fact, human beings are free at all. "It passes for a good plea," he mused, "that a man is not free at all, if he be not as *free to will* as he is to *act what he wills*" (*Understanding* 325). A generation later, Montesquieu followed Locke's lead and elaborated perhaps the most explicit formulation of the relationship between law, desire, and the self, writing that, "in a State, that is, in a society in which there are laws, liberty can only consist in being able to do what one ought to want, and in not being forced to do what one ought not to want" (2.XI.iii.162). Locke's and Montesquieu's formulations of liberty confound the obligations that citizens owe to themselves and those they owe to the state; the indeterminacy accordingly established between individual and civil desires and duties demonstrates how societal power conditions the most fundamental and personal elements of selfhood. The discursive structuring and concomitant control of desire, liberty, and subjectivity delimit both nature and identity by causing specific varieties of the self and its interactions with others to appear natural and uncontrived. As Timothy Reiss has observed, the production in early modern Europe of specific, determinately political points of view as universal and matter-of-fact is a feature of modernism: "The production of discourse, its objects, and its relation by the *I* of enunciation that originated it, in secret, in power, and with the complicity of a knowing elite, was gradually occulted: discourse became the common, transparent, and objective property of all, while the enunciating I was hypostatized as individual will" (360).

Usually by stressing the effect that the rapidly growing market economy had on the way people perceived their relationship to the world, theorists have traced the development of what has come to be called bourgeois individualism. In general, critics have regarded the seventeenth and eighteenth centuries as crucial to the development of the modern individual because radical changes in the deployment of social and economic power caused people to reconsider the personal characteristics they considered valuable. Beginning as far back, perhaps, as Adam Smith's *Inquiry into the Nature and Causes of the Wealth of Nations* (1776), the debates surrounding the evolution of the modern subject have primarily considered economic considerations to be principally responsible for generating new strains of subjectivity.[7] In the past few decades, however, it has become apparent that analyses of identity and social interaction based strictly on class minimize or disregard completely other, equally significant components of subjectivity. When we consider that individuals' identities are shaped by a wide range of social interactions, it appears especially crucial to examine the many elements of subjectivity that are frequently contested in the determination of community association.[8] As the feminist criticism of the early 1970s, with its overriding emphasis on gender, amply confirms, models of analysis that attempt to demonstrate that subjects are formed only through a single vector of power make visible some determinates of personhood while simultaneously obscuring others.

Present work in what is now loosely known as cultural studies has recognized the multiple components of subjectivity that categorize culture, but it has also tended to be markedly ahistorical: theoretical studies of the forms of subjectivity that antedate the middle years of the twentieth century, particularly the liminal varieties and the politics associated with them, have been few. In the introduction to their influential collection of essays, *The New Eighteenth Century*, Felicity Nussbaum and Laura Brown ask, "Why has eighteenth-century English literary studies often ignored or resisted new theoretical approaches, and why, in turn, have theorists neglected the materials of the eighteenth century?" (5). In addition to historicizing cultural studies, this volume extends their query to include other national literatures as well.

For a long time, eighteenth-century studies had been restricted to a textual formalism, born of the New Criticism, that refused examination of the ideological implications of cultural artifacts and practices. It may be that scholars who had expended the effort to accrue considerable cultural capital, in the form of tremendous erudition, felt reluctant to see it devalued by any discrediting of its universal applicability. The politics of canon formation, in which specific writers are deemed "excellent" while others—generally women or people of color—languish unnoticed, is but one example of how traditional cultural capital devalues. In *Illicit Sex*, we submit eighteenth-century culture to the most recent theoretical approaches, and we consider implicitly the politics obtaining in studying both dominant and marginal groups.

In the past ten years, several critics of eighteenth-century literature and culture have advanced theories that tacitly concern the development of bourgeois subjectivity, and each theory offers a partial explanation for the acquisition of a certain conception of self and society that has come to be described as bourgeois. In addition to Nussbaum and Brown's widely influential book, there have been a number of other book-length studies that bring contemporary critical discourse and the politics of identity formation to bear on eighteenth-century culture. *Misogyny in Literature*, edited by Katherine Anne Ackley, *Eroticism and the Body Politic*, edited by Lynn Hunt, *Hidden from History*, edited by Martin Duberman, Martha Vicinus, and George Chauncey Jr., and *The Ideology of Conduct*, edited by Nancy Armstrong and Leonard Tennenhouse, deal in part with eighteenth-century concerns from the perspectives elaborated above. Kristina Straub's *Sexual Suspects: Eighteenth-Century Players and Sexual Ideology* analyzes how public perceptions of the immorality of actors and actresses influenced gender expectations in the eighteenth century. The collection *The Languages of the Psyche*, edited by G. S. Rousseau, offers several extended analyses of the conjunction of medical psychology, philosophy, and psychology as they pertain to the body in the eighteenth century. In *Sexual Underworlds of the Enlightenment*, G. S. Rousseau and Roy Porter have collected a series of essays that offer a fresh perspective of the sexual imagination and behavior of the time. *The Pursuit of Sodomy: Male Homosexuality in Renaissance and Enlightenment Europe*, a collection of essays edited by Kent Gerard and Gert Hekma, examines some of the now repressed instances of same-sex desire in early modern Europe, instances that nevertheless had profound influence on contemporary culture. These works provide much-needed qualifications and augmentations of the standard heteronormative readings of the century and undermine forever any attempt to place the Enlightenment Age solely within normative sexual bounds.

While not always directly or precisely concerned with the evolution of the bourgeois subject, other notable, substantive books expanded an understanding of the social, political, and ideological contexts that shape and are shaped by cultural production.[9] Terry Castle in *Masquerade and Civilization* proposes that the masked assemblies of the eighteenth century took on special significance, becoming a cultural symbol that called the rigid, codified order of the world into question and pointed toward the utopian transformative capacity of humankind. Castle shows that the slow demise of the carnival is concomitant with the growth of the psychological self and the realistic fiction that accompanies it. In *The Origins of the English Novel*, Michael McKeon provides a dialectical genre study of the novel, revealing the interchange and reversals in progressive and conservative ideological positions. McKeon traces the steady alienation of self from society and points out the contradictory qualities that attend the assumption of this new individuality. In *Between Men*, Eve Kosofsky Sedgwick finds in the years between Restoration drama and Gothic novels new constructions of and restrictions on sociosexual behaviors, emphasizing the evolution of the category of the homosexual in the formation of the modern sexual self. Felicity Nussbaum argues in *The Autobiographical Subject* that autobiographical writings by women writers of the eighteenth century furnish an ideological ground on which to contain as well as disrupt conventional notions of female character and heterosexual differentiation.

Illicit Sex continues along the lines of inquiry opened up by these works, but it more specifically addresses the politics of ordinary, day-to-day individual identity. It fills in many of the gaps in the existing theoretical apparatus by providing historical antecedents to modern conceptions of the politics of identity. It helps situate the forerunners of particular modern subjectivities determined through gender, race, national identity and sexual orientation by pinpointing some of the conditions in which they emerged. The pertinent critical determinants of this newly reconfigured individual are: the consolidation of the bourgeoisie as a new social class with its attendant morality; a concomitant reformation of gender apprehensions, correlating the ascent of a new economic mode and its restructuring of labor, as well as a dramatic shift in the configuration of the family and the transmission of property; a renewed interest in foreign lands, both for tourism and for colonization, that contributed to the formation of distinct racial identities; an accompanying fascination with the putatively "natural" human being, one unspoiled by civilization and consequently outside of the influence of culture; and an intensely invigorated study of science and the human body, which led not only to the study of sexual difference but also to new theorizing about sexual behavior, sexual desire, and the meaning of same-sex and other "perverse" relations.

The essays that constitute *Illicit Sex* excavate both the processes that create hegemonic subjective identity and the subjects excluded from full cultural participation. They analyze the ideological assumptions implicit in such seemingly natural categories as "white" or "female" or "heterosexual," and they unmask the social work that operates both to cause identity to seem natural and to disenfranchise marginal subjective positions. Because these marginal positions emerge from a dominant culture that paradoxically authorizes them as illegitimate, they are frequently exoticized and eroticized; their marginality thus appears as a contradictory system of support and transgression of a dominant order. Many arguments in this volume focus on the ways in which new and inchoate categories of identity serve to define and engage contemporary concerns about moral behavior, sexual relations, and social changes. In "Englishness 'A'muck': De Quincey's *Confessions*," Rajani Sudan illustrates how the constitution of national English identity in Thomas De Quincey's *Confessions* depends on a certain notion of the foreign, particularly of France, but even more problematically of the Orient. Sudan contends that De Quincey's construction of this national and cultural identity employs the language of xenophobia and gynophobia in a system of othering, a process that creates a series of foreign bodies in order to cast them out. De Quincey's attempts at recuperating himself within his autobiographical project as well as within an English identity are as a consequence made at the expense of appropriating and discounting foreign spoils, a gesture that raises the problem of representing the (English) self as a nationally and culturally discrete subject in relation to a series of foreign others. The mediator between the resulting dynamics of opposition is the figure of the woman. Following out the collapse of the erotic and the exotic in De Quincey's narrative, Sudan uncovers the ways in which De Quincey embodies his recuperative (English) vision in the feminine, and how women function as a peculiarly transparent and transgressive body through which male nationalism can be read.

In "The 'French Threat' in Anti-Jacobin Novels of the 1790s," Nancy Johnson finds as well that the foreign and the female play a determining role in the construction of a proper English familial self. Examining five representative novels, Johnson finds a pervasive concern with the monitoring of desire, the containment of passion, the importance of filial obedience, and the social obligation of marriage. She argues that, although the legislation of desire in these novels is often cloaked in the language of Christian morality, the need to restrict intimate behavior and protect the structure of the family betrays an attempt to maintain the existing distribution of wealth, to control the acquisition and transmission of property, and to preserve the political authority of the already propertied. Efforts to concentrate wealth, such as the practice of primogeniture and the legal restrictions on married women's property, Johnson notes, were regarded as essential to national security. All endeavors to change traditional notions of property and government were greeted with immediate alarm and decisive narrative rebuttals. The anxiety the Anti-Jacobin writers expressed in their focus on unwieldy passions and licentious rakes who espouse French principles and endanger the family, Johnson affirms, was a reaction to the reconceptualization of ownership and the gradual empowerment of the individual.

David R. Evans also analyzes the constitution of a national self in terms of a relation to the foreign, but his essay focuses on incorporation rather than on rejection. In "Desiring the Foreign Self: Identity (Com)-modification and the Early Grand Tour," Evans looks closely at a number of the best-known seventeenth-century works on foreign travel to illustrate how travel literature as a whole attempted to restructure two inevitably linked types of authority: institutional and personal. In underscoring both the public, politically oriented and the private, socially centered enhancements that experience abroad could provide, travel writers conceived of travel as a form of education—an education limited to a select few. Insistence on the essential nature of the nobility by such writers as Henry Peacham, Evans explains, circulated the idea that social hierarchy was a God-given fact of existence, not a social construction. Identity, as defined by social status, could never be achieved, only inherited. As Evans remarks, however, one of the signal characteristics of the seventeenth century was that England's ruling assumptions came increasingly under an attack that revealed their fundamentally constructed nature. Thus, the strategy of publishing books of travel theory and accounts of foreign journeys that was vital to figuring travel in terms of cultural or what Pierre Bourdieu calls "symbolic" capital ultimately contained the seeds of its own destruction. Evans shows that by creating the desire to go abroad and the consequent capacity to remodel one's social identity, travel writers rather quickly and effectively undermined their own hegemonic act.

Sudan, Johnson, and Evans address the early modern belief in the implicit otherness of foreigners, a belief that informs or aids in the construction of national and personal identity. In a related undertaking, Thomas DiPiero considers the political application of the foreign, specifically Montesquieu's use of the harem as the model of despotic rule in *The Spirit of Laws* and *The Persian Letters*. The sort of sexual, moral, and political control that the sultan exercises in the harem and that the despot is presumed to wield in despotism, DiPiero posits in "The Spirit of Laws (of Desire)," correlates the models of patriarchal authority and conforms to the versions of the traditional nuclear family that are found in contemporary discussions of modern social practice. Western representations of the harem attempt with striking insistence to define and prevent illicit sex. DiPiero notes that the position of the eunuchs in the harem demonstrates that the question of sexuality and subjective identification depends on characteristics that extend far beyond the simple male/female binary opposition operating in our culture. Pointing out that gender and race inflect one another at the most fundamental level, he speculates about whether sexual difference—in particular as it pertains to masculine hegemony—exhausts the ways in which we can theorize the formation of identity and the power relations contingent upon it. In examining how other phenomena of sexual identity structure the way we construct and perceive gender, DiPiero helps to elucidate the foundation and workings of the complex and socially malleable cultural institutions of patriarchy and family.

Kathryn Temple discusses the battle to place women "in law," to imagine a female juridical identity, fought over and against those powerful cultural institutions of patriarchy and family. The formation of this identity began, Temple contends, not with a direct onslaught of the legal system but obliquely, in eighteenth-century Gothic novels and other texts. In "Imagining Justice: Gender and Juridical Space in the Gothic Novel," Temple looks at the ways in which novels by Mary Wollstonecraft and Ann Radcliffe play out women's exclusion from law across what many critics have seen as a radical/conservative divide. The primary difference in these representations of the relationship between women and law lies not in the change they desire or promote, Temple argues, but in the ways they struggle with the economy of body and discourse. As her readings of Mary Wollstonecraft's and Ann Radcliffe's courtroom scenes demonstrate, successful discursive interventions tend to sacrifice bodily presence, while physical participation compels discursive concessions. Temple's analysis of the two texts finds a gendered resistance to the Enlightenment's propaganda of universal inclusion. Temple establishes that only after complex, even tortured, reworkings of the meanings of gender and legal admission do women manage to take their places in juridical space, and the accession exacts a substantive price.

In "The Politics of 'Passing': The Scandalous Memoir and the Novel," Catherine Craft-Fairchild proves less sanguine than Temple about eighteenth-century attempts to construct an independent female identity. Craft-Fairchild argues that recent critical claims concerning the subversive potential of female transvestitism are overly optimistic. The transgression of cross-dressing (factual and fictional), Craft-Fairchild maintains, even when employed to form lasting homosexual or homosocial bonds between women, did not undermine eighteenth-century ideologies of domestic femininity in quite the way that twentieth-century feminists might hope. If the cross-dressed woman remained, at some level, undomesticatable, her transgression of the boundaries set for female sexuality and conduct did not—as John Cleland, Henry Fielding, and other male writers feared   produce widespread or lasting effects. Ultimately, sensational narrative accounts of cross-dressed or "unnatural" women reinforced ideas about what constituted natural femininity. Both biographical and autobiographical accounts of eighteenth-century female cross-dressers employ rhetorical strategies to domesticate the transgressive woman, to make her deviations appear as outgrowths of her "natural" feminine impulses. By the end of the eighteenth century, Craft-Fairchild observes, narratives of notorious women were actually used to shore up gender and class boundaries.

Robert Bataille elaborates on another method for the cultural reinscription of notorious women. Arguing that the reform and control of sexuality in mid-eighteenth-century London centers upon the establishment of a charity, Bataille recounts the history of the Magdalen House, an asylum designed to reform prostitutes and wayward girls by turning them into useful servants, productive workers and, ultimately, into wives and mothers. In "The Magdalen Charity for the Reform of Prostitutes: A Foucauldian Moment," Bataille shows how the Magdalen House creates what Foucault calls in *Discipline and Punish* a disciplinary space. Reformer Jonas Hanway first promoted the creation of the house as an institution necessary for Britain's economic survival, reasoning with passionate syllogistic force that England can succeed in war only if good wives might be reconstructed from deserted girls and reformed prostitutes. The actual functioning of the house, Bataille notes, as seen in its rules and regulations, attempted to discipline its female subjects and inculcate in them a kind of training so that once they were released the women could perform this useful, regimented role in society. Bataille finds that taken altogether, the various proposals for the establishment of the house and later on the reports of the charity form something very similar to a penal-sexual discourse and exemplify what Foucault calls "local centers" of "power-knowledge." The development of this local center amended the discourse of reform to conform to new economic interests, established the notion of reconstruction as a viable enterprise, and in the process refigured the bodies of wayward girls into the form of productive wives.

Although the transgressive potential of cross-dressing slowly transformed into its opposite, and certain aberrant sexual conduct, social performance, and gender behavior were converted into proper deportment by emerging corrective institutions, the cultural threat to patriarchal order posed by same-sex desire was steadily acquiring shape and distinction. Both Irene Fizer and George E. Haggerty confirm the imaginative power of this evolving identity. In "Women 'Off' the Market: Feminine Economies in the Eighteenth-Century Convent Novel," Irene Fizer claims that the convent was not merely a mysterious and constraining enclosure but (also) a site of different knowledge. It was the paradigmatic site where sexual difference could be theorized. Using Luce Irigary's provocative essay "Women On the Market" as a theoretical ground, Fizer reads Denis Diderot's *La Religieuse* as the narrative of a woman who operates as an "uneconomic" figure—a woman who has placed herself off the market. Fizer points out that in writing this novel Diderot was continuing an eighteenth-century tradition of convent pornography, pornography that was specifically directed to and exchanged among men. Fizer contends, however, that feminine sexuality becomes a term in and of itself in *La Religieuse*, rather than a term appended to or mediated by a phallic economy. There is no defining or central sexual category in the novel—rather, multiple models of female sexuality are placed into a comparative context. The nun becomes an indisputably independent entity—a financially, emotionally, and sexually autonomous being, answerable only to a(n absent) spiritual father. Remarking that Diderot's convent novel has an unintended effect—the nun's sexuality takes on an intrinsically feminine value—Fizer submits that by rendering sexuality among women its exclusive term, *La Religieuse* marks the convent as a site where an alternate economic order of exchange among women emerges.

Private, restricted spaces may have permitted the evolution of a fictional same-sex social and sexual economy, but public manifestations of same-sex desires found no such utopic havens. A social outcast, the unwitting pedophilic trailblazer William Beckford lived most of his adult life in exile, both at home and abroad. His public acknowledgment of his pederastic desire made him unfit for society. Although eighteenth-century usage made little distinction between the terms *pæderasty* and *sodomy*, George E. Haggerty claims in "Beckford's Pæderasty" that there is a sense in which William Beckford became for his generation, in Byron's phrase, "the Apostle of Pæderasty," and his novel *Vathek*, a primer in the examination of man-boy love. Haggerty proposes that Beckford's unwitting self-exposure led to a form of social opprobrium that defined for an entire generation what it was to be a social outlaw. Beckford played a crucial role in the popular evocation of a sexual identity, Haggerty contends, one that was distinct from the various sodomitical labels that were current at the time. In examining Beckford's case, Haggerty explores the implication of this evocatory role in Beckford's novel, in his diaries and letters, and in accounts of his life that were circulated in the popular press and in private anecdotes of his scandalous behavior. These public and personal writings intimate a new way of conceptualizing sexuality—an apprehension not merely of the performance of acts but of a relationship. In this sense, Haggerty submits, these homophobic accounts of unnatural, ungrammatical sexuality can be seen to reveal the first move toward something like a modern conception of sexuality.

William F. Edmiston's essay considers the move toward a modern conception of sexuality as well, challenging but not dismissing Michel Foucault's assertion in *The History of Sexuality* of a decisive shift in nineteenth-century European thought from viewing same-sex desire as a matter of prohibited *acts* (in which anyone might engage) to viewing it as a function of a stable definition of *identity*, dependent on personality even in the absence of sexual acts. According to Foucault, Edmiston relates, the sodomite had been a contemporary aberration, whereas the homosexual would become a nineteenth-century species. Eve Sedgwick in *Epistemology of the Closet* interprets this putative change as an intrusion into the universalizing discourse of sodomitic acts by a minoritizing understanding of sexual identity. Sedgwick rejects Foucault's view of the supersession of one model over another, Edmiston explains, and posits instead the contemporaneous existence of different models of same-sex desire. In "Shifting Ground: Sade, Same-Sex Desire, and the One-, Two-, and Three-Sex Models," Edmiston calls attention to an important and for the most part overlooked point: the marquis de Sade posited one of the first third-sex models of sexual desire to be found in Western literature. Balancing the opposing contentions of Sedgwick and Foucault and employing theories advanced by Thomas Laqueur and Randolph Trumbach, Edmiston rereads the works of Sade to tease out Sade's conceptions of same-sex desire. The two logics that Foucault finds distinct and sequential coexist, overlap, and contradict in Sade's writings, making it impossible to determine if a transition is taking place. Edmiston concludes that the works of Sade do not and cannot offer proof of the Foucauldian shift, but they do bear witness to a late eighteenth-century coexistence of at least two discourses concerning same-sex desire, with no evidence of strong dominance of one over the other.

Craig Patterson is even more unwilling than Edmiston to locate what Sedgwick in *Epistemology of the Closet* names the "Great Paradigm Shift" from homosexual acts to homosexual identity. To search for such a moment is as Sedgwick suggests an exercise in folly, Patterson attests in "The Rage of Caliban: Eighteenth-Century Molly Houses and the Twentieth-Century Search for Sexual Identity," and yet this search has assumed a level representational playing field, as if the representational character of texts remains unchanged across historical periods. Patterson is skeptical of recent critical studies that find the appearance of molly houses in the early eighteenth century to herald an important shift in the organization and meaning of same-sex sexual activity and the molly to represent a new type of sodomite. And while Patterson is sympathetic to these modified constructionist attempts to qualify Foucault's polemical statement that the homosexual is a product of the nineteenth century, he is leery of critical claims of identity based on early eighteenth-century publications concerning molly houses and sodomites, works that tend to represent external acts rather than internal states. The chief difficulty with this modified constructionist hypothesis, Patterson contends, lies in the degree of what one might call literary mediation that bedevils the texts that support the claims. A small number of uniformly ironic and markedly vitriolic texts have been used to support the contention of a new sexual identity without any regard to the generic and rhetorical conventions that operate within these texts. Patterson considers a number of these hostile accounts and concludes in part that although we may write a history of antisodomite rhetoric, a history of sodomy before the nineteenth century must necessarily be incomplete. Patterson confirms that early eighteenth-century London witnessed the emergence of sodomitical subcultures, but he warns that the only history that can be written of them must of necessity deal in external acts rather than internal states or identities.

Jones DeRitter also investigates the threat of another suddenly perceptible form of deviance: unwitting incest. The new urban individual—separated from family and friends, from established routines, and from accustomed circumstances—becomes susceptible to all that rigid family structure formerly prohibited and prevented. The eighteenth-century realist paradigm of unwitting incest, DeRitter explains, emerges as both an encapsulation and a metaphorical reinvention of a certain broadly based social anxiety. In "Blaming the Audience, Blaming the Gods: Unwitting Incest in Three Eighteenth-Century English Novels," DeRitter looks at three instances of this accidental condition or the threat of it. In Daniel

DeFoe's *Moll Flanders*, Henry Fielding's *Tom Jones*, and Fanny Burney's *Evelina*, DeRitter suggests, the paradigm of unwitting incest provided writers with a way of placing new methods of reconstructing and validating individual identities in competition with the determining force of the traditional family structure. DeRitter detects in the authors' treatment of the subject an assertion of both the literal priority of family relationships and the figurative priority of an increasingly obsolete socioeconomic system that would presumably offer each of these fictional characters a more stable social identity in exchange for a more restricted set of options. Indeed, the very fact that the authors employ this narrative device constitutes an expression of allegiance to an increasingly outmoded social system. In each of these accounts DeRitter discovers that the old arbiter of destiny, the representative of the traditional social order, appears at first to be entirely absent, but in the conclusion of each case it reasserts itself in a shocking and decided manner.

Pat Gill addresses the troubled relation of the estranged individual to patriarchal family and state structure as well. In "Revolutionary Integrity in Otway's *Venice Preserved*," Gill claims that Thomas Otway's persistent intermingling of public and private realms, his resolute refusal to let one be subordinated to or independent of the other, is a first in English drama. Gill contends that Otway affords a psychological displacement of the political onto the personal, a displacement that we now find very familiar and may well be one of the decisive markers of the move to a modern conception of a differentiated self. The world of *Venice Preserved* is a dark, dangerous, anxious one, riddled by corruption, depravity, lawlessness, social unrest, and state paralysis. The weird sexually charged relationships, the fanatic sacrifice of oneself and one's friends for a government that no longer upholds moral principles, and the radically personal sense of righteousness that secures neither social honors nor private recompense make the play seem strangely current, Gill argues, and afford an early glimpse of what will come to be known as a modern view of the world. The characters' alienated sense of themselves, their torturous gender negotiations between the (female) realm of domestic concerns and the (male) realm of public action, and their tragic failure to conform the operations of government to traditional models of justice and equity all unmoor meaning and authority from social reality while allowing the male protagonists to form a sense, however tenuous and troubled, of personal integrity and moral validity, a sense achieved only by the displacement of moral guilt onto women. *Venice Preserved* introduces a revolutionary conception of self-evaluation to respond to a world that no longer provides reliable, cogent moral precepts,

Gill asserts, adding that in so doing the play staged the gender displacements that as modern subjects we still continue to live out.

The early modern era reveals a particularly anxious insistence and heightened intensity concerning questions of gender, race, class, and their convergence. The contributors to this volume all assume a complex and contradictory relation between a system of representation and the construction of sexual and gender difference. Each contributor is attentive to the historical conditions that situate men and women, the marginal and the mainstream, differently with regard to the forces of literary and cultural production. All argue that when sex and gender, two slippery, highly permeable categories, are introduced into critical discussions, they tend to unsettle even the most systematic evaluation of culture and cultural theory. In elaborating the contention that these categories are assigned meanings by the complicated interaction of historically conditioned narratives, *Illicit Sex* provides ways of reading that are especially attuned to the discourses of identity and how these discourses inflect decisions about and definitions of gender roles, disciplinary boundaries, and marginal(ized) discourses. In the process of unfolding the transformations of cultural narratives that both reflect and inform newly politicized identities, *Illicit Sex* points to the tenacious endurance of both the material consequences and the political resonances of those narratives in the cultural practices of today.

NOTES

1. The *libertins érudits* of the seventeenth century offer the most striking early example of this phenomenon. For more detailed information, see in particular the studies by Antoine Adam, Joan DeJean, and René Pintard.

2. Readers are referred to the relevant works of Nietzsche, Hegel, Marx, and Freud. Some recent writers who offer sustained discussions on the philosophy and consequences of the Enlightenment: Jacques Derrida, especially *Positions* and *Margins of Philosophy*; Michel Foucault, especially *The Order of Things* and *Power/Knowledge: Selected Interviews and Other Writings 1972–1977*; Richard Rorty; Jane Flax; and Terry Eagleton in *Ideology*.

3. Particularly comprehensive explorations of the political, philosophical, and ideological consequences of emergent capitalism, Puritan thought, and the aftermath of the Civil War can be found in the works of Leo Strauss, C. B. Macpherson, J. G. A. Pocock, Christopher Hill, and Robert P. Kraynak.

4. For precise, well-documented investigations that employ a contextual approach in their discussion of literary works, see Michael McKeon, *Politics and Poetry* and *The Origins of the English Novel*; Barbara K. Lewalski; Annabel Paterson; Susan Staves; Steven Zwicker; and Graham Parry.

5. Some of the contemporary writings that indicate the problems and divisions in this period include Edmund Hickeringill, Gilbert Burnet, and John Locke.

6. Robert Markley provides the most comprehensive study of the ideological transformations of dramatic style in Restoration comedy. His explorations of the ways in which stylistic structures describe, respond to, and suppress the trauma of historical changes are compelling and provocative.

7. The most notable analyses in this vein include Ernst Cassirer, Lucien Goldmann, Lionel Gossman, Paul Hazard, and Fernand Braudel.

8. Kobena Mercer, writing in a different context, has formulated the relationship between subjectivity and group membership by writing that "identities are in crisis because traditional structures of membership and belonging inscribed in relation of class, party, and nation-state have been called into question" (124).

9. Notable works on this topic include those by Nancy K. Miller, Terry Eagleton, Lennard Davis, and Mary Poovey.

WORKS CITED

Ackley, Katherine Anne. *Misogyny in Literature: An Essay Collection.* New York: Garland, 1992.

Adam, Antoine. *Les Libertins au XVIIe siècle.* Paris: Buchet, 1964.

Armstrong, Nancy, and Leonard Tennenhouse, eds. *The Ideology of Conduct: Essays in Literature and the History of Sexuality.* New York: Methuen, 1987.

Braudel, Fernand. *Civilization and Capitalism, Fifteenth–Eighteenth Century.* New York: Harper and Row, 1981.

Burnet, Gilbert. *History of My Own Time.* London, 1818.

Cassirer, Ernst. *The Philosophy of the Enlightenment.* Trans. Fritz Koelln and James Pettegrove. Princeton: Princeton UP, 1951.

Castle, Terry. *Masquerade and Civilization: The Carnivalesque in Eighteenth-Century English Culture and Fiction.* Stanford: Stanford UP, 1986.

Davis, Lennard. *Factual Fictions: The Origins of the English Novel.* New York: Columbia UP, 1983.

DeJean, Joan. *Libertine Strategies: Freedom and the Novel in Seventeenth-Century France.* Columbus: Ohio State UP, 1981.

Derrida, Jacques. *Margins of Philosophy.* Trans. Alan Bass. Chicago: U of Chicago P, 1982.

———. *Positions.* Trans. Alan Bass. Chicago: U of Chicago P, 1981.

Diderot, Denis. *Supplément au voyage de Bougainville.* Paris: Garnier-Flammarion, 1972.

Duberman, Martin Bauml, Martha Vicinus, and George Chauncey Jr., eds. *Hidden from History: Reclaiming the Gay and Lesbian Past.* New York: New American Library, 1989.

Eagleton, Terry. *Ideology.* London: Verso, 1991.

———. *The Rape of Clarissa.* Minneapolis: U of Minnesota P, 1982.

Flax, Jane. *Thinking Fragments: Psychoanalysis, Feminism, and Postmodernism in the Contemporary West.* Berkeley and Los Angeles: U of California P, 1990.

Foucault, Michel. *The Order of Things.* New York: Pantheon, 1970.

————. *Power/Knowledge: Selected Interviews and Other Writings 1972–1977*. Ed. Colin Gordon. New York: Pantheon, 1980.

Gerard, Kent, and Gert Hekma, eds. *The Pursuit of Sodomy: Male Homosexuality in Renaissance and Enlightenment Europe*. New York: Harrington Park P, 1989.

Goldmann, Lucien. *The Philosophy of the Enlightenment*. Cambridge: MIT P, 1973.

Gossman, Lionel. *French Society and Culture*. Englewood Cliffs, N.J.: Prentice-Hall, 1972.

Hazard, Paul. *La Crise de la conscience européenne, 1680–1715*. Paris: Fayard, 1961.

Hickeringill, Edmund. *The History of Whiggism*. London, 1682.

Hill, Christopher. *Some Intellectual Consequences of the English Revolution*. Madison: U of Wisconsin P, 1980.

Hobbes, Thomas. *Leviathan*. New York: Penguin, 1968.

Hunt, Lynn. *Eroticism and the Body Politic*. Baltimore: Johns Hopkins UP, 1991.

Kraynak, Robert P. *History and Modernity in the Thought of Thomas Hobbes*. Ithaca: Cornell UP, 1990.

Lewalski, Barbara K. *Protestant Poetics and the Seventeenth-Century Lyric*. Princeton: Princeton UP, 1979.

Locke, John. *An Essay Concerning Human Understanding*. New York: Dover, 1959.
————. *Two Treatises of Government*. Cambridge: Cambridge UP, 1960.

Macpherson, C. B. *The Political Theory of Possessive Individualism*. London: Oxford UP, 1962.

Marcuse, Herbert. *Negations: Essays in Critical Theory*. Trans. Jeremy J. Shapiro. London: Free Association Books, 1988.

Markley, Robert. *Two-Edg'd Weapons: Style and Ideology in the Comedies of Etherege, Wycherley, and Congreve*. Oxford: Clarendon P, 1988.

McKeon, Michael. *The Origins of the English Novel 1600–1740*. Baltimore: Johns Hopkins UP, 1987.
————. *Politics and Poetry in Restoration England: The Case of Dryden's Annus Mirabilis*. Cambridge: Cambridge UP, 1975.

Mercer, Kobena. "'1968': Periodizing Politics and Identity." *Cultural Studies*. Ed. Lawrence Grossberg, Cary Nelson, and Paula Treichler. New York: Routledge, 1992. 424–49.

Miller, Nancy K. *The Heroine's Text: Readings in the French and English Novel, 1722–1782*. New York: Columbia UP, 1980.

Montesquieu, Charles-Louis de Secondat. *De l'Esprit des Lois. Oeuvres complètes*. 2 vols. Paris: Bibliothèque de la Pléiade, 1958.

Nussbaum, Felicity. *The Autobiographical Subject: Gender and Ideology in Eighteenth-Century England*. Baltimore: Johns Hopkins UP, 1989.

Nussbaum, Felicity, and Laura Brown. "Revising Critical Practices." *The New Eighteenth Century: Theory, Politics, English Literature*. Ed. Nussbaum and Brown. New York: Methuen, 1987.

Parry, Graham. *The Seventeenth Century: The Intellectual and Cultural Context of English Literature 1603–1700*. London: Longman, 1989.

Paterson, Annabel. *Censorship and Interpretation: The Conditions of Writing and Reading in Early Modern England*. Madison: U of Wisconsin P, 1984.

Pintard, René. *Le Libertinage érudit dans la première moitié du dix-septième siècle.* Paris: Boivin, 1943.

Pocock, J. G. A. *The Machiavellian Moment: Florentine Political Thought and the Atlantic Republican Tradition.* Princeton: Princeton UP, 1975.

Poovey, Mary. *The Proper Lady and the Woman Writer: Ideology as Style in the Works of Mary Wollstonecraft, Mary Shelley, and Jane Austen.* Chicago: U of Chicago P, 1984.

Reiss, Timothy J. *The Discourse of Modernism.* Ithaca: Cornell UP, 1982.

Rorty, Richard. *Philosophy and the Mirror of Nature.* Princeton: Princeton UP, 1979.

Rousseau, G. S., ed. *The Languages of the Psyche: Mind and Body in Enlightenment Thought.* Berkeley and Los Angeles: U of California P, 1990.

Rousseau, G. S., and Roy Porter, eds. *Sexual Underworlds of the Enlightenment.* Chapel Hill: U of North Carolina P, 1988.

Rousseau, Jean-Jacques. *Discours sur les sciences et les arts.* Paris: Garnier-Flammarion, 1971.

Sedgwick, Eve Kosofsky. *Between Men: English Literature and Male Homosocial Desire.* New York: Columbia UP, 1985.

———. *Epistemology of the Closet.* Berkeley and Los Angeles: U of California P, 1990.

Smith, Adam. *Inquiry into the Nature and Causes of the Wealth of Nations.* New York: Modern Library, 1937.

Staves, Susan. *Players' Scepters: Fictions of Authority in the Restoration.* Lincoln: U of Nebraska P, 1979.

Straub, Kristina. *Sexual Suspects: Eighteenth-Century Players and Sexual Ideology.* Princeton: Princeton UP, 1992.

Strauss, Leo. *Natural Right and History.* Chicago: U of Chicago P, 1953.

Zwicker, Steven. *Politics and Language in Dryden's Poetry.* Princeton: Princeton UP, 1984.

1 Disciplining the Subject

The Spirit of
Laws (of Desire)

Thomas DiPiero

Montesquieu's *Persian Letters* features a harem full of beautiful women and the eunuchs who guard them. In one of the novel's most frequently cited passages, the chief white eunuch laments his exchange of passion for fortune and tranquillity: "my first master formed the cruel design to confer his wives to me, and thus obliged me, through seductions accompanied by a thousand threats, to separate myself forever from myself" [me séparer pour jamais de moi-même] (33).[1] This brief passage has spawned a great deal of consideration of the eunuch's body and of the significance it has for his relationship to his master and the master's wives. Generally holding the eunuch to be not simply a violently mutilated male but a debased reject whose genital damage assigns him to some abstract third sex, many of Montesquieu's readers literalize in the eunuch's castration the social forces traversing his body. Much like the Persian Usbek, who claims that eunuchs "consent to be tyrannized by the stronger, as long as they can afflict the weak" (70), recent readers of the *Persian Letters* have attempted to excavate the relationship Montesquieu's work delineates among the body, desire, and the law that controls them.[2]

At issue here is the extent to which the control and regulation of the body correlates an attendant control and regulation of desire. The women in the harem and the eunuchs in charge of them live under the domination of a powerful despot who manages their lives far more fully than their simple imprisonment would warrant. The despot in control of the harem and its inhabitants derives his power less from the physical constraints he places on them than from the ideological force their sharply disciplined and administered desire produces. The despot's wives and the eunuchs who represent him in his absence appear to derive their identities nearly exclusively by imitating a form of desire prescribed for them in their specific political and sexual circumstances.

I propose to investigate the manner in which the regulation of desire that Montesquieu examines in his *Persian Letters* and *Spirit of Laws* underwrites the specific identities that the subjects he depicts might adopt. Montesquieu seems fascinated with the idea of an absolutist regime—which might explain his interest in the Persian harem—and equally compelled by the apparent impossibility of maintaining one. His fictive and political writings interrogate the consequences of absolutism, repeatedly suggesting that despotic states—whether civic governments or kinship relations—must always buckle under their own internal contradiction. To this more or less traditional way of reading Montesquieu's works, I would like to add the dimension of personal identity. How do subjects in any sort of regime regulated by law find for themselves a consciousness, one born of the forms of desire produced through the processes of legitimation the law undertakes? How, in other words, is a subject's irreducible perception of self informed by the kinds of desire both made available and prohibited by the law under which it lives? What, finally, can Montesquieu's early foray into the ideological dimension of subjective formation tell us about the politics of identity? A detailed analysis of the *Persian Letters* and the dialogue this novel maintains with Montesquieu's later *Spirit of Laws* shows that he construes absolutism as both a necessary and—paradoxically—impossible fiction. The fiction of absolutism, I argue, is one of a seamless cultural unity, and it is one that performs its ideological work primarily by naturalizing specific forms of sexual desire while simultaneously delegitimizing others.

Montesquieu's *Persian Letters* and *Spirit of Laws* respond to one another over issues relating directly to this problem. The *Persian Letters*, which has traditionally been considered a sort of trial run for Montesquieu's later political and sociological treatises, nevertheless mobilizes two concepts that inform the great majority of his work: the relation of law to desire,

and the effect of historical contingency on idealism. Usbek implicitly leg-
islates his wives' and his eunuchs' desire and, consequently, portions of
their identity, but he cannot for all his power prevent his subjects from
breaking the law of desire he has attempted to establish: the hermetically
closed world of the harem ultimately breaks down in the end when the
sultan's substitutes, the eunuchs, are unable to maintain control. In a similar vein, the *Spirit of Laws* searches for the irreducible logic of law, the cultural truth it reveals when people can become conscious of the tensions
and forces that oppose and unite them in social interaction, but that truth
is fleeting and inconsistent. If Montesquieu's work strives to disarticulate
an empirically observable sociology from an ideologically invested conviction—what human law *is* as opposed to what it *ought to be*—it also investigates how subjects in any system of governance are subjected first and
foremost by a legitimized form of desire, one that structures the specific
features of identity that individuals can embody.

By the eighteenth century, Orientalism and in particular the harem had already been established as fruitful arenas for the examination of sexual and
cultural difference. Jean-Baptiste Tavernier traveled throughout Turkey
and Persia and published his tales in 1676; Jean Chardin's three-volume
Voyage en Perse et aux Indes Orientales appeared in 1711, and his narrative
served as one of Montesquieu's sources for the *Spirit of Laws*. One early
account of travel and of the harem, that of Michel Baudier in 1626, manifests Europeans' ambivalent fascination with the strict sexual discipline
maintained there:[3]

> The order observed in the safeguarding of the women is painstaking.
> Not only are the women who enter [the harem] carefully examined,
> but so also are the eunuchs returning from the city. Furthermore, spe-
> cial care is taken with animals: the Sultanas are not allowed to keep
> monkeys or medium-sized male dogs. Fruits are only sent to them with
> great circumspection: if their appetite calls for somewhat elongated
> squash, cucumbers or other similar foods, they are cut up at the door
> into round slices, such that not the slightest occasion to commit an im-
> pure act might be allowed them, so debased was the opinion of their
> continence. (qtd. in Grosrichard 177)[4]

The comical litany of bestial and vegetable substitutes for the penis implies
that women—or at least those in the harem—will have sex with anything
as long as it has a penis or something remotely resembling one. The possi-

bilities for feminine impurity that this passage relates would seem to turn exclusively around the exclusion of the sultan: in his absence, his wives will apparently turn to whatever they can find that might stand in for him (or at least a part of him). What appears absolutely intolerable here is the wives' experiencing pleasure through any means other than with the sultan.

The harem, we have come to expect, exists for the purpose of confining the sultan's women, and specifically for keeping them out of sight and out of touch from other men. It might thus seem odd to classify as impure an act that, strictly speaking, does not compromise the sultanas' fidelity to the sultan. Yet, in the highly politicized sexual economy of the harem, in which the despot reigned over everything, including desire, errant attractions constituted treason.[5] Women in the harem had no identity apart from a being-for-the-sultan. While the prohibition of what amounts to dildos might appear gratuitous, the prohibition of penis substitutes makes them appear highly craved; consequently, it accomplishes the feat of causing all feminine desire to complement the sultan's.

However, it is not only sexual practices involving a substitute for the sultan's penis that are prohibited: lesbianism and even its temptations are proscribed in the harem as well. One of Usbek's wives, Zéphis, is punished for vaguely specified sensual activities with a slave girl, whom she describes as having "adroit hands [which] carry ornaments and graces everywhere" (28). The black eunuch who takes the slave away from her, she writes, "looks upon my confidences with her as criminal, and, because he is bored behind the door where I always send him, dares to suppose that he has seen or heard things that I cannot even imagine" (28). The prohibition of any feminine desire not directed to the sultan's body organizes all feminine desire around the sultan and, consequently, as phallic. It creates an economy of desire that not only mimics and complements his own but also revolves directly around the sultan himself.

The *Persian Letters* poses the question of how the disciplined feminine body can encode ideology. It also establishes early on that the eunuchs' genital mutilation separates them not only from themselves, as Usbek's chief white eunuch euphemistically puts it, but also from traditional, valorized forms of masculinity. Fatmé, one of Usbek's wives, writes, "I don't include in the category of men these horrible eunuchs whose least imperfection is that they are not at all men" (30–31). The chief white eunuch agrees that he is something less than a man—he demonstrates it, in fact, when he writes, "I become a man again on the occasions when I command [the women]" (34). There is certainly nothing unprecedented in the implicit claim here that the penis is the measure of the man; the intact male body has long been a traditional parameter for standardizing ideologically legitimate forms of subjectivity. The real issue here, however, would seem to be not whether genital organization establishes gender, but how specific features of social identity relate to the body and the forms of desire that traverse it.

In the harem that Montesquieu's *Persian Letters* depicts, genital mutilation is a symptom, and not a cause, of the eunuchs' disenfranchisement. The sultan's fully intact body symbolizes, rather than in some abstract way causes, his complete control over his subjects, in particular over their sexual functions. It is consequently crucial not to miss the point of the chief eunuch's remark that to become a eunuch is to "separate himself forever from himself": this remark has little to do with his relationship to his genitalia (as though his entire sense of self were located precisely in his penis) and nearly everything to do with the way in which his own desires are alienated from him. Specifically, like the women he guards, the eunuch must renounce his own desires. As is the case with the women in the harem, the fact that the eunuch may lack the physical means to express his desires carries far less importance than the ideological manipulation of *how* he desires. To be precise, the eunuch is constrained to desire like the sultan—or, perhaps more accurately, *in the place of the sultan*—without, nevertheless, having his desire ever coincide precisely with that of the sultan.

The chief black eunuch illustrates this point when he writes to Usbek about the acquisition of a new wife. A group of Armenians bring a young slave to the harem, and the eunuch takes her into its innermost recesses. He writes:

> I undressed her and examined her with the eyes of a judge, and the more I examined her, the greater I found her charms to be. A virginal modesty seemed to want to hide them from my view: I saw precisely what it cost her to obey; she blushed at being seen completely naked, even in front of me, who, exempt from the passions that might alarm her modesty, am insensitive to this sex's empire. . . .
>
> As soon as I had judged her worthy of you, I lowered my eyes; I gave her a mantle of scarlet, and I placed on her finger a gold ring. I prostrated myself at her feet, and adored her as the queen of your heart. I paid the Armenians, and sheltered her from all eyes. (136)

The black eunuch here stands in for his master until the precise moment at which the slave girl becomes his master's wife. Scrutinizing her as his master would in order to determine whether she might make an appropriate addition to the harem, and standing in for the master in what amounts to a wedding ceremony, he shields her from all view, including his own, the instant the marriage takes place and the business transaction is completed. Paradoxically, the eunuch's castration makes him more like the master than dissimilar: because he is unable to consummate sexual desire, he remains continually enthralled, unable to inhabit a sexuality other than the one his master hands down. Zélis, one of Usbek's wives, quotes her master to him in this regard, underscoring the master's regulation of the eunuch's enjoyment: "I have heard you say a thousand times that eunuchs enjoy a sort of voluptuousness with women that is unknown to us . . . ; that in this state one is in a sort of third sense, in which one merely, so to speak, changes pleasures" (96).

The eunuch's castration consequently extends beyond the mutilation of his body and well into the structural definition of his psyche. That is, his desires are not entirely thwarted, but subjugated. They become, effectively, the metaphor for his master's: the head eunuch writes, in fact, "although I guard [the women] for another, the pleasure of making myself obeyed gives me a secret joy: when I deprive them of everything, it seems to me that it is for me, and I derive from this an indirect satisfaction" (34). The chief black eunuch here must desire *as though* he were the sultan, and he must desire *for* the sultan. He must not only abandon a part of himself but accept as integral to his own identity a desire that must always remain, for all intents and purposes, alienated. It is this alienated desire— here, the sultan's particular penchant for specific kinds of women—that the eunuch must internalize at the expense of his own desire. He gives up part of himself, and what he gets in return is a consistency of identity that affords him a place in the culture as it is organized. Béatrice Durand-Sendrail succinctly specifies how the eunuch's insertion into the master's symbolic domain comes at a price when she remarks that "castration is the price of his lucidity" (76). I might suggest turning Durand-Sendrail's phrase around, however. I might claim, in fact, that lucidity is the price of castration, and that only through a "separation from self" can one achieve a genuine consciousness of self. Without this separation from self, consciousness coincides completely with itself; the lack of differentiation that allows us to perceive ourselves as simultaneously self and other would foreclose identity in a solipsism so absolute the self would exist without ever really being aware of itself as self.[6]

The specific relationship between law and desire that Montesquieu's works articulate thus extends beyond a vision of law as simple prohibition. Instead of regulating the women's and the eunuchs' desires merely by drastically limiting the means by which they might express them, the law of the harem radically structures desire in a manner that configures self-identity. The eunuchs in the *Persian Letters*, as we have seen, consider themselves nugatory extensions of their master. The master's wives fare only slightly better in their quest for autonomous identity—the price of their freedom from the master's constraining commandments is death. The law that Montesquieu describes regulates behavior, to be sure, but the regulation of behavior is an *effect* of the way it structures knowledge and belief in the culture in which it is deployed. If the despot's law in the harem regulates his extended family, so too does the father's prerogative superintend the Parisian family. As Rica explains it to an unidentified correspondent: "According to the law observed here [Paris], every child born in marriage is considered [*censé*] to belong to the husband. He might well have good reasons for not believing it, but the law believes for him, and it relieves him from examination and from doubt" (145). In the *Spirit of Laws* Montesquieu makes the following similar observation: "One considers that any child conceived in marriage is legitimate; the law has confidence in the mother as if she were modesty itself" (329). The law of the father thinks and believes *for* its subjects. Attempting to subvert the possibility that feminine sexuality might find expression through means other than with a legal spouse, European paternal law simply dictates that all progeny resulting from a married woman *must* be her husband's. Potentially illegitimate children are legitimized through what is nothing more than a legal fiction.

It is precisely through the question of legitimized forms of desire that the *Persian Letters* fathoms the issue of cultural individuation and suggests, as do key passages of the *Spirit of Laws*, that human desire is the final and stable cause of empirical law. Montesquieu goes to great lengths to assert an internal consistency in law, and as many readers have shown, he does so by associating human law with the idea of scientific, natural law. Louis Althusser has written that the modern meaning of unchanging, inviolate scientific law emerged in the sixteenth and seventeenth centuries, but that law never really divested itself of the moral and ideological imperatives associated with it in its religious contexts, in which, he maintains, people viewed the law "as a *commandment*" (31). Montesquieu tried to apply to human law, Althusser and others argue, a Newtonian notion of physical determinism or necessity.[7] By so doing he attempted to locate a kernel of stable social meaning within the oftentimes irrational or random applications of the law as force and sought to disarticulate from the concept of an unchanging, unmotivated "nature" the politically invested qualities attributed to it.

It is in this respect that Montesquieu's notion of nature differs somewhat from that proposed by Voltaire, Berkeley, Condillac, or Diderot. For a great many eighteenth-century thinkers, nature can only be defined as a tautology. Voltaire's Micromégas, for example, speaks for some of those thinkers when he impatiently castigates those who would define nature through metaphor: "Nature is like nature. Why look for comparisons?" (133). Montesquieu tried to escape from the redundancy of "nature is nature," however, by positing the idea that nature *has* (a) nature, and that that nature is expressly linked to human reason. In the preface to the *Spirit of Laws* he writes, "I posited principles, and I saw particular cases conform to them as of their own accord. I saw as well that the histories of all nations are only the results of this; and that each particular law is tied to another law, or that it depends on another, more general law" (229). The dizzying web of interconnected laws expresses a rational core fundamentally accessible in the last instance to those who would attempt to fathom the complexities of their interrelations. We can explain nature's organizing principle, Montesquieu claims, if we simply excavate all of the interrelations uniting history, law, and culture. As Montesquieu's famous definition of law has it, "Laws . . . are the necessary relationships which derive from the nature of things. . . . There is an originary reason; and laws are the relationships found between it and different beings, and the relationships among these different beings" (232).

Montesquieu is often cited as the founder of modern jurisprudence and political science because he strives to abandon the idealism that had characterized earlier political theorizing. He seeks to amass an illustrative quantity of historical data that might illuminate the motivations informing human political activity. To do this, he construes empirical law as a corollary of natural law by juxtaposing statements such as "Man, as a physical being, is, just like other bodies, governed by invariable laws" (234), with "Law, in general, is human reason, in as much as it governs all the people of the earth" (237). Montesquieu's attempt to demystify the sorts of political activity that had previously been blithely attributed to natural order or divine will casts nature not as an unknowable thing, an idea that Kant would later explore, but as a vastly complicated yet ultimately knowable repository in which things and events that have yet to be understood await their eventual elucidation. His views on nature as both cause and effect of human activity have incited Bernard Valette to wonder, "does the idea of nature flow from an observation of reality (what one might call 'the nature of things') or from an overly systematic, subjective vision, the result of our fears and desires?" (43).

As Valette suggests, Montesquieu intimates that nature, reason, and human law are ultimately linked to desire, and that human desire is the linchpin anchoring identity to culture. While his analysis of the influence that climate, history, and material living conditions have on the structure of laws leads him to theorize the legal differences distinguishing despotic, monarchic, and democratic states, he nevertheless establishes as a fundamental alliance among those states a culturally specific and hence unifying desire. If it is the case, for example, that in despotism "law is only what the prince wants" (300), it is also the case that in monarchies and democracies alike (distinguished from despotism by the fact that they have laws extending beyond the simple will of the despot), "liberty can only consist in being able to do what one ought to want [ce que l'on doit vouloir], and in not being forced to do what one ought not to want [ce que l'on ne doit pas vouloir]" (395). Consequently, despite Montesquieu's attempts to distinguish among despotism, monarchy, and democracy, law in any of the forms of government he analyzes reproduces a legitimized form of desire that underwrites the fundamental structures of the society. Significantly, as we saw in Rica's version of the Parisian law that believes for its subjects, people obey the legitimized laws of desire without even knowing it. Montesquieu makes that point quite explicitly when he writes about obedience, desire, and the will of the ruler: "Extreme obedience supposes ignorance on the part of he who obeys; it even supposes ignorance on the part of he who commands. There is no call for him to deliberate, to doubt, or to reason. He only has to want" (265). By circumscribing the very forms and kinds of desire subjects may have, law regulates human identity far more effectively than simple discipline and containment.

Up until now I have caused a sort of dialogue to exist between the *Persian Letters* and the *Spirit of Laws* without specifying how or why a fictive and a sociological work might interact. I am operating under the assumption that the two works are both largely sociological and largely fictional—and not fictitious, the difference, as I later show, is crucial. It concerns the manner in which plausible stories of the way things ought to be are passed off as the way things truly are. A nefarious narratological realism consequently buffers empirical history from ideologically invested idealism. The sociology of a work such as the *Persian Letters* seems self-evident. Regardless of the quantity of dispassionate empirical observation of his own culture that we think Montesquieu actually engaged in, it does not require a great deal of imagination, or even goodwill, to perform the famous "retour secret que nous faisons sur nous-mêmes" that Rica describes (104), and thus to ascribe to the novel a certain kind of social criticism. There are enough putatively naive but overbearingly transparent "Persian" accounts of Parisian behavior to test the patience of readers who had hoped to maintain for themselves the work's fictionality. More to the point, however, the accounts of life in the Orient have a decidedly Parisian cast. While it is beyond the scope of this essay to detail the Western configurations that Montesquieu applies to the Persian harem,[8] it is crucial to stress the fact that the despotism Montesquieu describes in the *Persian Letters* as well as in the *Spirit of Laws* bears a striking resemblance to the traditional Western nuclear family.

Montesquieu himself fairly explicitly made the connection between despotism and reigning views of the family, and it is fairly clear that much of what he attributes to Persia in the *Persian Letters* is simply a defamiliarized account of his own culture. In the despotic state, he avers, "each house is a separate empire" (265), curiously evoking the origin of the word *despot* (a Greek term for household). Although Montesquieu refutes the idea that a monarchic government is most natural because it most closely mimics paternal power, he never questions the legitimacy of patriarchy: he leaves unchallenged the notion that "nature established paternal power" (237).[9] Maintaining an age-old opposition between masculine culture and feminine nature, he argues that "reason dictates that when there is a marriage the children follow the condition of the father; and that when there is not, they can concern only the mother" (684). Moreover, Montesquieu further naturalizes the cultural contingency of masculine hegemony when he equates paternity with reason and, consequently, the law: "Laws must not be subtle. They are made for people of mediocre intelligence: they are not an art of logic, but a father's simple reason" (878). The *Persian Letters* and the *Spirit of Laws* attempt to organize human subjectivity around the pole of sexual difference, in which paternal figures administer law and feminine or feminized subjects are constrained by it.

I am not citing Montesquieu's privileging of a patriarchal form of reason and desire simply to rehearse the notion that particular forms of masculinity compose the standard of legal subjectivity. What I want to suggest is that Montesquieu affords us an early glimpse of the manner in which categories of identity are produced in early modern culture's juridical subjects. The *Persian Letters* and the *Spirit of Laws* show how individuality or personality, which fascinated Enlightenment thinkers who sought to disarticulate human essence from its specific cultural manifestations, came into being precisely in response to legal fictions specifying what one might and might not be. I want to argue that Montesquieu shows how, to borrow a phrase from Judith Butler, the *being* of identity is an effect (32).[10] Legitimized categories of being are produced at intersections of social tensions; specific forms of constraint on behavior and of the management of desire help structure the identity characteristics available in a given culture at a given historical moment. Montesquieu's works do not simply juxtapose two putatively diverse and unrelated cultures by way of illustrating the roles that various characters literally or metaphorically occupy. Rather, the *Persian Letters* and the *Spirit of Laws* provide glimpses not only of the beings of identity that patriarchal law produces, but something of the spirit of those beings as well. In other words, if these two works concern themselves with how absolutism structures family and civic relations, they also seem frustrated by an inability to decide just what it is or how it works. Specifically, in both of these works, Montesquieu seems to be trying to determine whether absolutism is, fundamentally, detrimental or necessary to the public good; he seems to wonder, in fact, whether absolutism is impossible to avoid, or impossible to imagine.

With the emphasis in Montesquieu's work on the role of law and desire now sketched out, I would like to look at the manner in which absolutism's regimentation of subjectivity depends not on containment or constraint, but on representation and identification. Specifically, Montesquieu's concern with domestic and civil absolutism casts their representation, and not their reality, as one of the mode's most salient features. Dena Goodman argues that in Montesquieu's work we see "the frustration and the pathos of the individual who struggles to break out of the entanglements of the social web, which keep the individual the center of Montesquieu's representation of a social world that cannot be mastered" (23). If this world cannot be mastered, it seems to me that it fares only slightly better when it needs to be represented. The fiction of seamless, monolithic, and apodictic control that the *Persian Letters* and the *Spirit of Laws* advance, I would like to suggest, produces more authority and domination than it describes. In other words, the ideologically significant aspects of the absolutism that Montesquieu describes do not necessarily antedate the description itself. Control is exercised, consequently, on an unconscious level that circumscribes the sites of subjectivity and radically delimits the way in which subjects can think about themselves.

Montesquieu is not alone in rendering problematic the discursive and the material nature of despotic control. In fact, his version of despotism seems curiously to anticipate the sort of patriarchal control that Sigmund Freud theorized in *Totem and Taboo* and *The Ego and the Id*. In the myth of the primal horde, Freud stressed the perennial generational struggle sundering the father from his sons. That struggle is premised on each son's desire to be like his father and reserve feminine sexuality exclusively for himself, and the son's inability to fill the father's role. In his fable of the primal horde and the sons' murder of the father, Freud points out that not only did the sons fail to usurp the father's province, but that the father became even more powerful, owing to the force exerted by the murderers' guilt, after his death. The brothers collaborated to fix a social order based on the fear and admiration of the dead and hence more powerful father, the mere memory of whose erotic control continued to exert its influence on the sons even after the man himself had been eliminated. While attempting to forestall the possibility that a single man determine the sexual and social identity of their group, the brothers constructed in place of any real ruler an abstract and imaginary patriarch. The patriarch they construct is an ideal representation of masculine power and control that each of them would like to embody. For that very reason, however, each must make certain that the patriarch remain forever abstract and imaginary.

The patriarch in Freud's myth remains, consequently, a purely discursive construction, but the discursive power invested in him is strong enough to govern the sexual and kinship behavior of an entire culture. Montesquieu's despot enjoys a barely more concrete status, but his power is similarly real and widespread. Commenting on the despot's largely covert governing, Montesquieu argues in the *Spirit of Laws* that "fortunately, men in [a despotism] are such that they require nothing more than a name to govern them" (293). In the *Persian Letters*, Usbek makes a similar point when he writes that Asian despots hide themselves because "they want to make themselves more respected; but they make royalty, and not the king, more respected, and they attach their subjects' loyalty not to a specific person, but to the throne" (166). The despot's power, in other words, increases in proportion to its abstraction; it expands in its province as the magnitude of its mythology grows and its reality takes shelter from the light of day. Furthermore, distribution of power in Montesquieu's political theory, like that in Freud's psychoanthropology, follows specific avenues in which particular males substitute for the abstract but centrally powerful male. Describing the administration of despotic government, for example, Montesquieu writes, "the vizier is the despot himself, and each particular officer is the vizier" (299).

But the similarities between Freud's mythical, prehistoric account of the origins and ramifications of patrilinearity and Montesquieu's depiction of patriarchal despotism do not end with their shared emphasis on the name of the father. Freud's primeval patriarchy and Montesquieu's foreign despotism both underscore their own virtual impossibility. In the case of Freud, the myth of the primal horde posits male sexuality and masculinity as reproducing themselves around a patriarchal figure of phallic control and plenitude discursively produced by men who willingly subordinate themselves to it. The discursive construction of a patriarch whose power derives from the sons' guilt is formulated to be an inaccessible representation of unattainable social control. It is a purely fictional account that bonds together the male members of the group. If this story guarantees that no man ever attains the power and status of the primal patriarch, it serves its purpose by protecting the men from one another.

Montesquieu's despotism is, similarly, discursively constructed yet practically unfeasible. Montesquieu, of course, characterizes the three basic types of political regime by the principle that motivates them. When the principle is corrupted, the regime crumbles. Of despotism's corruption, Montesquieu writes:

> The principle of the despotic government is continually corrupted, because it is corrupt by its very nature. Other governments perish because specific events violate their principles. But the despotic government perishes because of its interior vice, when accidental causes do not prevent its principle from becoming corrupted. It only continues when circumstances deriving from the weather, religion or the people force it to follow a given order. (357)

Although despotism is by its nature corrupt, its very corruption is continually corrupted. It only perishes, Montesquieu claims, in the paradoxical situation in which it is prevented from becoming further corrupted, and thus from following its true nature. Herein lies the paradox of Montesquieu's political theory: its goal is to characterize the nature or essence of the specific political regimes that populate the earth, but it turns out that for despotism, the regime that threatens the others and that for Montesquieu characterizes the traditional family, there is no nature. Despotism is continually corrupted; it consequently continually changes, despite Montesquieu's claim that it "is uniform everywhere: since only passions are required to establish it, everyone is good for that" (297). Like the primal father in Freud's myth, despotism seems to exist only as a discursively constructed entity, one that provides power to those who describe it and evoke its awesome presence. Despotism, it would seem, has no consistency or identity of its own. It exists in Montesquieu's scheme solely as the foil for democracy, as the dangerous other into which more egalitarian forms of rule seem poised to collapse.

I want to pause for a moment to underscore the similarities between the psychoanalytic and political descriptions of patriarchal authority, but also to emphasize that I am not interested here in what might appear to be pure coincidence. The analogy I am pursuing is an identificatory one in which men accede to positions of tremendous power by virtue of their association with an always absent or fictional patriarchal figure. Both Freud's and Montesquieu's descriptions of patriarchy present logically plausible but pragmatically impossible scenarios of autocracy. Both function as foils highlighting the ostensible egalitarianism of what appears to be both the primal horde's and the despotism's other: a benevolent democracy that is, nevertheless, patriarchal. Both the political and the psychoanalytic theories construct an impossibly powerful and necessarily hidden or absent patriarch that performs the purely logical function of providing the upper limit of masculine domination, a domination based almost exclusively on sexual appetite. I might, in fact, push the analogy between Freud's and Montesquieu's patriarchal models even further by noting that both theorize male identification with the patriarch. Psychoanalysis stipulates the position of masculine gender identity as one of identification with the father, be he the primal variety or simply the biological one. Montesquieu's despotism offers a series of viziers and eunuchs responsible for administering the despot's wishes, and as we saw they must learn to identify absolutely with him. Consequently, a series of metaphoric and metonymic substitutions allows these men to incarnate the absent despot's complete authority.

I argue above that in the domestic and political despotisms that Montesquieu describes desire is always the desire of the patriarch, a desire that, split along a bipolar gender identification, becomes highly institutionalized: in despotism "the law being only what the prince wants, and the prince only wanting what he knows, there must be an infinity of people who want for him and like him" (300). I want to turn here to the issue of how the impossible, fictional despotic patriarchs that both Montesquieu and Freud relate attain their power. As paradoxical as it might first appear, these despots derive their power not because they exist prior to and thus exert control over the narrations that describe them. They exist purely as powerful fictions. Concerning the power of fiction in the *Persian Letters*, Paul Valéry wrote in 1930, "it is necessary that the era of order be the empire of *fictions*—for there is no power capable of founding order on the force of bodies on bodies alone. Fictive forces are necessary" (53). In this vein, as I now show, it is in large part the *telling* of the story that confers patriarchal power.

I might illustrate the manner in which the story's telling accomplishes the phenomenon it purports to describe by returning briefly to Freud. It is important to keep in mind that Freud deploys his heuristic tale to provide an originary moment, mythical or not, in Western culture—the moment at which what amounts to the Oedipalization of a group of males radically transforms culture by introducing the incest taboo. The turning point in the story of the primal horde is the brothers' resolution to kill and consume the father. Freud briefly recounts the circumstances leading up to this act in a brief parenthetical phrase: "(Some cultural advance, perhaps command over some new weapon, had given them a sense of superior strength)" (*Totem and Taboo* 141–42). Surprisingly, Freud describes a cultural change that acts as an instigator in a tale that purportedly relates what for all intents and purposes is the origin of culture. This means that the story of the primal horde cannot explain what happened prior to the moment at which the brothers banded together, because our cultural understanding is limited to what came afterward. In other words, owing to the way in which we understand sexual difference and kinship relations, we have no way to conceptualize relations except through the filter of an incest taboo. In fact, even Freud's description of the brothers *before* the crucial murder of the father is overdetermined by modern, phallic notions of male behavior: "Each of them would have wished, like his father, to have all the women for himself" (*Totem and Taboo* 144).

The patriarch in Freud's story is, as I have mentioned, a fiction constructed by the brothers. The paradox here is that since he was killed by the band of brothers, he himself never underwent the process of acculturation that transformed his sons into incest-fearing, Oedipalized men. This means that not only is the father a purely discursive structure, but his figure represents the extreme limit of cultural understanding; his reality lies somewhere beyond the limit of representation. Neither a culturally defined male nor even a verifiable subject, the father is a discursive figure that lies, paradoxically, beyond language. As if to anticipate Freud in this matter, Montesquieu's definition of man—"man is a creature who obeys a creature who wants" (260)—endlessly defers the question of who or what the final desiring creature is and what it wants.

The same is true of Montesquieu's despot, be he the head of a family or of an empire. Montesquieu explicitly cites the legal fiction whose representation maintains patriarchal control—he writes, in fact, that "in well-policed societies, the father is he whom laws, through the ceremony of marriage, have declared must be such [devoir être tel], because they find in him the person that they seek" (683). Were I to pursue the psychoanalytic aspects of this notion, I might point out the similarities between Montesquieu's version of the father and Jacques Lacan's.[11] What is absolutely crucial by any account, however, is the discursive, ultimately fictional, and fundamentally impossible position the despot and despotism occupy. Despite Montesquieu's insistence on rejecting idealism—he notes that "it is necessary to clarify history through law and law through history" (943)—he remains absolutely unable to provide a concrete definition of despotism. Maintaining that "in the domain of law one has to reason from reality to reality, and not from reality to figure or from figure to reality" (878), Montesquieu nevertheless can only define despotism through metaphor: "When the savages of Louisiana want fruit, they cut down the tree at the base, and gather the fruit. That is despotic government" (292).

When Louis Althusser analyzes Montesquieu's description of despotism he writes, "No doubt 'despotism' is a caricature. But its object is to terrify and to edify by its very horribleness" (83). What I am trying to demonstrate, however, is not that despotism is some sort of a joke in Montesquieu's political philosophy, but that the sort of apodictic structures that we use to define the upper limit of political power and force only exist in our defining structures themselves and not in any political reality. Language and fiction are much more efficient tools to bolster behavior and identity than is force. As Montesquieu's fiction and sociology show, defamiliarizing representations of social and sexual structures that cast one in terms of the other provide neat models for identification. The representation of the harem, with its women and eunuchs totally subjected to the despot's wishes, provides an apt metaphor for the sexual division of power and for masculine identification with paternal figures. Yet, by way of a conclusion, I would like to complicate that neat binary gender division with which most contemporary commentators seem to be so comfortable.

As I mentioned above, nearly all of Montesquieu's readers who treat the question of gender and the harem cast the eunuchs on the side of the women. Yet, what most commentators have failed to account for is the fact that in the *Persian Letters* and in historical accounts of the harem's structure, the eunuchs are divided, both physically and administratively, by race. It is the "black eunuchs" who live in the harem proper and who come into close physical contact with the women, while the "white eunuchs" occupy the margins of the harem, excluded from its secret interiors. The "white eunuchs" are those principally responsible for carrying out the despot's orders. It is they who, like the vizier, enjoy the phallic privilege of executing commands while nevertheless remaining submissive to the despot himself. In addition, according to at least one early account—that of Jean Chardin, in 1686—white eunuchs suffer a less severe form of genital mutilation than black eunuchs. Chardin writes that white eunuchs "were simply snipped" (*taillés*), whereas black eunuchs "were completely gutted" (*on a tout coupé à fleur de ventre*) (qtd. in Grosrichard 185).[12]

The point I want to draw from this is not that of whether, because they lack male genitals, the eunuchs classify as men or women. The issue here is that gender is never *simply* gender and that the question of sexuality or subjective identification depends on characteristics operating in a culture that extend far beyond the simple male/female binary opposition. In the case of the eunuchs, whether or not it is correct, from a biological or genetic point of view, to call them male has little to do with the fact that their gender is related in an explicit fashion to their race. Zachi, one of Usbek's wives in the *Persian Letters*, receives a severe reprimand from her husband specifically for receiving a *white* eunuch in her chambers, a reprimand that underscores the complex interaction between race and gender operating here. The point here is that gender is inflected by race, that these two crucial components of subjectivity inform one another at the most basic level.

Yet, the question of the despot's relationship to the engendering of his subjects remains a difficult one. Isn't he, after all, ultimately in control of the criteria that collude to endow his subjects with a specific identity? Who structures his identity, his desire? I want to avoid making the obvious tautological assumption that the patriarchy forms the patriarchy, which is tantamount to arguing that there is something natural or essential about masculine hegemony. This sort of argument construes patriarchal power as awesomely monolithic and apodictically potent, something Montesquieu never imagined even for despotism, given that he argues that its principle—fear—is corrupted as much as that of any other form of government. The point here is that we need to understand how other phenomena of subjectivity structure the way we construct and perceive gender, race, and by extension, subjectivity. I suggest one way of disarticulating the knot of features contributing to identity by looking briefly at the question of race, but one might just as easily look at the way issues concerning class or sexuality inform Montesquieu's notion of authority. The task at hand is to unravel the cultural investments inhering in the metaphors of gender and patriarchy. Like those guarding the harem and the animals and fruits admitted there in the passage from Baudier I cite above, we frequently look too hard at the manifest content of much cultural activity, often forgetting that, for all their ethereal abstraction, you can still get screwed by your metaphors.

NOTES

1. All translations, unless otherwise noted, are my own.

2. In 1930, for example, Paul Valéry wrote that "there is no doubt that there is a deep and secret reason for the almost obligatory presence of these characters [eunuchs] so cruelly separated from so many things, and in some ways from themselves" (73). In a similar vein, Roger Kempf writes that the eunuchs occupy the "forefront" of the novel and calls them hideous, dehumanized parasites whose bodies are reduced to pure functionality. Tzvetan Todorov argues that the eunuch is "neither man nor woman," but that he is simultaneously master and slave (314).

3. Montesquieu himself was not immune to the fascination with sexual desire and the harem. Noting that "reason demands that the master's power not extend beyond the things in his service; slavery must serve utility, and not voluptuousness," he also observed that harems in Turkey, Persia, China, and Japan contributed to the admirable morality of the women there. See the *Esprit des Lois*, 499, 517.

4. The first edition of Michel Baudier's *Histoire générale du sérail et de la cour du Grand Seigneur, empereur des Turcs* was published in 1623.

5. Grosrichard writes, concerning the economy of desire and the despot's power: "That this structure [of power] supposes and imposes a rigorous economy of desire and of the relationship between the sexes, that the despot reigns, through a love that is inseparable from fear, only over a people of women, and by means of a middle term consisting of castrated men, deserves our attention" (38–39).

6. Or, as Slavoj Zizek puts it, following Hegel, "if . . . self-consciousness is self-consciousness only through the mediation of another self-consciousness, then my self-awareness—precisely insofar as this self-awareness is not the same as self-transparency—causes the emergence of a decentered 'it thinks.' When the split between 'I am' and 'it thinks' is translated into the standard motif of intersubjectivity, what gets lost is the radical *asymmetry* of the two terms" (68).

For a different reading of self-consciousness and the integrated psyche, see Kathy E. Ferguson, who argues, "In many respects feminisms arose as a protest against the absorption of difference into pretentious and bloated unities. Yet some kinds of feminism perpetuate this sin against otherness by absorbing the variegated worlds of women, and on occasion of all oppressed peoples and beings, into a unified field called 'woman,' 'women,' 'the feminine,' or 'feminism.' While sometimes this move takes place out of ignorance or a disregard for particularities of time and place, often it reflects a desire not unlike Hegel's: to find something recognizable in that which is unlike the self so as to find solid grounds for understanding self and world, and to create a shared basis for political action" (57).

7. Jean Goldzinck writes, "In this perspective, Montesquieu founds positivistic political science, and he submits history, societies, jurisprudence, and politics to the rigorous determinism of nature's sciences" (108).

8. But see Grosrichard, especially 35–45; Said; Alloula; Singerman; Hundert; and Romanowski for detailed considerations on Montesquieu's treatment of the harem.

9. Montesquieu bases his argument against the equation father=king on the issue of succession of power in the family and in the monarchy: "For if the father's power is related to government by an individual, after the death of the father the power of the brothers, or, after the death of the brothers, the power of first cousins, bears a relationship to a government by several. Political power necessarily entails the union of several families" (*Esprit des Lois* 237).

10. Butler is referring to the manner in which specific forms of sexuality are generally construed as normative and hence "before" power structures. "The presumption here," she writes, "is that the 'being' of gender is *an effect*, an object of a genealogical investigation that maps out the political parameters of its construction in the mode of ontology" (32).

11. "The only function of the father . . . is to be a myth, always and uniquely the Name-of-the-Father, that is, nothing but the dead father, as Freud explains in *Totem and Taboo*." Lacan, *Le Séminaire, livre VII* (356–57). See also *Le Séminaire, livre III* (223–26).

12. The *Voyages en Perse* is a reissue of the *Journal du voyage du chevalier Chardin en Perse et aux Indes orientales* (London, 1686, Amsterdam, 1711).

WORKS CITED

Alloula, Malek. *The Colonial Harem*. Minneapolis: U of Minnesota P, 1986.

Althusser, Louis. *Politics and History: Montesquieu, Rousseau, Hegel and Marx*. Trans. Ben Brewster. London: NLB, 1972.

Butler, Judith. *Gender Trouble*. New York: Routledge, 1990.

Durand-Sendrail, Béatrice. "Mirage des Lumières: Politique du regard dans les *Lettres persanes*." *L'Esprit Créateur* 28.4 (1988): 69–81.

Ferguson, Kathy E. *The Man Question: Visions of Subjectivity in Feminist Theory*. Berkeley and Los Angelos: U of California P, 1993.

Freud, Sigmund. *The Ego and the Id*. Trans. James Strachey. New York: Norton, 1960.

———. *Totem and Taboo*. Trans. James Strachey. London: Routledge, 1965.

Goldzinck, Jean. "Sur le chaptire 1, du livre 1, de *l'Esprit des Lois* de Montesquieu." *Analyses et réflexions sur Montesquieu, De l'Esprit des Lois: La nature et la loi*. Ed. Joël Askénazi. Paris: Edition Marketing, 1987. 107–19.

Goodman, Dena. *Criticism in Action: Enlightenment Experiments in Political Writing*. Ithaca: Cornell UP, 1989.

Grosrichard, Alain. *Structure du sérail*. Paris: Seuil, 1979.

Hundert, E. J. "Sexual Politics and the Allegory of Identity in Montesquieu's *Persian Letters*." *The Eighteenth Century: Theory and Interpretation* 31.2 (1990): 101–15.

Kempf, Roger. "*Lettres persanes* ou le corps absent." *Tel Quel* 22 (1965): 81–86.

Lacan, Jacques. *Le Séminaire, livre VII: L'Ethique de la psychanalyse*. Paris: Seuil, 1986.

———. *Le Séminaire, livre III: Les Psychoses*. Paris: Seuil, 1981.

Montesquieu, Charles-Louis de Secondat. *Esprit des Lois* (Spirit of Laws). *Oeuvres complètes*. Volume 2. Paris: Bibliothèque de la Pléiade, 1958. 225–995.

————. *Les Lettres persanes.* Paris: Garnier-Flammarion, 1964.

Romanowski, Sylvie. "La Quête du savoir dans les *Lettres persanes.*" *Eighteenth-Century Fiction* 3.2 (1991): 93–111.

Said, Edward. *Orientalism.* New York: Vintage, 1979.

Singerman, Alan J. "Réflexions sur une métaphore: Le sérail dans les *Lettres persanes.*" *Studies on Voltaire and the Eighteenth Century* 185 (1980): 181–98.

Todorov, Tzvetan. "Réflexions sur les *Lettres persanes.*" *Romanic Review* 74.3 (1983): 306–15.

Valéry, Paul. *Variété II.* Paris: Gallimard, 1930.

Valette, Bernard. "L'Idée de nature." *Analyses et réflexions sur Montesquieu,* De l'Esprit des lois: *La nature et la loi.* Ed. Joël Askénazi. Paris: Edition Marketing, 1987: 42–49.

Voltaire. "Micromégas." *Romans et contes.* Ed. René Pomeau. Paris: Garnier-Flammarion, 1966.

Zizek, Slavoj. *Tarrying with the Negative: Kant, Hegel, and the Critique of Ideology.* Durham: Duke UP, 1993.

The Politics of "Passing"

The Scandalous Memoir and the Novel

Catherine Craft-Fairchild

In an 1893 account of several "women adventurers," Ménie
Muriel Dowie offered what, for the nineteenth century, was the
quintessential comment on female cross-dressing:

> Allowed now to understand the world in which they live,
> and the conditions of its and of their own being, there is no
> longer any need for them [women] to put on the garb of
> men in order to live, to work, to achieve, to breathe the outer
> air.
>   . . . They do well to keep to their own clothes. An air of
> masculinity, however slight, goes against the woman who
> would be successful in the eye of the public and on plat-
> forms. (xx–xxii)

Dowie asserted that the "ladies of the sabre" whose lives she
records are "a classic jest" whose "day is done" and whose "histories forgotten" (x). Marking them as lower-class "common"
wenches, Dowie dismissed them. True to her predictions, the
cross-dressed heroine of the eighteenth century gradually
vanished from the public record until she was recently un-
earthed by twentieth-century feminist critics eager to investigate women who deviated from the restrictive norms of their

age. Given the large number of eighteenth-century ballads and memoirs that depicted the cross-dressed woman, why would her exploits be so little known after this period?[1] A short but complicated answer is that she was sunk into oblivion by the very people who recorded her story.

In many cases, the cross-dressed woman's poverty required that she turn her adventures to account by composing and selling a narrative of them to the public; however, poverty's accompaniments, such as a weak education, frequently made it impossible for the woman to write that narrative herself. Typically, the female soldier/sailor issued from the lower classes.[2] Her transvestism,[3] disguising her as an equally lower-class man, allowed her to earn a living during the period in which she "passed" but did not permit her to overleap class boundaries. Once her transvestism was discovered and her hard-won male privileges annulled, her deviations from the cultural expectations for female delicacy diminished her chances of economic advancement through traditional channels (i.e., marriage). With economic need pressing her, the cross-dresser would often sell her story to a bookseller in the hopes of gaining a temporary maintenance. Marketed as novelistic productions, these works reproduced the woman's narrative in ways that would be both palatable to and instructive for audiences; in short, they reshaped the story of transgression to make it fit a domestic plot. Ménie Muriel Dowie's disheartening advice to women that "they do well to keep to their own clothes" became the underlying theme of many of the eighteenth-century scandalous memoirs penned by men. The novelistic conventions that shaped the cross-dresser's narrative brought the activities of the transgressive woman into line with prevailing norms while any of her deviations merely allowed her biographers to define more completely and precisely what the normative categories were.

Taken together, the cross-dresser's poverty, her loss of control of her own tale, and the transformation of that narrative at the hands of others made it difficult for the transgressive woman's life story to affect permanently her society's definition of the proper feminine role and made it easy for her biography to be overshadowed by less conflicted, more fully novelistic works—the eighteenth-century novels themselves.

Judith Butler writes in *Gender Trouble:*

Parody by itself is not subversive, and there must be a way to understand what makes certain kinds of parodic repetitions effectively disruptive, truly troubling, and which repetitions become domesticated and recirculated as instruments of cultural hegemony. A typology of actions would clearly not suffice, for parodic displacement, indeed, parodic laughter, depends on a context and reception in which subversive confusions can be fostered. (139)

Contemporary scholars are quick to point out the "subversive" effect of the eighteenth-century cross-dresser's transgressions. Much of the current critical thought on early female transvestism supports the notion that cross-dressing was individually empowering and collectively enabling for women. In *Masquerade and Civilization*, Terry Castle notes, "Historically speaking, the appropriation of the trappings of authority by those without it has usually been perceived as a threat to social structure. . . . [T]he woman sporting male attire was a symbolic figure . . . inevitably projecting . . . radical aspirations after power, sexual prestige, and masculine authority" (92, 256). Echoing Castle's observations, Felicity Nussbaum argues that the transvestism revealed in the "scandalous memoirs" of women like Charlotte Charke (actress, male impersonator, and daughter of actor and poet laureate Colley Cibber) and Hannah Snell (who donned male garments to become both a soldier and sailor) "undercut[s] the ideology of the gendered subject that eighteenth-century theorists of character were attempting so desperately to preserve" (198–99).

In *Gender Trouble*, Judith Butler elaborates how this "undercutting of the gendered subject" might be brought about. She emphasizes the constructedness of gender, arguing that "the various acts of gender create the idea of gender, and without those acts, there would be no gender at all. Gender is, thus, a construction that regularly conceals its genesis" (140). Gender, in Butler's terms, is a performance, a locus of acts and gestures given meaning and form through public and social discourse; gender is not an essence, but appears as one since its fabrication works to hide its fabric. Cross-dressing is subversive in that it "effectively mocks . . . the notion of a true gender identity" by highlighting the performative aspects of gender. Butler continues, "The performance of drag plays upon the distinction between the anatomy of the performer and the gender that is being performed. . . . *In imitating gender, drag implicitly reveals the imitative structure of gender itself*" (137).

Kristina Straub, in *Sexual Suspects*, argues that the exposure of the imitative structure of gender was one of the threats posed by the staged transvestism of female actresses playing eighteenth-century "breeches parts." The "'castrated' figure of the cross-dressed actress" (134) held a mirror up to masculinity, "reminding men of the tenuousness of the connection between the penis and phallic control" (136). The actress's elaborate "male" posturing and staging of her role "marks that role *as a role*, [and] gestures toward the artificiality—and tenuousness—of the masculinity that she . . . puts on" (140). In addition, "the actress in male dress summon[ed] up, in the very act of specularizing the feminine object of desire, the 'hateful' idea of a feminine sexual desire that exceeds the limits of 'normal' heterosexual romantic love" (134). In short, the "performative, 'unnatural' masculinity" of the cross-dressed actress "unsettle[d] newly dominant assumptions about gender as legitimized according to fixed and oppositional categories" (138). Her masquerade undermined the "apparent naturalness and stability" of both male and female heterosexual roles (135).

As the boundary between the public domain of men and the private domain of women solidified during the course of the eighteenth century, the threat to the polarization of gender posed by the cross-dresser became increasingly more important over time.[4] Straub, tracing the critical responses to the actresses' performances from the beginning of the century to its close, notices that critics became more and more hostile to female transvestism as the century wore on.[5] Early reviewers, writes Straub, "defined the 'safe' limits of the cross-dressed actress's ambiguous appeal; as a specular commodity, the gender and sexual confusion associated with the actress could be a source of pleasure as long as it did not contaminate or compromise dominant narratives of heterosexual desire" (130). Provided that the woman's masculine performance was confined to the stage and that her offstage heterosexuality was well-established, early critics found her acting enjoyable. By midcentury, a critical "discourse of containment" (131) strove to erase the ambiguities of the transvestism or to insist, "all logic and evidence to the contrary, that it confirms the very gender definitions it would seem to problematize" (133). Straub notes that, late in the eighteenth century, the cross-dressed actress was "made to serve the dominant construction of separate spheres for men and women even as she would seem to trespass against that separation" (134).

Straub outlines the growing hostility of reviewers in order to emphasize the purposeful slipperiness of Charlotte Charke's autobiographical memoir, a slipperiness that allowed her to elude categorization and critical damnation. Straub writes, "Refusing to resolve the sexual ambiguities of her textual performance by giving her audience either a heterosexually defined romantic heroine or a 'monstrous' [homosexual] female husband, Charke fails to participate in what was becoming the dominant construction of feminine sexuality: the woman as oppositional, defining other to male sexuality" (135).

While a few transgressive women—like Charke, Mary Anne Talbot, and Loreta Janeta Velazquez—wrote about their own adventures and managed to use the ambiguity of their position as cross-dressed heroines to their own advantage,[6] the greater number had their stories co-opted by others. Theater reviewers' growing disapproval of the cross-dressed actresses' onstage exploits, which culminated in an outright condemnation of breeches parts by the early nineteenth century (Marsden 21; Straub 131), finds a parallel in the memoirists' progressive suppression of the threat posed by women who cross-dressed offstage. Concerning theatrical transvestism, Straub writes, "By the end of the century, discourse about the cross-dressed actress is both more condemnatory of the practice . . . and more insistent that female cross-dressing . . . was mere travesty, an obvious parody which left gender boundaries unquestioned" (127). Similarly, late-century biographical accounts of women who "passed" as men ultimately insisted upon the impersonators' feminine inadequacy for the role. While the majority of critics who study the cross-dressed woman of the eighteenth century tend to pass quickly over the details leading up to her eventual dismissal and disappearance, I should like to linger over them a bit, since the history of the domestication of the transgressive woman within the scandalous memoirs offers a useful understanding of how women's seemingly subversive actions have been, and can continue to be, made to serve the dominant ideology.

There are at least two types of narratives concerning early transvestites: those that depict a woman who adopts male clothing to gain access to a lover and those that trace the adventures of the woman who cross-dresses to pursue her own interests. The first of these parallel the earliest and most enduring records of female cross-dressers: the popular ballads of women warriors.

In her extensive examination of this form, *Warrior Women and Popular Balladry, 1650–1850*, Dianne Dugaw notes that the vast majority of the 120 female-warrior ballads that she catalogs tend "to be an interrelated and coherent body of songs . . . with a prototypical internal structure" (91). Highly conventionalized, the ballads' typical progression may be mapped, writes Dugaw, as follows:

(1) a courtship and the threatened or actual separation of the heroine and her beloved; (2) discourse (usually a debate) during which the woman proposes that she disguise herself in soldier or sailor garb and

accompany her man to war; (3) various trials the masquerading woman undergoes to prove both her love and her valor; (4) various tests of love imposed on the heroine's lover (and in many ballads on her parents as well); and (5) (usually) happy resolutions of these events. (*Warrior Women* 92–93)

Narratives of the lives of female soldiers and sailors that follow the outline of the female warrior ballads tend to have fewer internal contradictions and tensions than the works that claim to vie with the novel. For example, the chapbook account of *The Surprising Life and Adventures of Maria Knowles* (c. 1810) by William Fairbank, and its offshoot, *The Life and Extraordinary Adventures of Susanna Cope, The British Female Soldier*, contain many of the motifs of the female-warrior ballads and scarcely seem to suggest that they represent factual, rather than fantastic, women.[7] Indeed, after relating the adventures of Susanna Cope, the anonymous author of the second work transforms the prose account into verse, creating a new ballad with the same plot structure as many earlier songs.

The plots of both narratives follow Dugaw's schematic closely: in each account, the tall and robust heroine falls in love with Cliff, a sergeant of the guards, and elopes in male clothing to enlist in his regiment when it is ordered away to battle. In both texts, the heroine makes such a smart appearance as a military man that several women fall in love with her (mistaken love being one of the tests of the female warrior's "masculinity" in the ballads). An elderly rich widow narrowly escapes marrying the disguised heroine—the female soldier accepts the old woman's presents but jilts her at the altar. In the account of Maria Knowles, the heroine is discovered when she is wounded in the thigh during an engagement against the French; the later memoir of Susanna Cope places the wound in the breast. The wounding of sexual organs seems to be a commonplace of the biographical narratives—an insistence, perhaps, that biology will "out," that discovery is inevitable. Several accounts achieve a prurient titillation by offering descriptions of the physician's exploration of these organs before he realizes that his patient is a woman.[8] Finally, the heroine's masculine exploits come to an end with her donning female clothing and marrying her sergeant in a public ceremony that places her firmly back into the feminine domestic sphere.[9]

The heroines of these accounts engage in unusual adventures that are interesting without being threatening to the eighteenth-century status quo. Their plots center on heterosexual courtship, while their wounding and exposure return them to properly feminine roles at the end of the tales. Brief and often amusing, narratives of this type were circulated as chapbooks and made no claims to high literary merit. Not aspiring to reach beyond the lower classes, ballads and chapbooks stood little chance of obtaining a permanent place in many middle- and upper-class homes, nor were they apt to alter the ideology of female delicacy and domesticity taking hold there.

The more influential accounts of cross-dressed women were those that bore a relationship to the emerging novel. Appealing to a broad range of readers, these had enough of a stamp of individuality to suggest the living women who inspired the tales. Employing novelistic techniques while at the same time laying claim to biographical "truth" (which the early novels did as well, thereby rendering "history" and "story" nearly indistinguishable), these several histories of female wanderlust and valor were the ones most likely to reach an educated audience. Although they may have served to suggest to some readers that perhaps a few women were capable of physical exertion and bravery in male-dominated domains, particularly warfare, the very novelistic structures that the narrators utilized undercut their presentation of female heroism and sexual ambiguity. Hence in these more substantial accounts, as in the ballads and chapbooks, the threat to the emerging ideology of "separate spheres" posed by the cross-dressers, whose lives drew attention to the artificiality of male and female roles, was subtly contained.

From the beginning of the eighteenth century to the early part of the nineteenth, certain changes in form appear in the scandalous memoirs that mirror stylistic and thematic changes occurring in the novel. A gradual transformation of the composition and tastes of the reading audience around midcentury brought about, and was in turn influenced by, a new refinement in popular printed material. Jane Spencer, in *The Rise of the Woman Novelist*, writing about the "change[s] in the literary market" notes that, "As the eighteenth century advanced the 'feminine' qualities of delicacy and propriety became more generally important to bourgeois society" (76, 75). Dianne Dugaw draws attention to the influence of Samuel Richardson in extending upper-class norms of female delicacy to middle- and lower-class characters: "Articulating a new concern with working- and middle-class women, Richardson's novels imagine for them aspirations to a genteel virtue closely connected to the task of holding sexuality in check. They prescribe and map a world of female delicacy and bodily constraint generalized to include servants, at least upwardly mobile ones like Pamela" ("Rambling Female Sailors" 184). Nancy Armstrong, in *Desire and Domestic Fiction,* turns Spencer's and Dugaw's arguments around, insisting that fictional representations of the domestic woman, such as Richardson's, did not so much record the actions of a creature already existent as they wrote that creature into being. She says, "[T]he domestic novel antedated—was indeed necessarily antecedent to—the way of life it represented" (9).

By rewriting the transgressive woman as a novelistic heroine, then, rather than the female champion of the ballads, the memoirist offered her to a leisured middle- to upper-class audience rather than a laboring lower-class one.[10] By matching the appeal of their female protagonists to the tastes and values of their audience, these writers also ensured that the tastes and values of their audience would be properly shaped by the examples of their heroines. Domesticating their cross-dressed central figure—offering the transgressive woman's life in a way that allowed it, in some measure, to conform to and uphold prevailing norms—meant wrenching her story into the one acceptable feminine form: the courtship and marriage plot.

The need to rewrite the female transvestite's life story increased in intensity over time. Nancy Armstrong argues that the definition of masculinity as worldly and public that emerged at midcentury developed in opposition to the increasingly rigid definition of femininity as inherently domestic and private. If masculine identity depended on the oppositional structuring of gender, then, as Kristina Straub insists, the cross-dresser's ambiguity needed to be erased. Thus, while earlier narratives of women's cross-dressing tended to assume that the female warrior could combine traits of masculinity with those of femininity, later works, like later theater reviews and later novels, establish far clearer boundaries between masculine and feminine abilities and conduct.

Texts concerned with female cross-dressing that appeared from the early to the mid-eighteenth century were not particularly self-conscious about the contradictions they presented. In his *General History of the Robberies and Murders of the Most Notorious Pyrates* (1724), for example, Daniel Defoe offers a matter-of-fact description of the swashbuckling lives of Mary Read and Anne Bonny, two female pirates. In reporting on the fierce fighting spirit that predominated in these two women, Defoe avoids any mention of how they should have behaved. In his sketch of Mary Read, for instance, Defoe writes, without further comment, "growing bold and strong, and having also a roving Mind, she enter'd herself on board a Man of War" (154). He notes, again without undercutting, "in Times of Action, no Person amongst them [the ship's crew] was more resolute, or ready to board or undertake any Thing that was hazardous, than she [Mary Read] and *Anne Bonny*" (156).

The plot of Defoe's narrative centers on courtship: both women were clearly heterosexual, having lovers on board ship. Anne Bonny became a female sailor in the first place because she eloped to go to sea with her lover, Rackam, the captain of the pirate vessel. Mary Read was publicly married to a fellow sailor and, after his death, fell in love with another shipmate on whose behalf she fought a duel. Unlike later writers who would emphasize them, Defoe does not draw attention to any contradictions between Read's "feminine" fears about her lover's safety and her "masculine" efforts to ensure that safety by killing her paramour's opponent: "she fought him at Sword and Pistol, and killed him upon the Spot. It is true, she had fought before . . . but now it was altogether in her Lover's Cause, she stood as it were betwixt him and Death, as if she could not live without him" (158). While it is apparent that Defoe does not display authorial discomfort over his heroine's behavior, it is equally true that the cross-dressed women in *A General History of the Pyrates* do not have any dangerous aspirations after "gentlemanly" status. Like the heroines of the female warrior ballads, Mary Read and Anne Bonny remain lower class, heterosexual, and explicable.

So, too, does Christian Davies in *The Life and Adventures of Mrs. Christian Davies, Commonly Called Mother Ross* (1740), attributed to Defoe but more likely the production of a hack writer.[11] In this narrative, Davies is depicted as the "good wife," enlisting in the army to search for a husband she knows to have been forcibly taken into the service. The 1742 abridgment, by one J. Wilson, "formerly a Surgeon in the Army," is prefaced with a character sketch of Davies that highlights her conjugal fidelity:

What can be a greater Proof of the sincerest Affection for her Husband, than leaving her native Country, crossing the Seas, and going through all the Fatigues and Hazards of a military Life in search of him? After she has found him, how inseparably does she attend him wherever his Duty calls him, and expose herself to a thousand Dangers merely to be near his Person! How immoderately does she lament his Death, and even prejudice her own Health and endanger her Life by indulging an excessive Grief on that occasion! (*The British Heroine* i)

The author of this prefatory character analysis—J. Peter Obrian—emphasizes heterosexual love in order to de-emphasize Davies' female transvestism. By mixing praise of her bravery with his commendations of her motherly and wifely attachments, Obrian "feminizes" Davies' masculine pursuits:

> The most lively Descriptions our Novels and Romances give us of great and virtuous Ladies, are but a faint Resemblance of this extraordinary Woman, who was in reality all that Fancy and Fiction have attributed to others. . . . She was a brave Soldier, a tender Mother, an affectionate Wife, a true Lover of her Country, and a Pattern of Patience under a continued Series of Misfortunes. In short, she was an Honour to the fair Sex, and highly worthy their Imitation. (*The British Heroine* ii)

Like many later writers, this male chronicler works hard to fit the transgressive woman's life into a novelistic framework. Unlike the later commentators, Obrian betrays no uneasiness over his juxtaposition of "brave Soldier" with "tender Mother" and "affectionate Wife." These roles, which would appear discordant to later commentators, perhaps did not seem so completely at odds during the first half of the eighteenth century, when an oppositional model of gender was not as firmly established and when lower-class women were not expected to have the delicacy and refinement of their betters.[12]

As in the case of Mary Read and Anne Bonny, both Davies' lower-class status and heterosexuality are emphasized by her biographer. When a young cadet resents her presence among the officers and comments against "making mean people familiar," Davies, dressed in male clothing, steals the affections of the gentleman's mistress away from him by promising to marry her (*Life and Adventures* 119–20). The cadet, discovering Davies' sex, merely "laughed heartily" and said, "I am glad I have not a more dangerous rival; come Kit, I'll give you and your husband a bottle and bird for dinner" (121). The initial disruption of gender roles in this anecdote is resolved by its comic closure; the financially strapped and publicly married female soldier is depicted as a laughable rival for a gentleman—she possesses no power to alter his class snobbery, thwart his desires, or replace him in romance with other women.

Stories of Davies' discovery and discharge further reduce the threat of her masculine performance. After the trepanning of her fractured skull and subsequent exposure of her breasts to the surgeon, Davies' cross-dressed career is ended. She remains in the camp as a sutler, aiding her first husband and then, after his death, wedding another soldier. Twice widowed, Davies returns to England to do as many warrior women did—beg a pension from the nobility. Davies' swaggering masculinity, while perhaps no joke to her peers, is a source of amusement to the aristocracy she petitions: when she engages in fisticuffs with another soldier, "the quality . . . returning from court . . . stopped their chariots to be spectators of the fray" and several were entertained enough to throw money into the street (*Life and Adventures* 175).

Since neither Davies herself nor her narrative make any claims to gentility, her cross-dressing remains at the level of comedy. Aligning itself with the still less-than-reputable early novel, the account of Davies' life offers a great deal of lower-class humor. In one instance, when Davies' landlord attempts to raise her rent, she "treated him with all the opprobrious terms . . . [she] could think of." Davies boasts of her abilities in swearing: "and though I say it myself, there are very few, if any, of the academy of Billingsgate, was a greater proficient in the piscatory salutations. I hope my readers will not attribute this to me as a piece of vanity, when they reflect that quite through this long account of myself, I have all along guarded against that weakness, and only related pure matters of fact" (*Life and Adventures* 181). When the same troublesome landlord brings a carpenter to cut down her trees, Davies "secured . . . [her] husband, that he might not have an assault sworn against him . . . and went out . . . with a resolution, if possible, to provoke him [her landlord] to strike . . . [her] first, and in such case, to belabour him to some purpose" (181). She ends up pummeling both rascals—the landlord and his carpenter—until she "was quite spent with thrashing [them]" (182). Within this episode, Davies' exaggerated male posturings have the potential to destabilize oppositional gender categories by showing up the performative, constructed nature of masculinity. Straub writes that such "performances in drag . . . call into question whether *anybody's* masculine postures are successful" (141). Several elements here combine, however, to diffuse Davies' threat: the mention of Davies' husband normalizes her sexuality, while the discussion of the dispute shows it to concern the home, Davies' "natural" sphere. Given the presence of the husband and the domestic setting, the altercation itself remains at the level of Punch-and-Judy comedy.

Undignified as a man, Davies is rendered inelegant as a woman. Her biographer does not allow the reader to take her seriously: when Davies gives over the masculine for the feminine, she is infantilized. After one noble benefactress gives her a cast-off hoop petticoat, Davies finds that "it requires as much dexterity to exercise as a musket" and wearing it made her "fancy . . . [herself] in a go-cart, used for children when they begin first to feel their legs" (185). She manages the hoop so awkwardly as she walks down the street as to bring upon herself the laughter of several nearby apprentices. From being the valiant soldier, Davies becomes "the sport of boys" (*Life and Adventures* 185).

Christian Davies' cross-dressing confirmed male power through her pretensions to it;[13] her exploits, rendered as lower class and comic, remained only a flatteringly exaggerated imitation of masculine authority. By midcentury, however, the cross-dressers' chroniclers were taking the transgressive women's lives more seriously. If *The Life and Adventures of Mrs. Christian Davies* relied on stories like that about Davies entertaining a group of gentlemen by vomiting on a dandy in order to "spread ruin and desolation over one side of his clothes; the colour of which changed to a dismal hue, and all the glory of the glittering lace sunk oppressed by an inundation of indigested wine" (169), later accounts of cross-dressed women eschewed vulgarity and lewdness in order to fit themselves to a more genteel audience. Like the novelist, who was gaining respectability as the century progressed, these writers aspired upward.

From the mid–eighteenth century onward, the biographers of female cross-dressers employed rhetorical strategies to domesticate the transgressive woman by making her deviations and "unnatural" behaviors appear as outgrowths of her "natural" feminine impulses. Such domestication, a staple of the more expensively printed accounts of transvestite heroines, gradually became a convention even of the chapbook renderings, indicating the trickling downward of upper-class mores for women. While the techniques used by chroniclers to domesticate female soldiers, sailors, or rogues went a long way toward making these figures palatable and edifying to a broad range of readers, they also fractured the narratives. Not only did the novelistic retooling of the heroine's life dilute the power of these works to make an ideological impact, they also reduced the clarity and therefore the longevity of the texts. Many aspects of these women's lives did not fit the traditional courtship/marriage plot of the novel; to force their narratives into those molds distorted the details of the stories these women had to tell. Several works, most notable among them the late-century *Female Review* by Herman Mann, are rendered nearly incoherent by their authors' desires to present a traditionally "feminine" female warrior. If incoherence, in locating the place of potential disruption of the structure of gender, makes these texts interesting for twentieth-century critics, it also contributed to their disappearance after their initial circulation.

The fissure in a text brought about when the robust activity and labor of the cross-dresser's life is crammed into the domestic plot is apparent as early as 1750 in the account of *The Female Soldier; Or, The Surprising Life and Adventures of Hannah Snell.* In her introduction to the work, Dianne Dugaw notes the "fascinating and tellingly incongruent texture" of the text:

> One discerns two not always congruous strains in Walker's rendition of Snell's adventures: on the one hand, a natively intrepid heroine and adventure-packed story in the style of lower-class street ballads, and on the other, a narrative voice from a very different context shaping and trying to make sense of this character and her life. . . . The narrator's reading identifies her in novelistic and sentimental terms. . . .
>
> Speaking to the novel-reading—as opposed to the ballad-singing— public, *The Female Soldier* brings to Snell's lower-class story the codes and expectations of a different audience. (Introduction vii, viii–ix)[14]

The anonymous author of *The Female Soldier* emphasizes that, though dressed as a man, Snell is still very much a woman. Enlisting to search for the husband who abandoned her, Snell reveals through her endeavors that "there are no Bounds to be set either to Love, Jealousy or Hatred, in the fe-male Mind" (7). When she finds that her husband has been executed, Snell is still the virtuous wife who "grieved at his cruel and untimely Fate" (26). Although serving both as a soldier and a sailor, according to the narrator, Snell is prey to all the "Disorders, Terrors and Distractions" (20) of "one of the tender Sex, who are afraid of Shaddows, and shudders at the Pressage of a Dream" (15). And, notwithstanding she is hardy enough to receive five hundred lashes without a whimper (8), to [wo]man the pump when her vessel takes on water during a severe storm (13), and to extract shot from her groin herself after she is wounded in battle (16), Snell is at the same time so delicate that "her Ears and her Eyes were often affected with the disagreeable Sound of horrible Oaths, and many lewd Actions and Gestures [of the men] . . . which however disagreeable it might ap-pear to her, yet she was forced to make a Virtue of Necessity, by openly conforming herself to those rude, indiscreet, and unwomanly Actions, which she silently dissavoured and contemned" (17). Snell is, in other words, despite her disguise and brave actions, "a Woman, whose mould is tender, delicate and unable to endure Fatigues, and who is terrified at the Name of Dangers" (34).

In passage after passage throughout the memoir, the narrator works diligently to maintain gender boundaries. While reporting several acts of martial valor by the female soldier, what the author finds most significant in Snell's life are the "many Inconveniences she had overcome, and the Difficulties she had surmounted, in preserving her Virtue untainted in the midst of so many vicious and prophane Actions . . . and that she had . . . come off Conqueress . . . unsullied and undefiled by any of these Temptations wherewith she had been assaulted" (21). As Dugaw notes, "the ethos of the newly emergent Richardsonian novel . . . ultimately informs *The Female Soldier*" (Introduction ix). The narrator ends by asserting that Snell's are "Virtues infinitely surpassing the Adventures and Virtues of our romantick *Pamella*. . . . This is a real *Pamella*" (41).

Extolling Snell's chastity serves as a way of glossing over the troublesome features of her life—her desire for adventure, her concern to receive her soldier's pay and "to get hold of all the Money she could before her Sex was discovered" (38), and her possibly erotic exploits with her own sex. In one instance, the author, rather than explaining what ensues when Hannah Snell "endeavoured to try if she could not act the Lover as well as the Soldier . . . [and] effected this her Amour so as to obtain the young Woman's Consent to marry her" (28), abruptly begins to applaud Snell's virtue in sleeping beside several male comrades at arms without forfeiting her chastity (28–29). By shifting the emphasis to Snell's preservation of her chastity against a crew of British tars eager "to satiate their brutish Appetites" (17), the author avoids the issue of same-sex desire and, to a certain extent, successfully domesticates the female soldier. Setting the account of Snell's life above "the fictitious and fabulous Stories of a *Pamella*" (40), the narrator can present Snell's heroism as merely an instance of commonplace feminine virtue occurring in an exceptional setting: "Here is the real *Pamella* to be found, who in the midst of thousands of the Martial Gentry, preserved her Chastity by the most virtuous Stratagems that could be devised" (40–41).

The late-eighteenth-century text by the American Herman Mann, *The Female Review: Life of Deborah Sampson, The Female Soldier in the War of the Revolution*, strains even harder to avoid dwelling on the unsavory aspects of the life of the warrior heroine. Explicitly acknowledging the appeal of fiction, Mann asserts his own effort to present a better-than-novelistic heroine: "I readily yield the palm of style to the rapturous and melting expressions of the novelist: But I must vie with him in one respect:—What he has painted in *embryo*, I have represented in *expansion*" (42). To render Sampson appealing to the class of reader who could afford a subscription to his work,[15] Mann endows his female warrior with strongly feminine traits, reporting, for example, that only "with extreme *modesty* and trembling *diffidence*" did Deborah Sampson reluctantly consent to "take a public *Review* of the most material circumstances and events of her life" (39).

Throughout the text, the language Mann uses to describe Sampson, "our fair Soldier" (155), ill accords with her five-foot-seven, masculine, thick-waisted appearance (134): at one point, for example, he refers to her as a "half adorable object of love" (161). In other instances, Mann writes, "she might, like Flora, have graced the damask rose. . . . a nymph, scarcely past her teens! . . . a young *female*, who might, doubtless, have shone conspicuous with others of her sex in their domestic sphere" (136–37, 206). Mann, more strongly than earlier authors of "scandalous memoirs," continuously expresses a desire to reconcile transgressive female behavior with normative femininity.

Mann is hampered in his effort to sanitize his account of Deborah Sampson by one inconvenient fact: she, unlike the other transvestites mentioned so far, did not cross-dress to pursue a lover or husband. Sampson adopted male clothing to satisfy a desire to travel and learn about the world, "swerv[ing] from . . . [her] sex's sphere for the sake of acquiring a little useful acquisition" (112). This desire to obtain some of the freedoms offered only to men renders Sampson truly transgressive and forces Mann to dwell upon trifling elements of her femininity to make her narrative more mainstream.[16] He notes, for example, that Sampson spins and sews her own suit of male clothes: "Ye sprightly Fair, what is there in your domestic department, that necessity, ingenuity and resolution cannot accomplish?" (116). Mann also emphasizes Sampson's frailty, insisting that it is difficult for her to counterfeit the man: "She, doubtless, had awkward gestures on her first assuming the garb of the man; and without doubt, more awkward feelings. . . . Perhaps, exclusive of other irregularities, we must announce the commencement of such an enterprise a great presumption in a *female*, on account of the inadequateness of her nature" (129, 134–35).

Although they revised the cross-dresser's story to render it less notorious, biographers could not domesticate every detail of her narrative. What they couldn't domesticate, however, they condemned. By discouraging female imitation of the transvestite's more daring escapades, male chroniclers used her deviations from the norms of proper feminine behavior to establish more firmly what those boundaries for the "weaker" sex were. Every biographer stressed that the exploits of the cross-dressed woman whose life he recounted were exceptional and could not be reenacted by the majority of women. The preface to the first edition of *The Life and Adventures of Mrs. Christian Davies*, for example, cautions that the "masculine air and behaviour" that Davies acquired in the camp, "however excusable in her, would hardly be so in any other of her sex" (xv). *The Female Soldier; Or, The Surprising Life and Adventures of Hannah Snell* begins by noting that "if Heroism, Fortitude, and a Soul equal to all the glorious Acts of War and Conquest, are Things so rare, and so much admired among Men; how much rarer, and consequently how much more are they to be admired among Women?" (2).

Perhaps because Deborah Sampson was not firmly attached to a lover or husband, Mann's *Female Review* must offer, not one or two reminders of the extraordinary nature of the female life it records, but dozens. Mann begins his dedication by insisting that *The Female Review* was written "not with intentions to encourage the like *paradigm* of FEMALE ENTER-PRISE." He repeats this warning again in the body of the narrative: "I cannot desire you [female readers] to adopt the example of our Heroine, should the like occasion again offer.... Whilst most females must recoil at the commencement of an undertaking of this nature, few can have resolution to attempt a second trial" (119–20). Continually throughout the text, Mann's authorial asides patronize his female readers, clearly separating them from his heroine:

> Suspicious ... that the FEMALE REVIEW would be a subject as *delicate*, especially for the Ladies, as it is *different* from their pursuits; I have studiously endeavored to meliorate every circumstance, that might seem too much tinctured with the rougher, masculine virtues....
>
> I shall here notice a heroic deed of this gallantress; which, while it deserves the applause of every patriot and veteran, must chill the blood of the tender and sensible female.
>
> ... Yet, where is the fair one, who could again hazard it! Methinks I see the crimson cheek of the female turning pallid, her vigorous limbs relaxing and tottering in the rehearsal of this eventful scene. (42, 149–50, 152)

Mann positively insists on separate spheres for male and female activity:

> Thus, Females, whilst you see the avidity of a maid in her teens confronting dangers and made a veteran example in *war*, you need only half the assiduity in your proper, *domestic sphere*, to render your charms completely irresistible....
>
> The reader keeps in view, I suppose, that all *female* courage is not jeoparded in this manner. I am perfectly enraptured with those females, who exhibit the most refined sensibility and skill in their sweet *domestic round*, and who can show a group of *well bred* boys and girls. (183, 204)

At the very end of the text, Mann becomes ridiculously offensive in his assertion of masculine superiority: describing Sampson being worsted at wrestling, Mann writes, "Let this be a memento [sic] to Columbia's daughters; that they may beware of too violent scuffles with our sex. We are athletic, haughty and unconquerable. Besides, your dislocated limbs are a piteous sight!" (235). Clearly, the author of *The Female Review* is determined to prevent the dashing adventures of his female soldier from blurring the distinctions between male and female abilities and roles; Herman Mann has no desire to alter the status quo.

In fact, Mann is far more anxious than earlier eighteenth-century chroniclers to condemn the female cross-dresser's "imposition on the masculine character" (194) and her "breach in female delicacy" (237), while at the same time he works to make her masquerade explicable in feminine terms. Mann's text, unlike the accounts of the female pirates, of Christian Davies, or even of Hannah Snell, shows a consciousness of the contradictions posed by the transvestite woman. By insisting on the temporary nature of Sampson's disguise—motivated by patriotism, her martial desires must naturally vanish with the end of the war—and using her own words to position her in the home, Mann reduces her threat: "I cannot learn, she has the least wish to usurp the prerogatives of our sex. For, she has often said, that nothing appears more beautiful in the *domestic round,* than when the husband takes the lead, with discretion, and is followed by his consort, with an amiable acquiescence" (250).

Again, perhaps because her economic status does not admit of any other way for her to obtain a steady and adequate income, Sampson is finally submerged in marriage and traditional domesticity. Mann seems eager to note of his robust heroine that "she exhibits, perhaps, an unusual degree of contentment, with an honest farmer, and three endearing children, confined to a homely cot, and a hard-earned little farm" (250).

Confining Sampson to this homely fireside is narratively difficult; like other female warriors, her life story continually threatens to cross the boundaries established for her sex, boundaries that became firmer and more important to all classes of women as the eighteenth century neared its close. Hélène Cixous and Catherine Clément write in *The Newly Born Woman,* "deviants . . . all occupy challenging positions foreseen by the social bodies, challenging functions within the scope of all cultures. That doesn't change the structures, however. On the contrary, it makes them comfortable" (155). Both the challenge to the ideology of gender difference and the comfort of narrative accommodation to that ideology are apparent in the biographical accounts of eighteenth-century cross-dressed women.

1. Dianne Dugaw catalogs more than 120 separate female warrior ballads—see "The Female Warrior Heroine in Anglo-American Popular Balladry." Cross-dressing captured the public imagination in the eighteenth century: along with the ballads, accounts crop up in pamphlets, memoirs, newspapers, and novels. British and American fictions that contain a prominent cross-dressed female character include Mary Davys's *The Accomplished Rake* (1727), John Cleland's *Fanny Hill* (1748–1749), Elizabeth Inchbald's *A Simple Story* (1791), the anonymous *The History of Constantius and Pulchera* (1794), Charles Brockden Brown's *Ormond* (1799), Maria Edgeworth's *Belinda* (1801), and Frances Burney's *The Wanderer* (1814). In the theater, the popularity of transvestite roles for actresses during the Restoration and eighteenth century also attests to the cross-dresser's early appeal. (See Pat Rogers.)

Although she was as often condemned as applauded in the eighteenth century, the cross-dresser was frequently discussed; by the nineteenth century, however, her narrative was marginalized. While Ellen Clayton would entitle her work *Female Warriors: Memorials of Female Valour and Heroism, from the Mythological Ages to the Present Era*, the more typical titles of collections that contain accounts of female soldiers and sailors indicate the progressive decline in status of the warrior heroine: *Kirby's Wonderful and Eccentric Museum; or, Magazine of Remarkable Characters; including all the Curiosities of Nature and Art, from the Remotest Period to the Present Time* (1803–1820); James Caulfield's *Portraits, Memoirs, and Characters, of Remarkable Persons* (1819–1820); Thomas Carter's *Curiosities of War and Military Studies* (1860); John Ashton's *Eighteenth Century Waifs* (1887); and Dowie's *Women Adventurers* (1893). While the cross-dressed heroine didn't disappear entirely, she became a ghostly figure haunting a few pages of obscure works. (For a fuller discussion of her treatment in the nineteenth century, see Julie Wheelwright's "Amazons and Military Maids.")

2. The temporary form of cross-dressing—transvestite costume at masquerades—was popular with all stations of men and women (see Castle 46–47, 63–64, and Ribeiro). With regard to more permanent forms of cross-dressing, however, class becomes one (but by no means the only) factor that distinguishes the transvestism of men from that of women. The best-known cross-dressed men were from the ranks of the upper classes—examples include the Chevalier D'Eon, Edward Hyde, and some members of the notorious molly clubs. By contrast, nearly all of the female cross-dressers whose lives were recorded were members of the lower classes. Commenting on the frequent appearance and popularity of the "unconventional woman" in the eighteenth century, Ménie Muriel Dowie notes, "Rarely . . . was she of the better class" (xviii). For discussions of male cross-dressing during the period, see Peter Ackroyd; Randolph Trumbach's "The Birth of the Queen"; Marjorie Garber, especially pages 259–66; and Gary Kates.

3. The word *transvestite*, in the aftermath of Havelock Ellis's *Studies in the Psychology of Sex*, today generally refers to individuals who find erotic stimulation in wearing the clothes of the opposite gender and who may have a psychosexual compulsion to do so. I am not using the word in this sense, since eighteenth-century female cross-dressing was more often than not undertaken primarily for economic and social, rather than sexual, reasons. In instances where homoerotic unions occurred,

eighteenth-century understandings of homosexuality were different from our modern conceptions of lesbianism (see Trumbach's "London's Sapphists"). Throughout this essay, then, I use the terms *transvestism* and *cross-dressing* interchangeably to mean this earlier type of passing as the opposite sex. The terms would find their closest twentieth-century equivalent in what Ellis refers to as "pseudo-transvestism" in which the "cross-dressing is adopted, not out of psychic compulsion but from convenience or interest or occupational grounds" (14).

4. Thomas Laqueur traces this polarization of gender as it gradually surfaces in the medical treatises of the period. Laqueur argues that "the old model, in which men and women were arrayed according to their degree of metaphysical perfection, their vital heat, along an axis whose telos was male, gave way by the late eighteenth century to a new model of radical dimorphism, of biological divergence. An anatomy and physiology of incommensurability replaced a metaphysics of hierarchy in the representation of woman in relation to man" (5–6). In short, Laqueur concludes, "the female body came to be understood no longer as a lesser version of the male's (a one-sex model) but as its incommensurable opposite (a two-sex model)" (viii). The stability of this system of representation depended upon, and continues to depend upon, maintaining a visible line of demarcation between men and women.

5. Jean Marsden addresses this temporal shift as well. Examining the reasons why late-century actress Dorothy Jordan aroused the ire of critics like Leigh Hunt through her success in breeches roles, Marsden writes, "The disappearance of the cross-dressed woman in popular culture can be seen as part of a new understanding of gender as comprising two distinct and immutable sexes. . . . To the late eighteenth and early nineteenth century, the specter of androgyny undermined a social system that featured extreme polarization of the sexes, thus calling into question the gender differentiation on which that system was based" (23).

6. In "The Politics of 'Passing' in the Eighteenth Century," I argue that the tantalizing ambiguities left unexplained in the autobiographies of cross-dressed women may be purposeful—by refusing to submit herself to clear gender categorization, the writer allocates to herself free discursive space.

7. Although the chapbooks are not dated, it is fairly clear that the account of Susanna Cope is an abridgment of the fuller and more detailed *Surprising Life and Adventures of Maria Knowles*. For example, while the Cope chapbook ends with the marriage of heroine and hero, the Knowles chapbook includes the description of Cliff's death from yellow fever and his widow's return to England.

Dugaw also asserts that the Cope chapbook is a later version of the Knowles account: see *Warrior Women* 185–87.

8. Cathy Davidson emphasizes that, "Since the crossdressed picara retains her power only as long as its inauthentic basis is not revealed either literally or figuratively, the novels often flirt, almost pornographically, with the threat of exposure" (181).

9. "The devotees of love—those who went in search of or with a husband or lover—were sometimes remarried in an elaborate ceremony that not only reunited the couple but reaffirmed their appropriate roles" (Wheelwright, *Amazons and Military Maids* 89).

10. While early accounts of female cross-dressers tend to appear in chapbooks, later volumes were often published handsomely by subscription. Walker, for example,

published both a cheap 46–page unillustrated octavo and an expensive 187–page illustrated novelistic version of the life of Hannah Snell (Dugaw, Introduction v). Herman Mann's *The Female Review* was one of a few early American works published by subscription (Davidson 26–27, 265 n. 17).

11. Defoe's recent biographer, Paula Backscheider, acknowledges the difficulty of offering a definitive canon (xiv). She does not include *The Life and Adventures of Mrs. Christian Davies* in her bibliography of works by Defoe.

12. In "Balladry's Female Warriors," Dianne Dugaw offers several examples of women who ride, box, and fight duels to prove that "the age in which the ballads flourished not only recognized in but expected of women the same physical toughness and energy we find in the female warrior" (3).

13. Writing about *Women and Fashion*, Caroline Evans and Minna Thornton state, "In masculine fantasy, the sexually aggressive lesbian figure makes the same gesture as the sexually aggressive man, confirming his power in her pretensions to it" (86). See also Lynne Friedli's remarks in "Passing Women": "The 'exceptional' women merely reinforced the distance between the roles of men and women normally, and the adoption of masculinity in *clearly defined circumstances* can be seen to confirm the value of being male" (243).

14. Dugaw repeats these assertions, in a somewhat different form, as she analyzes the decline of the warrior-heroine tradition in her article "Rambling Female Sailors": "Walker's account veneers this gritty 'truth,' imagining Snell in the sentimental terms of upper-class literary tradition. . . . The timorous 'tenderness,' the socially marked 'femininity' of these literary types stands at odds with the facts of Snell's rambunctious story" (184). In this article and in her study "'Wild Beasts' and 'Excellent Friends,'" Dugaw dwells upon the fact that "An increasingly commanding concept of female delicacy pulled against and ultimately put an end to the conventions and convictions which made possible the celebrated sailing and soldiering of these cross-dressing women" ("Rambling Female Sailors" 193). But, with the exception of her discussion of *The Female Soldier*, Dugaw doesn't trace the relationship between these narratives and the early novel.

15. "[R]arely were [American] publishers able to find an adequate number of subscribers for novels, and only four early novels were published bound with subscription lists." Mann's *Female Review* was one of these (Davidson 265 n. 17).

16. Lynne Friedli notes that the inclusion of "quotations" from the heroine "provides a plural reading"—Sampson's voice, which "challenges the restrictions of the female sphere," is contradicted by the narrator's efforts at containment (see "Passing Women" 243, and "Women Who Dressed as Men" 27).

WORKS CITED

Ackroyd, Peter. *Dressing Up—Transvestism and Drag: The History of an Obsession.* New York: Simon and Schuster, 1979.

Armstrong, Nancy. *Desire and Domestic Fiction: A Political History of the Novel.* New York: Oxford UP, 1987.

Ashton, John. *Eighteenth Century Waifs: Essays on Social Life and Biography of the Eighteenth Century.* London: Hurst and Blackett, 1887.

Backscheider, Paula R. *Daniel Defoe: His Life.* Baltimore: Johns Hopkins UP, 1989.

Brown, Charles Brockden. *Ormond.* 1799. Ed. Ernest Marchand. New York: Hafner, 1937.

Burney, Frances. *The Wanderer; or, Female Difficulties.* 1814. Ed. Margaret Anne Doody, Robert L. Mack, and Peter Sabor. New York: Oxford UP, 1991.

Butler, Judith. *Gender Trouble: Feminism and the Subversion of Identity.* New York: Routledge, 1990.

Carter, Thomas. *Curiosities of War and Military Studies: Anecdotal, Descriptive, and Statistical.* London: Groombridge and Sons, 1860.

Castle, Terry. *Masquerade and Civilization: The Carnivalesque in Eighteenth-Century English Culture and Fiction.* Stanford: Stanford UP, 1986.

Caulfield, James. *Portraits, Memoirs, and Characters, of Remarkable Persons, from the Revolution in 1688 to the End of the Reign of George II.* 4 vols. London: T. H. Whiteley, 1819–1820.

Charke, Charlotte. *A Narrative of the Life of Mrs. Charlotte Charke.* 1755. Ed. Leonard R. N. Ashley. Gainesville: Scholars' Facsimiles and Reprints, 1969.

Cixous, Hélène, and Catherine Clément. *The Newly Born Woman.* Trans. Betsy Wing. Minneapolis: U of Minnesota P, 1986.

Clayton, Ellen C. *Female Warriors: Memorials of Female Valour and Heroism, from the Mythological Ages to the Present Era.* 2 vols. London: Tinsley Brothers, 1879.

Cleland, John. *Fanny Hill; or, Memoirs of a Woman of Pleasure.* 1748–1749. Ed. Peter Wagner. New York: Penguin, 1985.

Craft-Fairchild, Catherine. "The Politics of 'Passing' in the Eighteenth Century: Sexy Ghosts and Scandalous Memoirs." American Society for Eighteenth-Century Studies Conf. Omni Charleston Place Hotel, Charleston, S.C. 12 March 1994.

Davidson, Cathy N. *Revolution and the Word: The Rise of the Novel in America.* New York: Oxford UP, 1986.

Davys, Mary. *The Accomplished Rake; or, Modern Fine Gentleman.* 1727. *Four Before Richardson: Selected English Novels, 1720–1727.* Ed. William H. McBurney. Lincoln: U of Nebraska P, 1963. 233–373.

Defoe, Daniel. *A General History of the Robberies and Murders of the Most Notorious Pyrates.* 1724. Ed. Manuel Schonhorn. London: J. M. Dent, 1972.

———. *The Life and Adventures of Mrs. Christian Davies, Commonly Called Mother Ross.* 1740. Ed. Sir John Fortescue. London: Peter Davies, 1928.

Dowie, Ménie Muriel, ed. *Women Adventurers: The Lives of Madame Velazquez, Hannah Snell, Mary Anne Talbot, and Mrs. Christian Davies.* The Adventure Ser. 15. London: T. Fisher Unwin, 1893.

Dugaw, Dianne. "Balladry's Female Warriors: Women, Warfare, and Disguise in the Eighteenth Century." *Eighteenth-Century Life* 9.2 (1985): 1–20.

———. "The Female Warrior Heroine in Anglo-American Popular Balladry." Diss. U of California–Los Angeles, 1982.

———. Introduction. *The Female Soldier.* 1750. Los Angeles: William Andrews Clark Memorial Library, 1989. v–xiii.

———. "'Rambling Female Sailors': The Rise and Fall of the Seafaring Heroine." *International Journal of Maritime History* 4.1 (1992): 179–94.

————. *Warrior Women and Popular Balladry, 1650–1850.* Cambridge: Cambridge UP, 1989.

————. "'Wild Beasts' and 'Excellent Friends': Gender, Class and the Female Warrior, 1750–1830." *Jack Tar in History: Essays in the History of Maritime Life and Labour.* Ed. Colin Howell and Richard J. Twomey. Fredericton, New Brunswick: Acadiensis, 1991. 132–42.

Edgeworth, Maria. *Belinda.* 1801. Ed. Kathryn J. Kirkpatrick. New York: Oxford UP, 1994.

Ellis, Havelock. "Eonism." *Studies in the Psychology of Sex.* Vol. 7. Philadelphia: F. A. Davis, 1928. 1–110.

Epstein, Julia, and Kristina Straub, eds. *Body Guards: The Cultural Politics of Gender Ambiguity.* New York: Routledge, 1991.

Evans, Caroline, and Minna Thornton. *Women and Fashion: A New Look.* London: Quartet, 1989.

Fairbank, William. *The Surprising Life and Adventures of Maria Knowles.* Newcastle: M. Angus and Son, n.d.

The Female Soldier; Or, The Surprising Life and Adventures of Hannah Snell. 1750. Los Angeles: William Andrews Clark Memorial Library, 1989.

Friedli, Lynne. "'Passing Women'—A Study of Gender Boundaries in the Eighteenth Century." *Sexual Underworlds of the Enlightenment.* Ed. G. S. Rousseau and Roy Porter. Chapel Hill: U of North Carolina P, 1988. 234–60.

————. "Women Who Dressed as Men." *Trouble and Strife* 6 (1985): 25–29.

Garber, Marjorie. *Vested Interests: Cross-Dressing and Cultural Anxiety.* New York: Routledge, 1992; New York: HarperCollins, 1993.

The History of Constantius and Pulchera, or Constancy Rewarded: An American Novel. Boston: n.p., 1794.

Inchbald, Elizabeth. *A Simple Story.* 1791. Ed. J. M. S. Tompkins. Introd. Jane Spencer. New York: Oxford UP, 1988.

Kates, Gary. "D'Eon Returns to France: Gender and Power in 1777." *Body Guards: The Cultural Politics of Gender Ambiguity.* Ed. Julia Epstein and Kristina Straub. New York: Routledge, 1991. 167–94.

Kirby's Wonderful and Eccentric Museum; or, Magazine of Remarkable Characters; including all the Curiosities of Nature and Art, from the Remotest Period to the Present Time. 6 vols. London: R. S. Kirby, 1803–1820.

Laqueur, Thomas. *Making Sex: Body and Gender from the Greeks to Freud.* Cambridge: Harvard UP, 1990.

The Life and Extraordinary Adventures of Susanna Cope, The British Female Soldier. London: J. Pitts, n.d.

Mann, Herman. *The Female Review: Life of Deborah Sampson, The Female Soldier in the War of the Revolution.* 1797. Ed. John Adams Vinton. Boston: J. K. Wiggin and Wm. Parsons Lunt, 1866. New York: Arno, 1972.

Marsden, Jean I. "Modesty Unshackled: Dorothy Jordan and the Dangers of Cross-Dressing." *Studies in Eighteenth-Century Culture* 22 (1992): 21–35.

Nussbaum, Felicity. *The Autobiographical Subject: Gender and Ideology in Eighteenth-Century England.* Baltimore: Johns Hopkins UP, 1989.

Ribeiro, Aileen. *The Dress Worn at Masquerades in England, 1730 to 1790, and Its Relation to Fancy Dress in Portraiture.* New York: Garland, 1984.

Rogers, Pat. "The Breeches Part." *Sexuality in Eighteenth-Century Britain.* Ed. Paul-Gabriel Boucé. Manchester: Manchester UP; Totowa, N.J.: Barnes and Noble, 1982. 244–58.

Spencer, Jane. *The Rise of the Woman Novelist: From Aphra Behn to Jane Austen.* Oxford: Basil Blackwell, 1986.

Straub, Kristina. *Sexual Suspects: Eighteenth-Century Players and Sexual Ideology.* Princeton: Princeton UP, 1992.

Trumbach, Randolph. "The Birth of the Queen: Sodomy and the Emergence of Gender Equality in Modern Culture, 1660–1750." *Hidden from History: Reclaiming the Gay and Lesbian Past.* Ed. Martin Bauml Duberman, Martha Vicinus, and George Chauncey Jr. New York: New American Library, 1989. 129–40.

———. "London's Sapphists: From Three Sexes to Four Genders in the Making of Modern Culture." *Body Guards: The Cultural Politics of Gender Ambiguity.* Ed. Julia Epstein and Kristina Straub. New York: Routledge, 1991. 112–41.

Wheelwright, Julie. "'Amazons and Military Maids': An Examination of Female Military Heroines in British Literature and the Changing Construction of Gender." *Women's Studies International Forum* 10.5 (1987): 489–502.

———. *Amazons and Military Maids: Women Who Dressed as Men in the Pursuit of Life, Liberty and Happiness.* London: Pandora, 1989.

Wilson, J. *The British Heroine: or, An Abridgment of the Life and Adventures of Mrs. Christian Davies, Commonly Call'd Mother Ross.* London: T. Cooper, 1742.

Imagining Justice
Gender and Juridical Space in the Gothic Novel

Kathryn Temple

My dear E——
It is the peculiar exemption, and, I may say, advantage, of the Female sex, to
be relieved from all those cares and anxieties of public life, which begin with our
earliest age, and end not, but with the close of our existence. You will be never
called upon to take a part in those awful responsibilities, to which the juror, the
magistrate, or the legislator, are constantly liable; and even in those acts, relating
to which the laws have laid down positive enactments, if you are not protected by
the law itself from feeling the evils of your own imprudence, you have a father, a
brother, or a husband, to assist, advise, or control you. To you, therefore, a know-
ledge of the laws and constitution of your country may not be so indispensably
requisite; and you may pass through life, often without inconvenience, and gener-
ally without reproach, if you are ignorant of the institutions under which you live.
—*Sir John Eardley-Wilmot*, An Abridgment of
Blackstone's Commentaries on the Laws of England

Gender, the Gothic, and Juridical Space

John Eardley-Wilmot's public letter to the privatized "E" imagines an impenetrable barrier between his daughter's domestic concerns
and the Gothicized "awful" responsibilities associated with law.[1] As he
tells his daughter, he wishes not to train her in law but to "adorn your
mind with useful knowledge . . . as will eventually render you a cheerful

companion"(3). Underscoring the distance between the domestic world of the "cheerful companion" and the institutional world of the law by naming "E" not at all in a project dedicated to her, Eardley-Wilmot draws on the Gothic lexicon of "anxiety," "awe," and death ("the close of our existence") to elaborate his version of separate spheres ideology.[2]

In placing his abridgment of William Blackstone's great Enlightenment text in a Gothic setting, Eardley-Wilmot chose a genre oppositional to Blackstone's intent. In 1765 Blackstone had represented the *Commentaries* as replacing Gothic constructions of the law with a coherent and integrated model or "map" based on reason (1: 35).[3] Blackstone imagined law in a new way, as accessible to a much greater range of people.[4] As Blackstone enthused in his oft-quoted discussion of the problems accompanying legal fictions: "We inherit an old Gothic castle, erected in the days of chivalry, but fitted up for a modern inhabitant. The moated ramparts, the embattled towers, and the trophied halls, are magnificent and venerable, but useless. The inferior apartments, now converted into rooms of convenience, are cheerful and commodious, though their approaches are winding and difficult" (3: 268). Eardley-Wilmot—writing for "the use and advance of female education" rather than for the audience of "gentlemen" Blackstone imagines—seizes Blackstone's spatial metaphor and realizes its potential for constructing the relationship between law and women. Emphasizing the winding and difficult nature of the barrier between "E" and the enlightened space of the law, Eardley-Wilmot distances and protects her from the "anxiety" associated with entry into courtrooms and legislatures by providing her with an array of fathers, brothers, and husbands to "assist, advise," and somewhat more ominously "control" her.

Eardley-Wilmot's imaginative reconstruction of Blackstone's *Commentaries* exposes the collision between gender and the Enlightenment construction of law implicit in Blackstone's work. But the *Abridgment*'s self-conscious novelistic signposting also reveals a representational bond between the law and the Gothic novel. For as Eardley-Wilmot's Gothicization of law suggests, the Gothic aesthetic provides a particularly powerful discursive arena for contests over women's relationship to law. What Robert Miles calls the "ideological business of the Gothic aesthetic" (40) turns out to include the particularized "business" of the gendering of law.

Like the Gothic novelists I discuss below, both Blackstone's *Commentaries* and Eardley-Wilmot's *Abridgment* offer readers fictionalized versions of the law, constructions that themselves attempt to redistribute the tensions surrounding women's role in Enlightenment forms of government. Reading Eardley-Wilmot, one might assume a legal status—never actually found in black letter law—for the "peculiar exemption" he claimed for his daughter. Such a status, however, is difficult to find in the sources lawyers and judges relied upon. Although Frederic William Maitland and Frederick Pollock reference the ancient legal doctrine that "a woman can never be outlawed for a woman is never in law" (482), they mark the doctrine as an oddity. The statement serves more as an early example of the intersection between spatial metaphors and gender than as an assertion of legal principle. Even the authoritative Blackstone's assertion that women were excused from jury service "by defect of sex" was contradicted by his successor Robert Chambers, who argued that rules removing women from public life are "strange doctrines" (1: 264). As J. H. Baker explains in his authoritative history of English law, "There were doubts in later times about the exercise of public functions by women, though the doubts arose from the rarity of its occurrence rather than from abstract legal principles" (530). Indeed, Pollock and Maitland unequivocally state that no law "makes any general statement as to the position of women" (482).

Recent historical research has confirmed not only that positive law failed to exclude women, but also that women actively participated in legal events much more frequently than stereotypical notions of women's place might suggest. As Jennifer Kermode and Garthine Walker point out in their collection of essays on women and law covering the period from 1550 to 1750, "[W]omen were far from being passive victims or bystanders, and it is no longer adequate to discuss their experiences with the simple paradigm of active/passive or public/private. We find women moving easily from one to the other, indeed exploiting the paradoxes between the two as they constructed stories which utilized or manipulated convention for their own ends." Given the complexity of women's actual historical status and activity, the "peculiar exemption" Eardley-Wilmot assumes for his daughter cannot derive from observations of practice, nor from custom, precedent, or statute. Instead, his work takes its place as one among many cultural imaginings about women, law, and public life.

In the search for the origins of women's exclusion from public life, including the public life of the law, literary historians have turned to the novel for evidence of the cultural construction of separate spheres ideology. Nancy Armstrong connects the exclusion from public life to the novelistic construction of women as powerful domestic subjects, while John Zomchick asserts that both legal and fictional narratives "construct a normative female subject with a sexuality dedicated to the production of domestic tranquility" ("Penetration" 535). Like Armstrong and Zomchick,

I see fiction—along with many other texts—as instrumental to producing the public-private split. Typically, novels imagine women as domestic and privatized subjects who operate outside the law. While novelistic characters like Samuel Richardson's Clarissa could write wills privately, they could not imagine themselves entering the public space of courtrooms. By the end of the century, a woman's willingness to "go to law" marked her as the sort of lower-class "man-woman" that Frances Burney creates in Evelina's notorious grandmother, Mme. Duval.

That Mary Wollstonecraft and Ann Radcliffe—despite their ideological differences—turn almost simultaneously to problems of law, space, and gender in their 1797 novels, *The Wrongs of Woman* and *The Italian*, points both to the power of domesticity and to certain underinvestigated moments of resistance to that power.[5] Through the Gothic, women writers avoided a direct onslaught on the monolithically imagined legal system yet commented obliquely on their exclusion.[6] John Bender, who argues in *Imagining the Penitentiary* that fiction can inspire new and different modes of thinking, notes that the noun "novella" originally meant an "addition to the legal code" (11). Bender quotes David E. Wellbery on the ways fiction can help us imagine change: "Literary texts often represent innovative and problematic codifications from which reduced codes are later abstracted in such a way that they can generate subsequent materializations" (*Imagining the Penitentiary* 257, n. 17). As they engaged with the tensions surrounding the struggle to "generate" such materializations, women authors as different as Wollstonecraft and Radcliffe used fiction to imagine alternatives to the arbitrary exclusion assumed in the dominant culture.

Given Blackstone's and Eardley-Wilmot's use of Gothic space in plotting law, how are we to read similar moments in *The Wrongs of Woman* and *The Italian?* In all four authors' works, sites of struggle over the gendered juridical are literalized as legal spaces that invite, deny, or resist entry to variously gendered bodies. In Wollstonecraft's *The Wrongs of Woman* the use of the discourse of sensibility—a discourse tied here to the female body not only through the senses but also through references to maternity—ultimately results in Maria's expulsion from juridical culture. In Radcliffe's *The Italian*, an "equivocal being" makes its way through the Gothic frame of the Inquisitorial hallways to an enclosed Enlightenment version of the English legal system.[7] These novels, both published at the historically charged moment after the excesses of the French Revolution and before domesticity's universal hegemony, play out concerns about women's exclusion from law across what many critics have seen as a radical/conservative divide. But the primary difference in their representations of the relationship between women and law lies not in the degree of change they desire or promote, but in the ways they struggle with the economy of body and discourse. As readings of Wollstonecraft's and Radcliffe's courtroom scenes demonstrate, successful discursive interventions tend to sacrifice bodily presence, while bodily entry exacts discursive sacrifices. A reading of the two texts together points to a gendered resistance to the Enlightenment propaganda of universal inclusion. Only after complex, even tortured, reworkings of the meanings of gender and entry do women manage to take their places in juridical space. Moreover, those who enter inevitably pay a price, losing either body or discourse as a result.

The Wrongs of Woman:
Sentimental Discourse and the Disappearing Body

As if speaking of Wollstonecraft, Bakhtin notes "the significance of legal-criminal categories in the novel, and the various ways they are used—as specific forms for uncovering and making private life public" (124). Throughout *The Wrongs of Woman,* Wollstonecraft consistently problematizes the boundaries between private and public as she narrates Maria's varying abilities to access public forums. Although it is not until the novel's conclusive courtroom scene that Maria's private problems are finally transformed into public ones, concerns about the relationships between private and public, "woman" and the institutional space of law, govern the work.

Wollstonecraft frames the novel as one that seeks to make women's private concerns public. Her preface proclaims that "the history ought rather to be considered, as of woman, than of an individual" (73). The novel begins with Maria's illegal incarceration in a private madhouse; much of the narrative concerns itself with her attempts to breach this illegal privatization through literal or literary escape. In addition to seeking physical escape, Maria pursues imaginative access to the public world—partly through reading, but also through writing letters to her child. The text within a text created by these maternal letters marks Wollstonecraft's conflation of sentimental discourse and the female body. The attachment of text to body implied by Maria's frequent references to childbearing, nursing, and bodily separation further creates a narrative situation that allows bodies of text to stand in for literalized bodies. Given these devices, it can be said that Wollstonecraft does more than simply "embody" the sentiments as she claims in her preface; she imagines sentiments both as bodies and as bodies of words.

The Wollstonecraft who wrote the *Vindication of the Rights of Woman* in 1792 might have argued that Maria's sentimentality confines her to a private female sphere, an area demarcated by the radical difference between individualizing sentiment and generalizing legality. Such a reading would have seen the novel as relying on a characterization of woman that plays into masculine stereotypes. Replacing the "manly" persona that informed the *Vindication of the Rights of Woman* with a heroine more sentimental and passionate, Wollstonecraft seems in *Wrongs of Woman* to be arguing that female sensibility is both inevitable (since it is derived from inevitable biological processes) and self-destructive.[8] In the final scenes of the novel, the access Maria gains to juridical space is vexed by bodily absence on the one hand and the inappropriate nature of her discursive strategies on the other. In these scenes, Wollstonecraft underscores the differences between a naturalized sentimental female discourse and legal discourse, leaving us in the end with what may seem on the surface to be a deeply frustrating and unsuccessful collision between sentimental individuality and the discursive generality the law requires.

The work's denouement occurs in a courtroom that Maria enters neither in an institutional sense—she has not actually been sued—nor in person. Oddly unattached to any spatial referents, the courtroom exists here solely as discourse; we experience the judge, lawyers, and Maria as pure speech. Only Godwin's editing puts Maria's body into this space; without his bracketed notation that "She therefore eagerly put herself forward instead of desiring to be absent," Maria would have appeared in the scene only as "paper" (195).

Disconcertingly, at the very moment when she has been given the opportunity to demonstrate a "manly" reliance on reason, Maria's "paper" self relies on sentimentality and insists on the importance of women's subjective experience over that of black-letter law. Maria's argument, in its form, affect, and details, purposefully rejects the legal system, calling "the subterfuges of the law . . . disgraceful" on a number of different levels (195). A detailed analysis of this rejection on only the simplest level—that of linguistic and disciplinary expectations—reveals a number of key refusals to play the juridical game. Although Maria notes that there are cases other than her own in which a woman should be allowed to separate from her husband, she does not enumerate them, thus both rejecting argument by precedent and refusing to generalize her own case. Her decision not to argue about "whether the duties of the state are reciprocal" performs as a refusal to engage in the abstractions typical of legal discourse, while her rejection of any authority other than God's indicates her intent to obviate worldly hierarchies. When she demands that she be allowed to "regulate her conduct . . . by her own sense of right" (197), she places herself outside the legal system rather than within it. In contrast to the novelistic lawyer's tendency toward the abstract language of equivocation, Maria's diction is absolute. She labels her husband's behavior "an insult upon humanity" and "an act of atrocity." She leaves him "forever" (196). Maria's discursive refusal to engage with the linguistic and disciplinary expectations of the legal world allows the judge to classify her not as "Woman" but as one particularly difficult, possibly mad woman. When juxtaposed to Maria's sentimental argument, the lawyer's and judge's discourses adhere to the expectations of juridical culture; they are abstract, alien and alienating, depersonalized, and authoritarian—all characteristics legal linguists associate with effective legal discourse.[9] Her oration rejects both the law and legal discourse; while seeming to demand a public meeting with the law, she refuses to speak its public language.

The inefficacy of Maria's courtroom argument seems to play itself out in the various forms of silencing inflicted on Maria. In the larger frame narrative, Wollstonecraft provides evidence of a metaphoric silencing. After the opposing counsel's argument, she writes that "a strong sense of injustice had silenced every motion . . . in Maria" (195). Moreover, the notes Godwin appends to the text predict a final silencing rather than any more successful outcome (201–4). One reads, "Divorced by her husband—Her love unfaithful—Pregnancy—Miscarriage—Suicide." The only opening Wollstonecraft leaves for Maria returns her once again to the body but takes away her discursive ability. After a suicide attempt, Maria's response to the sight of her rescued child is to first vomit, then recover. Such silencings imply that Wollstonecraft is unable to imagine a female juridical presence; she never allows an embodied Maria into the courtroom and substitutes for her instead an ineffective essentialized discourse incapable of intersecting with juridical expectations. The Maria we glimpse after the juridical scene is dead, dying, or silent; if re-embodied, she is still unvoiced.

But Wollstonecraft's complex, even tortured machinations need not be read only as signs of her pessimism. Instead, they can be seen as attempts to solve a problem articulated in twentieth-century studies of legal discourse. In his 1987 study of legal linguistics, Peter Goodrich posits that the law's resistance to legal change lies in its linguistic structure. He argues: "The legal subject has very little choice; the law endeavours to condemn its subjects to choose, at best, between joining the ranks of a society for which they are not in fact responsible or destroying themselves, rhetorically if not always literally, in the authentic pursuit of fundamental social change" (191). Goodrich sees this as the inescapable conundrum posed by the structure of legal discourse. In his pessimistic view, one has only two choices: accept exclusion or capitulate.

Wollstonecraft's novel attempts to deal with the question implied by Goodrich's conclusion: How might one avoid the linguistic trap he imagines? How might an author critique legal discourse without joining it? How might one be "inside" and "outside" simultaneously? In *Wrongs of Woman* Wollstonecraft struggles both to prevent her critique of juridical culture from being recontained within a stabilizing juridical discursive structure and to pursue social change without destroying the female "self" either rhetorically or literally. Her rejection of metaphorical destruction persists throughout the work; although the conclusions appended to the work suggest the possibility of Maria's death, the novel itself resists physical dissolution as a means to closure.

Given the problem Goodrich lays out, Maria's seemingly ineffective speech can be reread as a feminized juridical text that interrupts and disrupts official juridical language. Appearing between the lawyer's and judge's texts, it simultaneously undoes all of the didactic oppositions— "reason vs. sentiment, practical vs. aesthetic, public vs. private, the masculine vs. the feminine" that John Bender lists as characteristic of Enlightenment thinking ("New History" 5). The unruly refusal of the text's multiple conclusions to cohere, even the appended endings that suggest numerous possible tragedies, serve not as dire predictions but rather as mirrors of the chaotic disorder Maria instigates in her challenge to the orderly world of Enlightenment law. Maria's bifurcated self, the separation of her discourse from her body and the use of that discourse to gain entry into legal space, itself produces this disruption, offering us a female juridical subject who, far from dedicated to domestic tranquillity, instead dedicates herself to disturbing the monolithic tranquillity of the Enlightenment legal system. Maria's fragmented and unsatisfactory placement in that system points not to Wollstonecraft's implication in the system, but instead to the stress caused by confronting the disjunction between Enlightenment theory and practice.

The Italian: "Bursting" Voices, Equivocal Bodies

Radcliffe's *The Italian* encodes a more subtle but no less complex attempt to bring women into the exclusionary space of law.[10] Whereas in

Romance of the Forest she naturalizes an equality-based relationship between women and law, her position in *The Italian* is more critical. Using "equivocal beings" to stand in for women, Radcliffe refuses to cede legal space to masculinity, manipulating instead the same complex economy of body and discourse that we have seen operating in Wollstonecraft's *Maria*. Critics have often overlooked this version of Radcliffe's resistance to domesticity because they have tended to see her "mixed" or "disjunctive" characters as examples of a flawed aesthetic[11] or have attributed to her a totalizing conservatism. Coral Ann Howells offers an antidote to both the aesthetic and conservative arguments when she suggests that our aesthetic pleasure derives precisely from the moments when Radcliffe's conservatism breaks down. What she finds "ultimately seductive" in Radcliffe "are those moments of aberration, those eccentric moments which evade the constraints of conventional narrative and social order, lifting the veil to reveal other possibilities not contained within the story at all" (151).

Certain of Radcliffe's aberrations, those Claudia Johnson calls her "equivocal beings," suggest that we need not burden her with the essentialist view of gender that has been presumed to accompany her "conservatism." The works of Catharine Macaulay, Wollstonecraft, and Mary Hays, among others, document the late eighteenth-century resurgence of the view that gender was constructed. In these and other works, theories of social constructivism coexisted with essentialist theories, an indication not of confusion but of ideological stress. As Mary Poovey points out: "It is not surprising that at the end of the eighteenth century the debate about woman's proper place and her peculiar power intensified, for as the paternalistic system began to lose its hegemony, women sensed the imminent destruction of both their dependent status and their power. Their response, predictably, was a deeply divided one" (310). Late eighteenth-century radical authors display not a simple rejection of traditional gender categories, but an acceptance of the fluid and changeable nature of those categories. Despite her reputed seclusion, Radcliffe could not have avoided confronting such issues. As Hays points out in a dark attack on the inconsistency of male attitudes, women's rejection of conventionally gendered behavior extended far beyond feminist tracts, reaching even into the streets and impacting on both fashion and public behavior (189–91).

Of course, the standard reading of the novel argues that Radcliffe *reinforces* rather than attacks the separate spheres ideology. Recognizing that Ellena waits "anxiously" in a convent described as a "large family" (300), while almost all of the male characters participate in an alienating scene of law distanced historically and geographically from late eighteenth-century England to the Italian Inquisition, such a reading points out that Radcliffe reinscribes cultural stereotypes about women and law. On the surface both these scenes and the ultimate end of the novel may seem to support an interpretation of Radcliffe as promoter of female domesticity. Ellena partakes of and eventually produces domestic tranquillity, while the men in the novel participate in the juridical world, examining evidence, meting out judgments, and finally leveling violence against nonconformers. Indeed, at the novel's conclusion all of the characters, male and female, have joined Ellena in domestic harmony, and the juridical setting is imagined as a distant and "diabolical" locale. As Nancy Armstrong has argued so convincingly, middle-class and domestic subjectivity conjoin here; by the end of the eighteenth century, middle-class harmony exists in isolation from public institutions.

But, as Patricia Meyer Spacks points out in "Female Orders of Narrative," endings aren't everything. Reading endings in isolation—without contextualizing them in their larger text—can produce skewed results. Examining Radcliffe's novel-length disruption of categories—male and female, public and private, English and Italian—as carefully as her ending allows a new interpretation of both the novel and its conclusion. Such a reading reveals a Radcliffe resistant to separate spheres ideology, particularly as that ideology is played out in juridical culture. Particularly important to this reading is the ironic narrative frame Radcliffe provides in the prefatory materials, a frame at least as important as her somewhat formulaic ending. This frame, in which the assassin is confined to the church while parishioners deliver food from the apparently more public yet domestic world, conflates public and private, the law and domesticity. The fact that the assassin seeks "shelter" from the law in the church, the very church that comes to represent "law" in the novel, hopelessly confuses the observant English traveler. "Of what avail are your laws," he asks the Italian friar on page two of the novel, hoping that "public" law can somehow exert a controlling force on what he sees as corrupt church law. The friar's response calls the distinction itself into question. Answering "if we were to shew no mercy to such unfortunate persons, assassinations are so frequent, that our cities would be half depopulated," the friar provides a public purpose for the church's "private" law, revealing—no matter how ironically—that the two are interactive rather than distinct.

By creating a sort of mobius strip in which church law (initially "Italian") and public law (initially "English") become indistinguishable, Radcliffe suggests as well the inextricable entanglement of the English traveler with the supposedly foreign Italian system. That a private Italian confession, given in a dark wood closet covered with a black canopy by a penitent "concealed from observation," should become a public object for an English reader, and that this publicizing of a private crime should be an "extraordinary . . . departure from the law," raises immediate questions about the nature of public and private in relation to a "law" meant to keep private confessions private. That the novel itself elaborates the confession, obtained only through a "departure from the law," suggests the work's subversive intent (4).

Radcliffe's disruptive mode extends to her treatment of gender categories. As Spacks notes, both men and women in *The Italian* take on cross-gendered characteristics: "The plot pits traditionally female qualities of emotion and attachment (here embodied in Vivaldi as well as in women) against traditionally male ambition and force (exemplified by Vivaldi's mother as well as by male characters)." In *The Italian*, Radcliffe's deployment of gendered behavior works not so much to promote a generalized feminization of the culture but to question the essentialism that would designate certain behaviors as male and certain behaviors as female.

As if to bear out the preface's disruption of the conventional connections between institutions and gender, throughout the novel Radcliffe refuses to classify juridical activities as "male" or "female." While she codes the confessing assassin of the preface male, the next confessing assassin we meet, Vivaldi's mother, is coded female. The Marchesa, a "man-woman" described as alternatively passionate and patient who "loved her son, rather as being the last of two illustrious houses . . . than with the fondness of a mother" (7–8), unashamedly aspires to "lose the mother in the strict severity of the judge" (111). Meanwhile, the primary couple in the novel, Ellena and Vivaldi, seem to have switched eighteenth-century gender roles: Ellena demonstrates rationality, restraint, and a fine sense of "justice," while Vivaldi's "prevailing weakness" turns out to be a "feminine" "susceptibility which renders you especially liable to superstition" (397). Juridical agents, both just and unjust, are represented in male and female forms that refuse to adhere to any preconceived notions of gender. The evil abbess of volume 1 can no more be awakened to a sense of justice than can her binary opposite, the abate who relinquishes power to her precisely because of his "mildness of temper and gentleness of nature" (127). The novel's female emblem of justice, the abbess of Santa della Pieta, is "loved as a mother, rather than feared as a judge" (300). Throughout the novel, Radcliffe mixes genders and spheres, providing us with men-women who participate in the law as well as with "feminine" men who delight in domestic life.

Recognizing the porous nature of gender boundaries in *The Italian* allows us to reinterpret the relationship Radcliffe creates between female author-ity and male servitude, between "*Ann* Radcliffe" and the masculine storytellers in the novel. In his study, "English Fiction from Below," Bruce Robbins notes the pervasive use of servants as authorial mouthpieces and as "figures of the people's subordination" (x, 25). Radcliffe draws on both of these devices when she engages in a sort of narrative transvestism[12] by allowing her voice to emanate from a male who also represents a subordinated class. In the character of the subordinate servant Paulo, an accomplished storyteller who even in prison demands "a light, and a pen and ink" (366), Radcliffe provides us with a feminized persona in a male body that represents both author and woman. Paulo challenges the rigid boundaries between masculine and feminine to disrupt both domestic and public tranquillity.

Radcliffe prepares us for Paulo's role in an early scene in the novel, the descent into the vaults of Paluzzi. Now, as later when Vivaldi descends to the Inquisitorial prison, Paulo takes Ellena's place, like Ellena serving as a devoted and subordinate companion to Vivaldi (70). Individualized by his "exquisite adaptation of his gesture to his idea"—the characterization points to Radcliffe's model for the Gothic novelist—Paulo carries the as yet unlit torch as well as the secret to the novel's denouement. Unlike Ellena, however, Paulo has a voice, a voice established immediately as that of a storyteller. In an amusing parody of Gothic narrative technique, Paulo begins telling Vivaldi a story variously described as "odd," "wonderful," and "extraordinary" (71), adjectives also applied to Radcliffe's story in the prefatory frame. While Paulo and Vivaldi descend into the vaults at Paluzzi, Paulo draws his story out, and his "reader," Vivaldi, makes many of the objections that readers have always made when subjected to Gothic conventions. Like Radcliffe's novel—which the Italian frame narrator notes "is much too long to be related now; that would occupy a week; I have it in writing and will send you the volume"—Paulo's story is "too long," as Vivaldi says, "too big to rest within your brain." In the end, Vivaldi dismisses the story, remarking that he "could not feel an interest concerning strangers; for he had already perceived, that it could not afford him information connected with Ellena."

Paulo's story, of course, provides an essential clue to the mystery that drives the novel. Rather than "strangers," he discusses the very confessor who will destroy Schedoni. By the end of the novel Radcliffe has revealed time and again not only that servants know more than their impatient masters, but also that servants control the narrative. "All in good time," says a fisherman before telling Vivaldi of Ellena's kidnapping, while later a guide threatens to keep his story to himself, warning Schedoni, "I don't like to be snapped up so" (277). On a less literal level, Radcliffe demonstrates the narrative control servants exercise through her use of servant's faces to provide the essential evidence revealing both Schedoni's and Olivia's identities. But the parallel Radcliffe draws between Paulo and Gothic author, between Vivaldi and Gothic reader, is most obvious when Vivaldi notes, "You have dropt the thread of your story" (80), and Paulo replies with a discussion of the secrecy of the confessional and the impossibility of ever discovering exactly what a penitent may have said. The discussion directs the reader to Radcliffe, who in framing the novel as a confession has had to deal with such problems herself. In providing us with the confession Paulo cannot obtain, she links herself to him through the very fact of the narrative.

As authorial transvestite, Paulo ignores traditional gender traits. When Paulo and Vivaldi enter the prisons of the Inquisition, again in the absence of Ellena, Radcliffe emphasizes his lack of "noble fortitude," comparing it to Vivaldi's courage. Foregrounded here are Paulo's "innocence," "devotion," and "faithfulness," all qualities we might have associated with a more activated Ellena. Foregrounded as well by constant references to "my master" and "my servant" is the nature of their relationship, one based in the dominance of Vivaldi and the emotional subservience Paulo exhibits. Like Vivaldi's relationship with Ellena, the relationship with Paulo is founded on love rather than money. When offered money and freedom at the end of the novel, Paulo refuses both, asking "what use if I am not to stay with you?" (407).

Unlike Ellena, Paulo adheres to his "master." While Ellena is spirited away, eventually finding safety if not freedom in a "home-like" convent, Paulo aggressively pursues his master into upper-class salons as well as into the Inquisitorial prison. Though able to approach the centers of power because of his physically determined body, Paulo is also—because of his disempowered position—free to critique them. Rejecting the "awe" Eardley-Wilmot associates with the legal system, Paulo "despised alike [the judges'] reprehension, their thundering menaces, and their more artful exhibitions. . . . [H]e left his examiners in a state of astonishment at his rashness, and indignation of his honesty, such as they had, probably, never experienced before" (305).

Unlike Wollstonecraft's *Maria, The Italian* imagines a resistant legal subject who not only challenges public tranquillity but also cries "oh, happy day," on the last page of the work. By providing readers with an "equivocal being"—a feminized male servant able to challenge the law precisely because he speaks from a compromised position—Radcliffe implies a female subject capable of entering the juridical space denied Ellena. But Radcliffe's intervention, like Wollstonecraft's, shows the signs of struggle endemic to attacks on the ideological fissures in Enlightenment constructions of law. In remaking gender so as to press a male servant into service as Vivaldi's partner, Radcliffe replicates on the level of class what she attacks on the level of gender.

Moreover, Radcliffe's representation of Paulo's participation utilizes the same tortured economy of body and discourse found in Wollstonecraft's trial scene. While a lengthy discussion of Radcliffe's use of Blackstonian imagery is precluded here, Paulo's breaching of the Gothic "winding and difficult" entries into the Enlightened and rational space of the final trial reveals both a commitment to the ideals of Enlightenment law reminiscent of *Romance of the Forest* and a critique of its exclusionary practices.[13] Paulo's efforts to participate fully—both physically and discursively—result in one of the more painful "comic" scenes in the novel. Although sequestered from Vivaldi during their incarceration, Paulo appears suddenly at the moment of trial. Serving no apparent narrative purpose, his presence at the trial can only function symbolically. Rather than exhibiting the "anxiety" Eardley-Wilmot assumes, Paulo responds vigorously to the legal "space" represented by the Inquisitorial trial. On the night of Vivaldi's trial, we find Paulo "bursting forth" verbally, struggling with his guards, and sobbing hysterically for Vivaldi. When the Inquisitorial officials place "violent hands on him," Vivaldi offers up Paulo's voice in exchange for his presence. Thus ensues a three-page attempt to quiet Paulo's insistence on speaking "so loud, that every word I say shall ring in the ears of all those old black devils on the benches yonder" (358). Only after Paulo's "compliance" is obtained does the trial commence. Paulo then remains perfectly silent until the hearing is over—testimony himself to the sacrifice of voice for presence.

Radcliffe's narrative strategy allows her to avoid Goodrich's linguistic double bind. Making of Paulo a questionably gendered voice of dissent who nevertheless must trade voice for presence, Radcliffe pursues a physical entry into juridical culture at the expense of a discursive one. Unlike Goodrich's figures, who either "join the ranks" or "destroy themselves, rhetorically if not always literally" (191), Radcliffe's Paulo keeps his discursive distance, managing like Maria to suggest the possibility of a disruptive female presence even if at the expense of discursive presence.

Given Radcliffe's preoccupation with entry and voice, we can newly interpret the ending of her work as resistant to privatization despite the ways it suggests the contours of English domesticity. While the novel ends in an English-Italian garden, Paulo's celebration of "liberty" (a loaded word given the historical moment at which the novel was published) dominates the final scenes as he lays claim to both Ellena's and Vivaldi's private domain and to the world at large. "Here we are all abroad once more! All at liberty! And may run, if we will, straight forward, from one end of the earth to the other, and back again without being stopped" (414). Moving rapidly from the Inquisitorial prisons to their roofs, to the moon, sky, and sea, Paulo's final utopic vision gives him full physical and discursive access to both the public and the private; in refusing to comply with an economy in which body and voice are traded off against each other, he suggests an alternative to Enlightenment ways of obscuring juridical exclusion.

NOTES

Financial support for this project was provided in part by the National Endowment for the Humanities. My experiences in Mary Jacobus's 1995 NEH Summer Seminar, "Feminism and Enlightenment: Women Writers in the 1790s," and the careful readings offered by participants, especially Betsy Bolton, Catherine Burroughs, and Marie McAllister, enriched this project immeasurably. I would also like to thank Deborah Kaplan, Sue Lanser, and the members of the Folger Colloquium "Women in the Eighteenth Century" for their help and advice.

1. The Harvard Law School Library attributes this tract to Sir John Eardley-Wilmot, bart., 1783–1847, although the tract's title page claims as author merely "A Barrister at Law." The author of the tract, called to the bar in 1806, was almost certainly the son of John Eardley Wilmot (1750–1815) who added the extra hyphenated "Eardley" to the family name in 1812 and was himself the son of the respected eighteenth-century Lord Chief Justice Sir John Eardley Wilmot (1709–1792). For the life of the Lord Chief Justice, see John Wilmot's *Memoirs*. For the life of his son and a reference to his grandson, see Margery Weiner.

2. Eardley-Wilmot's position is complicated by his simultaneous feminization of law. Quoting Hooker, he begins his treatise for women with the words, "Of Law, no less can be acknowledged, than that her seat is the bosom of God, her voice the harmony of the world. . . . Both angels and men . . . yet all with uniform consent, admiring her as the mother of their Peace and Joy." Rather than associating female subjectivity with law, however, this trope draws on the idea—expounded by Blackstone as well as European legal theorists—that law itself had a "natural" fount in a supreme being. Though that

"fount" might be feminine, attempts to order its flow relied on the "perfection of reason" attributed to a patriarchal God. See Lieberman's discussion of Blackstone.

3. In his introduction, "On the Study of the Law," Blackstone urges his readers to "consider his course as a general map of the law, marking out the shape of the country, it's connexions and boundaries, it's greater divisions and principal cities" (1: 35). Lieberman's first chapter provides an interesting discussion of Blackstone's publishing history as well as a defense of his status as an Enlightenment thinker. For a book-length discussion of Blackstone, see Daniel J. Boorstin. For a deconstructive view of Blackstone's work, see Duncan Kennedy.

4. I do not mean to imply that Blackstone wrote for laborers and farm workers. He directed his work toward "gentlemen of independent estates and fortune, the most useful as well as considerable body of men in the nation" (1: 7). Nevertheless, the *Commentaries*, produced initially as a series of lectures for undergraduates at Oxford beginning in 1743, were meant to make legal knowledge available to nonspecialists and thus were the first step in the demystification of legal discourse.

5. See Poovey, Durant, and Howells for discussions of Radcliffe's conservatism. Claudia Johnson questions the usefulness of such categories in relationship to gender, arguing that "writers such as Radcliffe and Burney, who do not challenge conservative principles on the level of theory, nevertheless consistently tarnish the authority of tearful fathers, brothers, and sweethearts on the level of narrative" (17).

6. As Lieberman argues, the eighteenth-century legal system was never as monolithic as Blackstone—or for that matter some twentieth-century legal historians—have imagined it to be. The investment in *imagining* the legal system as monolithic increased in the mid-eighteenth century. As John Richetti has noted in his discussion of Jurgen Habermas, the emergence of the public sphere depended in part on a new understanding of law, one in which "the law is conceived of as an embodiment of permanent and universal norms rather than as an imposition by the sovereign for securing order and power" (115).

7. Although I presented the core of the arguments elaborated in this essay in conference paper form as early as the 1993 Modern Language Convention, prior to my reading of Claudia Johnson's wonderfully complex work in *Equivocal Beings* published in 1995, my subsequent reworking of this material owes much to her book, particularly to her chapter on gender and politics in *The Italian*. Following Johnson, I have adopted Wollstonecraft's term for nonspecifically gendered bodies (Johnson 11). Like Johnson, I have not adopted Wollstonecraft's homophobia.

8. Recent years have seen an explosion of critical arguments surrounding eighteenth-century depictions of the relationship between sensibility and gender. Critics like Terry Eagleton have argued that the feminized male characters typical of eighteenth-century novels of sensibility reveal a "feminization" of discourse and of later eighteenth-century culture. Eagleton sees this development purely from a male perspective: "Male hegemony was to be sweetened but not undermined; women were to be exalted but not emancipated. The recourse to the feminine was always problematical—for how could the public sphere of male discourse model itself upon values drawn from an essentially private realm?" (95). But the construction of male characters who display "female" characteristics like sensitivity and subordination may point to an author's refusal to naturalize gender traits or even to a far more complex au-

thorial desire to deploy categories for particular reasons. See Claudia Johnson for a complex, interesting, and different take on Wollstonecraft's deployment of the "manly" and the "sentimental."

9. For one of the few book-length linguistic analyses of law, see Peter Goodrich.

10. Although Claudia Johnson notes that Radcliffe's "biography provides no comparably direct polemical point of entry into the social and political scene of the 1790s" (15), her biography seems more suggestive to me. Radcliffe's husband trained in law and was a parliamentary reporter before becoming the editor of the *English Chronicle*, suggesting that he at least, if not Radcliffe herself, occupied an insider/outsider position in regard to the legal profession (Murray 16).

11. See Elizabeth Napier for this position.

12. See Madeleine Kahn for a detailed discussion of this phenomenon as practiced by male authors who assumed female voices in their novels.

13. For a detailed and interesting reading of the Enlightened nature of Radcliffe's Inquisitorial tribunal, see Johnson 132–33.

WORKS CITED

Armstrong, Nancy. *Desire and Domestic Fiction: A Political History of the Novel*. New York: Oxford UP, 1987.

Baker, J. H. *An Introduction to English Legal History*. London: Butterworths, 1990.

Bakhtin, M. M. *The Dialogic Imagination*. Austin: U of Texas P, 1981.

Bender, John. *Imagining the Penitentiary: Fiction and the Architecture of Mind in Eighteenth-Century England*. Chicago: U of Chicago P, 1987.

———. "A New History of the Enlightenment?" *Eighteenth-Century Life* 16.1 (1992): 1–20.

Black, Henry Campbell. *Black's Law Dictionary*. 4th ed. St. Paul, Minn.: West, 1968.

Blackstone, William. *Commentaries on the Laws of England: A Facsimile of the First Edition of 1765–1769*. Intro. Stanley N. Katz. Chicago: U of Chicago P, 1979.

Boorstin, Daniel J. *The Mysterious Science of the Law*. Cambridge: Harvard UP, 1941.

Chambers, Robert. *A Course of Lectures on the English Law: 1767–1773*. Ed. Thomas M. Curley. Vol. 1. Madison: U of Wisconsin P, 1986.

Durant, David. "Ann Radcliffe and the Conservative Gothic." *SEL: Studies in English Literature* 22 (1982): 519–30.

Eagleton, Terry. *The Rape of Clarissa*. Minneapolis: U of Minneapolis P, 1982.

Eardley-Wilmot, Sir John. *An Abridgment of Blackstone's Commentaries on the Laws of England, in A Series of Letters from a Father to his Daughter. Chiefly Intended for the Use and Advancement of Female Education*. London: John Hatchard and Son, 1822.

Goodrich, Peter. *Legal Discourse: Studies in Linguistics, Rhetoric and Legal Analysis*. London: Macmillan, 1987.

Hays, Mary. *Appeal to the Men of Great Britain in Behalf of the Women*. 1797. New York: Garland Reprints, 1974.

Howells, Coral Ann. "The Pleasure of the Woman's Text: Ann Radcliffe's Subtle Transgressions in *The Mysteries of Udolpho* and *The Italian*." *Gothic Fictions: Prohibition/Transgression*. Ed. Kenneth W. Graham. New York: AMS, 1989. 151–62.

Johnson, Claudia L. *Equivocal Beings: Politics, Gender, and Sentimentality in the 1790s.* Chicago: U of Chicago P, 1995.

Kahn, Madeleine. *Narrative Transvestism: Rhetoric and Gender in the Eighteenth-Century English Novel.* Ithaca: Cornell UP, 1991.

Kennedy, Duncan. "The Structure of Blackstone's Commentaries." *Buffalo Law Review* 28 (1974): 209–21.

Kermode, Jennifer, and Garthine Walker, eds. *Women, Crime and the Courts in Early Modern England.* Chapel Hill: U of North Carolina P, 1994.

Laws Respecting Women. 1777. Dobbs Ferry, N.Y.: Oceana, 1974.

Lieberman, David. *The Province of Legislation Determined: Legal Theory in Eighteenth-Century Britain.* Cambridge: Cambridge UP, 1989.

Maitland, Frederic William, and Frederick Pollock. *The History of English Law.* 2d ed. Cambridge: Cambridge UP, 1923.

Manchester, A. H. *A Modern Legal History of England and Wales 1750–1950.* London: Butterworths, 1980.

Miles, Robert. "The Gothic Aesthetic: The Gothic as Discourse." *The Eighteenth Century: Theory and Interpretation* 32.1 (1991): 39–57.

Murray, E. B. *Ann Radcliffe.* New York: Twayne, 1972.

Napier, Elizabeth. *The Failure of the Gothic: Problems of Disjunction in an Eighteenth-Century Literary Form.* Oxford: Clarendon, 1987.

Poovey, Mary. "Ideology and *The Mysteries of Udolpho.*" *Criticism* 21.4 (1979): 307–30.

Radcliffe, Ann. *The Italian.* London: Oxford UP, 1968.

Richardson, W. C. *A History of the Inns of Court.* Baton Rouge: Claitor's, 1975.

Richetti, John. "The Public Sphere and the Eighteenth-Century Novel: Social Criticism and Narrative Enactment." *Eighteenth-Century Life* 16.3 (1992): 114–29.

Robbins, Bruce. *The Servant's Hand: English Fiction from Below.* New York: Columbia UP, 1986.

Spacks, Patricia Meyer. "Female Orders of Narrative: *Clarissa* and *The Italian.*" *Rhetorics of Order / Ordering Rhetorics in English Neoclassical Literature.* Ed. J. Douglas Canfield and J. Paul Hunter. Newark: U of Delaware P, 1989. 158–72.

Weiner, Margery. *John Eardley-Wilmot: A Man of His Time.* 1966 Bedwell Lecture of the Edmonton Hundred Historical Society, Edmonton, Alberta. EHHS Occasional Papers (New Series) no. 20, 1971.

Wilmot, John. *Memoirs of the Life of the Right Honourable Sir John Eardley Wilmot, Knt. Late Lord Chief Justice of the Court of Common Pleas.* 2d ed. London: J. Nichols and Son, 1811.

Wollstonecraft, Mary. *Mary, A Fiction and The Wrongs of Woman.* Ed. Gary Kelly. London: Oxford UP, 1976.

———. *A Vindication of the Rights of Woman.* Ed. Carol H. Poston. 2d. ed. New York: Norton, 1988.

Zomchick, John. *Family and the Law in Eighteenth-Century Fiction: The Public Conscience in the Private Sphere.* Cambridge: Cambridge UP, 1993.

———. "'A Penetration which Nothing Can Deceive': Gender and Juridical Discourse in Some Eighteenth-Century Narratives." *SEL: Studies in English Literature* 29.3 (1989): 535–61.

2

Changing
the
Subject

Women "Off" the Market

Feminine Economies in Diderot's
La Religieuse and the Convent Novel

Irene Fizer

The nun is uneconomical—she has placed herself off the market. If the bride, according to Levi-Strauss's terms, assents with her vow to serve as the mediating commodity for economic exchange between men, the nun pronounces with her vow a dissent.[1] Ritually exchanged by her father to the church fathers as the intended bride of Christ, the nun throws the paternal economy into a different relief when she renounces her commodity status during this betrothal. In taking her vow, she repudiates her intended part in sexual and symbolic reproduction—the continuation of the father's bloodline, name, and property. Shedding her patronym, she assumes a feminine name within the enclosure of the convent. A paradox opens. The nun is directly subjugate to God the father and Christ the bridegroom and bounded by the institution of theological law. Yet the nun is no longer the property of her male kin and, as a result, the economy of homosocial exchange must forfeit its claim to her. Her new name severs her from the patrilineal family and binds her into a female kinship system of mothers and sisters. Once the nun is defined as a female subject who cannot be exchanged on the market, existing as she does without a proper name and within a house of women, she enters a different model of sexual economy.

The nun became visible in the eighteenth-century French and English novel when the question of her status was tied to a new inquiry about feminine sexuality. Propelled by the burgeoning of natural history, a classificatory system of sexual difference, and by the elaboration of the regulatory institution, the asylum and the prison, the novel began to delineate an interior within which a particular inquiry could be staged: do women have an autonomous sexuality among themselves?[2] This was an inquiry interested not by the mechanics of sexual reproduction, but rather by the techniques of sexual pleasure. The female body had otherwise stood as the inferior supplement, or the inverted simulacrum, to the male.[3] Inside the institution, in the absence of a phallic model, a different ordering of feminine sexuality was needed. Within eighteenth-century fiction the institution was increasingly imagined as a space where the sexes were segregated and barred from contact, rather than massed together. The sexual behavior of women among women became an issue of continual narrative speculation. Eighteenth-century novels, whether prurient or sentimental, such as Montesquieu's *Persian Letters* (1721), Defoe's *The Fortunate Mistress [Roxana]* (1724), Richardson's *Clarissa* (1747–1748), and Cleland's *Memoirs of a Woman of Pleasure [Fanny Hill]* (1748), all offered to view the brothel and the harem as paradigmatic enclosures of the female sex. The brothel and the harem were narrated not only as arenas of sexual exchange between women and their male clients but also, and more markedly, as sites where women operated within their own sexual economies. By definition, the brothel and the harem service the market; yet, they are always perceived to contain an interior economy that the narrative seeks to document—an off-market economy of sexual pleasure that the women share only with one another and which is not for sale. The convent, as an all-female cult of the deity, likewise became a site for Denis Diderot in *La Religieuse [The Nun]* (1760; published 1780–1783) that could potentially yield a new knowledge of feminine sexual pleasure. The convent is reconceived as a sacrilegious parallel to the harem and the brothel, a laboratory where the man of letters theorizes sexual difference by rationalizing the sexual pleasures of women. This project depends, however, upon a system of exchange. Either the nun has to make her body available to his view or give up to him her body of knowledge about the convent. The nature of this transaction between the woman inside and the outside speculator in *La Religieuse* is my concern here.

As a text, *La Religieuse* shifts on and off the market—mediating between private manuscript culture and the eighteenth-century print market. While orienting the philosopher's gaze to the convent, Diderot was also writing out of eighteenth-century convent pornography. As a house of virgins designed to repel voyeurism but which incorporates surveillance as a structural condition, the convent was primed for pornographic inscription. The libertine genesis for *La Religieuse* has been scrupulously documented by Georges May, as Diderot confirmed that he had read and owned in his library a copy of the cleric Jean Barrin's *Vénus dans le Cloître; ou, La Religieuse en Chemise [Venus in the Cloister; or, the Nun in her Smock]* (published in 1692, 1719, and 1746), the most notorious and widely translated of the convent pornography novels of the eighteenth century.[4] The conventions of this pornography—the nubile novice sexually initiated, flagellation scenes, the lesbian mother superior—directly inform *La Religieuse*. Indeed, it can be argued that Diderot can imagine the convent only in hypersexualized terms: the nuns in *La Religieuse* do little other than requite or sublimate their desires. (Later in the eighteenth century, such women novelists as Germaine de Stael will write a vastly different convent novel, by reimagining the politics of gender within the convent.)[5] Robert Darnton has recently documented the market for pornographic prints and texts in prerevolutionary France.[6] Pornography retains a clandestine wrapping, however, no matter how openly it is sold; by definition, it is a black-market commodity. *La Religieuse*, carrying the taint of a covert sexual economy, was banned on the market as a pornographic text. Banned in France in 1824 and 1826, it was again the issue of controversy when the French Ministry of Information banned Jacques Rivette's film version in 1968 (qtd. in Furbank 217–31). Within this narrative nexus that merges pornographic with rationalist discourse, something fundamental about the novel is revealed—its erasure of the purported distance between a black market and the market proper. These markets, and their respective discourses, always operate in tandem, or in collusion, within *La Religieuse*.

To the genre of convent pornography Diderot also made a critical revision: he restricts his narrative almost exclusively to the nuns within the convent walls. The pornographic predecessor texts dwell upon the grates, walls, and doors of the convent, as the routes of sexual interchange. The generating narrative principle is most often trespass—the transgressive sexual coupling not among the nuns themselves but between the nuns and the priests and laymen outside.[7] By contrast, Diderot's interest is mobilized by the sexual mysteries of the convent's interior. The three convents in *La Religieuse* are nearly sealed shut, standing as self-contained feminine institutions. The nuns, having renounced heterosexual relations, develop a range of erotic practices wholly autonomous of men. By virtue of its closed libidinal economy, the convent in *La Religieuse* becomes a site for sexual pleasures known to women alone. Or known to one woman: the narrator. She writes under no name, or between names, as her given name Marie-Suzanne Simonin has been annulled and she has repudiated the feminine name assigned to her in the convent, Sœur Sainte-Suzanne. Although the three convents in *La Religieuse* have virtually no contact with the outside, they do transact an economy among themselves: they trade Suzanne, bartering over her dowry price. As a commodity exchanged between the convents, Suzanne becomes knowledgeable about the workings of multiple feminine sexual economies. Her revelation of this knowledge defines the structure of *La Religieuse:* a transaction between a nun, off the market, and her male reader, from whom she seeks a small monetary recompense in return for her text.

La Religieuse stands as a memoir of convent life sent by Suzanne to a potential patron, the marquis of Croismare. Addressing herself to the marquis, whom she has never met but whose benevolent aid she hopes to inspire, she begins her memoir with an offer.[8] In exchange for revealing everything about herself, with childlike candor, she will ensure that the marquis will send her a favorable reply:

> La réponse de M. le marquis de Croismare, s'il m'en fait une, me fournira les premières lignes de ce récit. . . . Mais il n'est pas à présumer qu'il se détermine à changer mon sort sans savoir qui je suis, et c'est ce motif qui me résout à vaincre mon amour-propre et ma répugnance, en entreprenant ces Mémoires, où je peins une partie de mes malheurs, sans talent et sans art, avec la naiveté d'un enfant de mon âge et la franchise de mon caractère. (39)
>
> [The reply of the Marquis de Croismare, if indeed he does reply to me, will provide the first lines of this story. . . . But it can hardly be presumed that he will decide to change my lot without knowing who I am, and it is with this motive that I resolve to conquer my self-love and my repugnance, in undertaking these Memoirs, where I paint a part of my misfortunes, without art or skill, but with the naivete of a child of my age and with the frankness of my character. (11)][9]

Forced into the convent at a marriageable age, Suzanne writes of her years of unceasing struggle to leave, and the economic destitution in which she finds herself now that she has finally and surreptitiously fled. Her earlier attempt to leave the convent by legal means, through the aid of a lawyer, Monsieur Manouri, had failed; her suit for release was repeatedly denied. More pointedly, M. Manouri had written and published an indictment of the convent system, based upon Suzanne's testimonials, but this memoir—the male auditor's secondhand rendering of the nun's story—had equally failed to be of profit to Suzanne or to gain her release. Near the end of her own memoir, she makes a direct economic request to the marquis for a private position as a servant:

> "Monsieur, hâtez-vous de me secourir. Vous me direz, sans doute: 'Enseignez-moi ce que je puis faire pour vous.' Le voici: mon ambition n'est pas grande. Il me faudrait une place de femme de chambre ou de femme de charge, ou même de simple domestique, pourvu que je vécusse ignorée dans une campagne. . . . Les gages n'y feront rien; de la sécurité, du repos, du pain, et de l'eau. Soyez très assuré qu'on sera satisfait de mon service." (206–7)
>
> ["Monsieur, help me quickly. Doubtless you will say to me: 'Tell me what I can do for you.' This: I have no great ambition. I should like a place as a lady's maid or housekeeper, or even as an ordinary servant, provided I could live in retirement in the country. . . . Wages are of no importance; safety, rest, bread, and water. You may be sure that I would provide satisfactory work." (192)]

Suzanne writes her memoir as a virtual untouchable, a defrocked nun without any economic means or tradable skills. Her memoir is a poignant record of negotiation between the two economies within which she was exchanged—the market economy and the convent system. Within both, she lacks any currency. The memoir, through which she seeks to obtain a menial wage, is the one property that she can produce from out of the convent. With nothing but time on her hands, she can write a potentially limitless text on the subject of women among themselves.

To the marquis, Suzanne will confess all yet without knowing all that she is confessing. She offers him a tantalizing proposition. that she, as a young woman in her twenties, has always remained innocent even while being initiated into a corporeal knowledge by other women. She portrays herself as the mediator of this knowledge, never as its practitioner. Her passions were exaggerated by the invariability of her state, but she can describe only the symptoms of desire without explicating their cause. For the marquis she will document feminine sexual practices in the convent, yet she avows that he knows far more about this particular subject than she herself possibly could—for only men know what women do when alone together: "En vérité, je ne suis pas un homme, et je ne sais ce qu'on peut imaginer d'une femme et d'une autre femme, et moins encore une femme seule" (103); [In truth, I am not a man, and I do not know what one can imagine about a woman and another woman, still less about a woman alone (82)]. Suzanne offers the marquis, therefore, the position of the classifier of feminine sexuality within the convent.

By design, her memoir is suffused with minute details of sexual practices, yet it entirely lacks a technical vocabulary of sex. It is the marquis who will, potentially, categorize Suzanne's data into a sexual science and ascribe to it a system of classification, a technical nomenclature. Moreover, he will determine how Suzanne knows what she knows; he will become the convent's epistemologist. The various sexual practices Suzanne describes have long been referenced in the critical literature as mysticism, sadism, and lesbianism.[10] Such terms, however, already presuppose a semantic coding of the novel. I name the convents in *La Religieuse* as schools of feminine sexual pleasures, that is, of mystical ecstasy (Longchamp under Madame de Moni), sublimation (Longchamp under Soeur Sainte-Christine), and homoerotic pleasure (Sainte-Eutrope under Madame ✳✳✳), because I cannot elude this narrative condition. I am proposing a language that can mediate in between Suzanne and the marquis, in between her description and his anticipated prescription. None of these terms, nor any approximations, appear in *La Religieuse;* they can only be imposed upon the novel from without. Every reader of *La Religieuse* falls into Suzanne's narrative exchange, for every reader is compelled to name what she will only ever describe. The memoir exists solely within this system of exchange: Suzanne offers the memoir to the marquis as a virginal commodity that he must agree to sexually encode.

To retain his novel within the cloister, Diderot constructs an irreconcilable narrative structure—as a male author writing a fictional memoir of convent life under the pseudonym of a nun for a male reader. On the one hand, *La Religieuse* offers to document sexual practices that are accessible only to women. On the other, the novel seeks to maintain that the knowledge of feminine sexuality is attainable only by men. That is, the nun may feel her own pleasure, but she knows nothing about it. However, this irreconciliation cannot be localized in Suzanne alone, or limited to her narrative prudery or hypocrisy. It is the crux of the novelist's project within the convent, as other readers have argued.[11] There, he gains an ultimate pleasure in mastery for he is displacing God as the nun's omniscient voyeur. He has a privileged access, penetrating both the hard architecture of the convent's walls and the soft architecture of the nun's habit. Yet, while his interpretative expertise is predicated upon the nun's sexual ignorance, he is bound to speak through her voice because his own authority cannot legitimately extend into the convent's interior. The nun, as an eighteenth-century woman inaccessible to the speculations of reason, must be incorporated into the Enlightenment project. She must be made to speak within its framing terms. (The metatextual history of *La Religieuse* is a remarkable mirror of this textual structure. Diderot wrote *La Religieuse* as a fake memoir of a nun that circulated among a group of his close friends. The memoir was intended to lure the real marquis de Croismare back to Paris, for the marquis had previously, but unsuccessfully, attempted to aid an actual nun seeking release from her vows. Circulated privately in 1760 as the "true" history of Suzanne, until the ruse was revealed, the text was later published by Diderot as a serial from 1781–1783, and posthumously published as a novel in 1796. For Diderot, therefore, *La Religieuse* originated as a closet text for a select group of readers, initiating them into the secrets of the cloister, rather than for print. Moreover, the nun's text served as the mediating conduit for an exchange between two men.)[12] Although structured as a narrative that continually denies the authority of the nun's text, *La Religieuse* also produces an alternate reading: that Suzanne knows of what she writes. Only she can verify the evidence obtained in the convent—and it is this possibility that the novel cannot fully contain. As Luce Irigaray writes: "But men insist that women can say nothing of their pleasure. Thereby they confess the limit of their own knowledge" (97). The convent—standing as the potential repository of a sexual knowledge exchanged only between women—always marks a representation of that limit.

In a critical rereading of Levi-Strauss's system of exchange, Irigaray muses about an alternate economic order among women. "The society we know, our own culture, is based upon the exchange of women. Without the exchange of women, we are told, we would fall back into the anarchy (?) of the natural world, the randomness (?) of the animal kingdom. The passage into the social order, into the symbolic order, into order as such, is assured by the fact that men, or groups of men, circulate women among themselves" (170). She ponders the potential workings of an off-market exchange: women would invest in their own pleasure from which, as commodities in an economy that valuates only the phallic standard, they are otherwise alienated. "For without the exploitation of women, what would become of the social order? What modifications would it undergo if women left behind their condition as commodities—subject to being produced, consumed, valorized, circulated, and so on, by men alone—and took part in elaborating and carrying out exchanges? Not by reproducing, by copying, the 'phallocratic' models that have the force of law today, but by socializing in a different way the relation to nature, matter, the body, language, and desire" (191). Reinscribing the terms of exchange when postulating this feminine economy, Irigaray leaves standing the notion of a market economy. She is admittedly idealizing a market without exploitation and loss, only equal exchange and mutual profit. Yet within this utopian scenario, she is asking: Do women remain the conduits of exchange between dominant and marginal markets? What is the extent to which women would copy and reinstitute phallocratic law as a regulator of their new economic order? What is the extent to which the structure of the dominant economy could be altered once women deliberately moved outside it? Theorized as a site where women have explicitly "left behind their condition as commodities," the convent puts Irigaray's hypothetical order into play.

Born a bastard daughter, Suzanne was never deemed eligible for exchange on the marriage market. She reveals her out-of-wedlock birth to the marquis on the memoir's opening page, albeit through a series of rhetorical questions that enable her to profess her innocence. Later, she confirms in the memoir that she was born illegitimate; thus, in writing the following sentences, she already knows to what she is confessing: "Vous l'avouerai-je, monsieur? Quelques discours échappés à mon père dans sa colère, car il était violent, quelques circonstances rassemblées à differents intervalles, des mots de voisins . . . m'en ont fait soupçonner une raison qui les excuserait un peu. Peut-être mon père avait-il quelque incertitude sur ma naissance; peut-être rappelais-je à ma mère une faute qu'elle avait commise; et l'ingratitude d'un homme qu'elle avait trop écouté; que sais-je?" (40); [Shall I admit it, my lord? Some observations that escaped my father in his wrath (for he was a violent-tempered man), some incidents collected at different times, the whispers of the neighbors . . . all made me suspect a reason. . . . Perhaps my father was not quite certain about my birth; maybe I recalled to my mother a fault she had committed, or the ingratitude of a man to whom she had too gladly listened. How can I know? (12)].

"Que sais-je?"—How can I know?—in this reflexive question Suzanne's narrative position is distilled. She testifies to her ignorance about the unsanctioned sexuality of women, a sexuality that takes place off the market and beyond the father's view. Yet, at the same time, she is describing that she was born out of her mother's act of fornication.[13] The bastard daughter is always already fallen. She is stigmatized not by her birth alone, for it is equally her inheritance of a forbidden sexual knowledge that purportedly corrupts her virtue. Suzanne was born knowing too much about the power of desire and the consummation of pleasure. Even before entering the convent, she disturbed the category by which a woman is placed on the marriage market—she was a virgin with a sexual knowledge. (When speaking about her father's wrath and his refusal to give her a dowry, she is referring to her stepfather. Her natural father never appears in the novel.) Once deemed unworthy as a bride, Suzanne is moved into the black markets where dowryless women were exchanged in the eighteenth century: the convent and, later, the brothel. That the convent system and prostitution undergirded the market economy in the eighteenth century is clear, cycling off women for whom no other economic provisions had been made or were possible. At the close of *La Religieuse* this slippage between the convent and brothel is overtly made: Suzanne is aided in her escape from the nunnery by a priest who exchanges her directly to a brothel, from which she must also flee. Impoverished and ill, she labors as an assistant laundress—the abject labor is the only alternative she can find to work in the brothel. As both an illegitimate daughter and as a defrocked nun, Suzanne cannot be legally exchanged on the market. When she is exchanged onto the black market, however, her sexual knowledge is at once contained and imminently exploitable.

Exogamous exchange—the transfer of the bride between the father and the male suitor—does not, therefore, operate as the novel's model of sexual economy. Suzanne is subject to a different order of exchange, for she is trafficked between women. Her mother, Madame Simonin, escorts and pays her dowry to the mother superior at the convent of Sainte-Marie; and, as Suzanne is transferred from one cloister to another, this ritual of her economic exchange remains in place. If the bride serves as a conduit for homosocial relations between men, and indeed as the material basis for all economic relations, then Suzanne, as a novice, becomes the conduit for such relations among women in *La Religieuse*. In its essential structure, the convent exchange of the novice imitates the giving away of the bride. While ostensibly Suzanne is marrying Christ, the transcendental bridegroom, the wedding that binds her to the convent is in actuality a marriage between women. Suzanne is given an opportunity to voice her assent or dissent to this ceremony that will alter her sexual status and transfer her from a patrilineal economy to a feminine economy. Unlike the bride, however, Suzanne's power to refuse her novitiate vows is negligible because she has already been given over to the convent before she speaks—she has already been brought over its threshold. During the ceremony, Suzanne repeatedly answers "no" when the vows are posed to her; despite her refusal to take vows, she is allowed neither to leave the convent nor to return to her family home. Restricted to the convent economy, she becomes an object of barter, a means by which the convents exchange with one another.[14]

Yet the commodification of Suzanne, as a woman exchanged among women, is not merely imitative of the dominant economy of marriage and inheritance. Once off the market, within the convent, Suzanne enters a different sexual economy. Neither a phallic standard nor a monetary standard, both of which regulate the system of exchange in the market economy, applies within the convent. In the convent, feminine sexual pleasure gains an intrinsic value beyond and apart from sexual reproduction.[15] In exchanging Suzanne and mediating through her body, the nuns in *La Religieuse* pass among themselves a knowledge of this pleasure. This sexual economy among women still requires and exploits an intermediary commodity—the novice. As a bride exchanged to serve the interests of a patriarchy, however, Suzanne would need to know nothing of her own sexual pleasure—or only enough to ensure her participation in the reproduction of an heir. Every patrilineal currency—whether property, income, or bloodline—would pass through her body without accruing to her. Never wavering from her desire to be released, Suzanne insists she has acquired a schooling in sexual pleasures within the convent against her will. Nonetheless, she is cognizant that her memoir of the cloister is the only commodity that she can offer in exchange to the marquis. *La Religieuse* structures not merely one anomalous off-market exchange in which women transact among themselves, but rather a complex system of exchange between the convents of Sainte-Marie, Longchamp, and Sainte-Eutrope. Serving as the medium of exchange within this convent economy, Suzanne also becomes heir to its knowledge.

Suzanne is initiated into the convent through the practice of mystical ecstasy. As Mme. de Moni, the mother superior at the Longchamp convent, summoned her visionary powers she invited the novices to imitate her. "Son dessein," Suzanne writes, "n'était pas de séduire; mais certainement c'est ce qu'elle faisait" (65); [Her intention was not to seduce; but certainly this was the consequence of her actions (40)]. The mystery of feminine mysticism to the outside observer lies with its invisibility— it cannot be proven upon the sexual anatomy. Only the female mystic herself sees what can be seen.[16] To document feminine mysticism for the marquis—to prove that it exists—Suzanne describes the moment of ecstatic union between herself, the other novices, and Mme. de Moni: "D'abord on l'écoutait; peu à peu on était entraîné, on s'unissait à elle;

l'âme tressaillait, et l'on partageait ses transports . . . on sortait de chez elle avec un coeur ardent, la joie et l'extase étaient peintes sur le visage, on versait des larmes si douces!" (65); [At first one listened, gradually one was swept along and united with her; the soul trembled and one shared her transports . . . one left her with a burning heart, joy and ecstasy were painted on the face; one shed such sweet tears! (40)]. The experience of ecstasy was collectively shared as the transports of mystical pleasure radiated from one woman to another. Suzanne thus delineates a sensation that passed through the interior of her own body, and which was then manifested on the beatific faces of Mme. de Moni and the other nuns.

Suspended between innocence and an initiation into the practice of pleasure, Suzanne avows that she did not feel, as did the other nuns, a "grand plaisir." Her own pleasure, she underscores, always stopped just short of consummation: "Ce n'est pas à ma seule expérience que je m'en rapporte, c'est à celle de toutes les religieuses. Quelques-unes m'ont dit qu'elles sentaient naître en elles le besoin d'être consolées comme celui d'un très grand plaisir; et je crois qu'il ne m'a manqué qu'un peu plus d'habitude, pour en venir là" (65); [This was not my experience alone but that of all the nuns. Some told me that they felt born in themselves the need to be consoled like the need for a very great pleasure—and I believe that I lacked only a little more practice to arrive at the same feeling (40)].

Under Sister Moni's tutelage, Suzanne also takes her vows. During the ceremony, she claims, she fell into a kind of unconscious stupor: "j'étais presque réduite à l'état d'automate. . . . J'ai prononcé des vœux, mais je n'en ai nulle mémoire, et je me suis trouvée religieuse aussi innocemment que je fus faite chrétienne" (69); [I was practically reduced to the state of an automaton. . . . I pronounced my vows, but have no memory of doing so, and I found myself a nun as innocently as I was made a Christian (44)]. Within the framework of her testimonial to the marquis, Suzanne is negotiating the larger question of the existence of feminine desire. Portraying herself as an automaton, a body programmed to act without consciousness, Suzanne negates in herself the very principle that she ascribes to Mme. de Moni. By documenting the practice of mystical ecstasy, Suzanne is bearing witness to a libidinal economy that operates only among women themselves and according to the power of their desire.

In *La Religieuse* mysticism opens the inquiry into feminine sexual pleasure by locating an engine of desire distinct from the body. Sadism becomes the direct narrative inversion of mysticism, for it acknowledges desire by sublimating the flesh. Under the new superior, Soeur Sainte-Christine, every nun at the Longchamp convent is given a hair belt and a

whip, as well as a strict schedule of flagellation and confession. By vehe-
mently protesting these rules, Suzanne unwittingly enables this sexual
economy to function, for a commodity of exchange is needed through
which all the other nuns will mediate their desires. Thus, rather than shut-
ting Suzanne into a locked cell, Soeur Sainte-Christine instructs the nuns
to ritualistically humiliate and torture Suzanne as she moves among them.
In excruciating succession, Suzanne is spat upon, disrobed, burned with
pincers, cut with glass, nearly drenched with waste, and starved. When
Suzanne falls prostrate on the chapel floor, Soeur Sainte-Christine ex-
horts the nuns: "'Marchez sur elle; ce n'est qu'un cadavre.' Quelques-unes
obéirent, et me foulèrent aux pieds; d'autres furent moins inhumaines;
mais aucune n'osa me tendre la main pour me relever" (102); ["Walk over
her. She is only a corpse." Some of the nuns obeyed, and trampled on me;
others were less inhuman; but none dared to stretch out a hand to lift
me up (80)]. Encircled by the nuns, Suzanne becomes an abjectified commodity through which they exchange with one another—she is tainted
and then passed among them.

Through her punished body Suzanne provides a symptomatology of
the feminine sex at the Longchamp convent. To the marquis, she recalls a
particular scene when she was accused by the nuns of a sexual "crime"—
the attempted seduction of another novice:

> Une des plus jeunes était au fond du corridor, j'allais à elle, et il n'y avait
> pas moyen de m'éviter. La frayeur la plus terrible la prit. . . . "Je suis per-
> due! Sœur Sainte-Suzanne, ne me faites point de mal". . . . Je ne saurais
> vous dire comme cette aventure fut travestie; on en fit l'histoire la plus
> criminelle: on dit que le démon de l'impureté s'était emparé de moi; on
> me supposa des desseins, des actions que je n'ose nommer, et des désirs
> bizarres auxquels on attribua le désordre évident dans lequel la jeune
> religieuse s'était trouvée. En vérité, je ne suis pas un homme, et je ne
> sais ce qu'on peut imaginer d'une femme et d'une autre femme, et moins
> encore d'une femme seule. (103)
>
> [One of the youngest [novices] was at the end of the corridor; I
> went towards her and she could not avoid me. A terrible fear overtook
> her. . . . "I am lost! Sister Suzanne, do not do me any harm." . . . I cannot
> adequately describe how this adventure was travestied; the most crimi-
> nal story possible was made of it. They said the demon of impurity had
> seized hold of me, and attributed to me designs and actions that I dare
> not name, and strange desires to which they attributed the evident dis-
> order in which the young nun was found. In truth, I am not a man, and

I do not know what one can imagine about one woman with another woman, still less about a woman alone. (82)]

This is a significant passage in the novel, as much as a revealing passage in the history of sexuality in the eighteenth century. A taxonomy and a nascent pathology of feminine sexuality is emerging, but it is not yet schematized into a science. When Suzanne writes "on me supposa des desseins, des actions que je n'ose nommer, et des désirs bizarres" [the nuns attributed to me designs and actions which I dare not name, and bizarre desires] her refusal to either name or imagine sexual practices between women is certainly, but not only, a semantic retreat. A classificatory system for feminine sexual practices does not yet exist here; the novel is working to produce such a system, to make it a working science. (To identify this practice as lesbianism, therefore, would be to impose a clinical term upon the novel that it cannot recognize.) *La Religieuse* always remains a casebook of symptoms provided by Suzanne for the marquis's diagnosis. As Suzanne confirms, the nuns know about the "désirs bizarres" that they project onto her, but their language of "termes obscurs" is equally inarticulate: "[C]es femmes ont le coeur bien corrompu: elles savent du moins qu'on commet seule des actions déshonnêtes, et moi je ne le sais pas; aussi n'ai-je jamais bien compris ce dont elles m'accusaient, et elles s'exprimaient en des termes si obscurs, que je n'ai jamais su ce qu'il y avait à leur repondre" (103); [These women must certainly have thoroughly corrupt hearts: at the very least, they know that these dishonorable actions can be committed all alone, and I do not know it; also I have never well understood what they were accusing me of, and they expressed themselves in terms so obscure, that I never knew how to answer them (82)]. Within this passage, the distribution of sexual knowledge to men and sexual ignorance to women is beginning to break down. Inside the convent, Suzanne, along with her accusers, has acquired a sexual knowledge of her own sex. What she denies that she has acquired is an epistemology, a language through which she can know that she knows. That language, she maintains, cannot be spoken between women within the convent; it can emerge only within the textual exchange between herself and the male reader. That language has yet to be coined.

Homoeroticism, deemed the most secret symptom of feminine sexuality in the convent, is placed at the close of *La Religieuse*, at the furthest remove from the economy outside. In the Sainte-Eutrope convent, the last to which Suzanne is exchanged, the mother superior, Mme. ✳✳✳, institutes a sexual economy oriented by pleasure alone. With her entire name censored with asterisks, the only such name in the novel, Mme. *** is nearly a pure sign of a femininity autonomous of the phallic order. (Suzanne, as the bastard daughter, and Mme. *** share a common namelessness according to a patrilineal system.) Urging Suzanne to begin a legal process against the Longchamp convent that would transfer her dowry to Sainte-Eutrope, Mme. *** asserts her proprietal claim over Suzanne within the convent economy. Mme. *** cultivates Suzanne more particularly, however, as a young woman who bears another kind of wealth—as one who knows about the sexual pleasures practiced in the other convents. Their sexual intimacy is sealed within a confessional frame, when Mme. *** requests that Suzanne recount her memories of convent life and she readily complies: "'Raconte, mon enfant,' dit-elle; j'attends, je me sens les dispositions les plus pressantes à m'attendrir.' ... Je commençai donc mon récit à peu près comme je viens de vous l'écrire. Je ne saurais vous dire l'effet qu'il produisit sur elle, les soupirs qu'elle poussa, les pleurs qu'elle versa" (159); ["Speak, my child" she said; "I am waiting, and I already feel the most pressing disposition to hear." ... So I began my story, rather similarly as I have written to you. I do not know how to explain to you the effect that it had upon her, the sighs that she heaved, the tears that she shed (142)]. Thus, as Suzanne now reveals in passing to the marquis, he is not, after all, her primary auditor. Mme. *** was the first recipient and solicitor of the memoir that she has sent him. Suzanne negotiates, as such, a suitable arrangement: she will live at Sainte-Eutrope as she pleases in exchange for spending time in private conference with Mme. ***. Suzanne agrees to answer anything that Mme. *** asks of her although she sets an irrevocable condition: she explicitly refuses to be initiated by Mme. *** into the *consciousness of desire*: "Je ne sais rien, et j'aime mieux ne rien savoir, que d'acquérir des connaissances qui me rendraient peut-être plus à plaindre que je ne le suis. Je n'ai point de désirs, et je n'en veux point chercher que je ne pourrais satisfaire" (163); [I know nothing and I would rather know nothing, than to acquire knowledge(s) that would perhaps make me more pitiful that I already am. I have no desires at all, and I do not search for what I cannot satisfy (146)]. The question, therefore, of what kind of language Suzanne and Mme. *** speak with one another—what kind of code will mediate the language of desire between them—is at the center of the Sainte-Eutrope section of *La Religieuse*.

Documenting these private sessions with Mme. *** for the marquis, Suzanne provides a meticulous description of erotic pleasure as it is manifested upon the female body, without ever giving this pleasure a name. She offers her own body as an anatomical specimen of desire, drawn by the lips of Mme. ✳✳✳:

> Elle baissa les yeux, rougit et soupira; en vérité, c'était comme un
> amant. . . . Je me penchai, et elle me baisa le front. . . . C'était toujours un
> baiser ou sur le front, ou sur le cou, ou sur les yeux, ou sur les joues,
> ou sur la bouche, ou sur les mains, ou sur la gorge, ou sur les bras, mais
> plus souvent sur la bouche. . . . En vérité je serais bien belle, si je
> méritais la plus petite partie des éloges qu'elle me donnait. (151)
>
> [She lowered her eyes, blushed and sighed; in truth, this was like a
> lover. . . . I bent down and she kissed my forehead. . . . There was always
> a kiss on the forehead, or on the neck, or on the eyes, or on the cheeks,
> or on the mouth, or on the hands, or on the neck, or on the arms, but
> most often on the mouth. . . . In truth I must have been very beautiful,
> if I merited the smallest part of the praises that she gave me. (133)]

Suzanne is constructing a triangulation of desire: she is the mediated object who herself feels nothing as she is exchanged through the gaze of Mme. ✳✳✳ to the marquis's view.

Always the passive participant, Suzanne reiterates this anatomical lesson upon the body of Mme. ✳✳✳. Bringing Mme. ✳✳✳ to orgasm with her own kisses, she transcribes the succession of clinical symptoms that she observed:

> Elle m'invitait à lui baiser le front, les joues, les yeux et la bouche, et je
> lui obéissais: je ne crois pas qu'il y eût du mal à cela. Cependant son
> plaisir s'accroissait, et comme je ne demandais pas mieux que d'ajouter
> à son bonheur d'une manière aussi innocente, je lui baisais encore le
> front, les joues, les yeux et la bouche. . . . Enfin il vint un moment, je ne
> sais si ce fût de plaisir ou de peine, où elle devint pâle comme la mort;
> ses yeux se fermèrent, tous son corps s'étendit avec violence . . . et elle
> me parut mourir en poussant un grand soupir. . . . Je crus qu'elle se
> trouvait mal, je voulais sortir, appeler. Elle entrouvit faiblement les
> yeux, et me dit d'une voix éteinte: "Innocente! ce n'est rien." (155)
>
> [She asked me to kiss her forehead, her cheeks, her eyes and her lips,
> and I obeyed her: I do not think there can have been any harm in that.
> Meanwhile her pleasure increased, and as I asked nothing better than
> to add to her happiness in a manner as innocent, I kissed her again on
> the forehead, the cheeks, the eyes, and the mouth. . . . Then came a mo-
> ment, I know not if it was pleasure or pain, when she turned pale as
> death; her eyes closed, all her body stiffened violently. . . . She seemed to

me to die, as she uttered a deep sigh. I got up quickly: I thought she was ill. I wished to go out and call for help. She opened her eyes fully and said in a dying voice: "Innocent! it is nothing." (138)][17]

As proof of an autonomous feminine sexual pleasure, this passage begs the question: Who is the theorist of this pleasure? Who will make the final accounting of it? Suzanne's authority over this sexual knowledge is never resolved, given the narrative conditions of *La Religieuse*. Suzanne produces a clinical casebook of feminine sexuality in the convent while her own pleasures remain either unconsummated or unknowable to her. Immediately after observing the climax of Mme. ✳✳✳, Suzanne climaxes in turn, but she knows how to describe only the process, not the aim: "Je ne sais pas ce qui se passait en moi; je craignais, je tremblais, le coeur me palpitait, j'avais de la peine à respirer, je me sentais troublée, oppressée, agitée, j'avais peur, il me semblait que les forces m'abandonnaient et que j'allais défaillir; cependant je ne saurais dire que ce fut de la peine que je ressentisse" (156); [I do not understand what went on inside me. I was afraid, I trembled, my heart thumped, I had difficulty in breathing, I felt disturbed, oppressed, agitated; I was frightened. I felt that my strength was abandoning me and that I was going to swoon; however, I cannot say that it was pain that I had sensed (139)]. When queried by Mme. ✳✳✳ she denies her experience: "'Mais est-ce que vous n'avez pas souffert?' 'Non'" (156); ["Have you suffered?" "No" (139)]. Between women in *La Religieuse*, there are never any shared terms with which they can affirm that the pleasure they felt was the same.

Does the nun always lose consciousness of her pleasure the moment it arises, thereby giving it away to the male reader? Offered as a memoir written from the convent for an outside speculator, *La Religieuse* also eludes this project of speculation. To the degree that a technical vocabulary of sexual pleasure is never articulated between women themselves, their pleasure remains their own; it has an intrinsic value that cannot be quantified or delimited by an exterior economy. Within the nun's text in *La Religieuse*, feminine sexuality becomes a term in and of itself, rather than a term contingent to or knowable by a phallocentric model of sexuality. The classification of that feminine pleasure can only be approximated in the commercialized arena of the market, where Suzanne's memoir will be read, cataloged, and given a price. *La Religieuse* seeks to document a new science of feminine sexuality, but it confronts a possibility inherently disruptive to its inquiry: a sexual knowledge shared between women off the market for which it can never give a fully authorized account.

After completing and rereading her hurriedly written memoir, Suzanne reflects in a short postscript on the potential profit that she hoped to realize by sending the text to the marquis. Writing now as a woman who has recognized that she has composed and sent a sexually explicit tale to a male reader, she asks a series of final questions. Has she actually engaged, during the course of writing the memoir, in a course of seduction? Has she appealed to the marquis's prurient, rather than benevolent, interests?

> P.S. . . . Serait-ce que nous croyons les hommes moins sensibles à la peinture de nos peines qu'à l'image de nos charmes, et nous promettrions-nous encore plus de facilité à les seduire qu'à les toucher? Je les connais trop peu et je ne me suis pas assez étudiée pour savoir cela. Cependant, si le marquis, à qui l'on accorde le tact le plus délicat, venait à se persuader que ce n'est pas à sa bienfaisance, mais à son vice que je m'addresse, que penserait-il de moi? Cette réflexion m'inquiète. En vérité, il aurait bien tort de m'imputer personnellement un instinct propre à tout mon sexe. Je suis une femme, peut-être un peu coquette, que sais-je? Mais c'est naturellement et sans artifice. (207–8)
>
> [P.S. . . . Can it be that we think men less moved by the picture of our sufferings than the image of our charms? Do we say to ourselves that it is easier to seduce them than to touch their feelings? I know them too little, and have studied myself too little to say. Still, what would the marquis, who is known to be a man of exquisite tact, think if he were persuaded that I was appealing not to his benevolent but to his basest instincts? The thought distresses me. In truth he would be wrong to impute to me personally an instinct common to all women. I am a woman, perhaps a bit of a coquette. How can I know? But this is naturally and without guile. (207–8)]

She answers her own interrogation about the memoir by posing a final question: "En vérité . . . que sais-je?" [In truth, how can I know?]. This same phrase both opens and closes the transcript of *La Religieuse*. For, in truth, Suzanne has written through her body, rather than through a body of knowledge. In the end, she lays claim to both. She may always know something more, that she keeps to herself.

NOTES

1. See Claude Levi-Strauss and also Gayle Rubin.

2. On the emergence of the prison and on natural history as a science of classification, see Foucault. See also Bender.

3. As Luce Irigaray writes in *This Sex Which Is Not One:* "Female sexuality has always been conceptualized on the basis of masculine parameters" (23).

4. Georges May's study is a remarkable documentation of the novel's cultural contexts.

5. Novels such as Anne Fuller's *The Convent* (1786), Ann Radcliffe's *The Italian* (1797), Germaine de Stael's *Delphine* (1802), Elizabeth Helme's *The Nun's Story* (1801), and Sydney Morgan's *The Novice of St. Dominick* (1804) only begin to catalog the extent to which eighteenth-century women writers took up the thematics of the convent, reimagining society in an all-female community.

6. Robert Darnton's study, thus, structures a print market that encompasses a plurality of discourses, rather than a separation between a "proper" book market and an underground or covert economy for books and prints.

7. Roger Thompson provides a detailed overview of convent pornography, based upon primary research. Along with *Venus in the Cloister*, Thompson cites *An Anatomy of the English Nunnery in Lisbon* (1684), *The Amorous Abbess, or Love in a Nunnery* (1684), and *The Adamite, or the Loves of Father Rock and His Intrigues with the Nuns* (1683), which were reprinted into the eighteenth century.

8. Thomas DiPiero, who reads Suzanne's proposition to the marquis as a daughter's seduction of the father, has informed my own reading (289–331).

9. The English translations are my own. The parenthetical page references following the English translations are from *Memoirs of a Nun*.

10. See, for example, Walter E. Rex and Carolyn Durham on lesbianism in the convent.

11. On the triangulation between Diderot, the marquis, and Suzanne, see Jack Undank. On Diderot's cross-dressing through Suzanne, see Beatrice Durand. Eve Kosofsky Sedgwick considers the problem of Suzanne's "unknowing" within terms complementary to but different from my own. Julie Hayes illuminates the critical framework within which the novel has been read through an incisive analysis of its narrative "slips" or lacunae.

12. This history is taken from Roland Desné's introduction to *La Religieuse*. See also Durand.

13. As a bastard, Suzanne is, in a profound sense, exclusively her mother's possession. Unlike her half-sisters, she can claim only a matrilineal line. By law, as her mother threatens her, she is nameless, without the right to the surname of Simonin: "your sisters have obtained by right a name which is yours through crime" (33), and "[i]f you survive me, you will remain without name, future, or estate" (34). Monsieur Simonin and the church fathers may sanction Suzanne's exchange into the convent by signing the legal documents, but the literal economic dealing is conducted between Madame Simonin and the mother superiors.

For other views of the relations between mothers and daughters in *La Religieuse* see Pierre Saint-Amand and Janet Todd. Todd notes Madame Simonin punishes Suzanne for refusing her vows by breaking her nose and the sexual nature of the nosebleed that flows over Suzanne's face. This nosebleed, I would argue, is a ritualistic defloration of Suzanne as she is exchanged between women.

14. As Pierre Fauchery writes in a brilliant study of the convent novel: "Les moyens mis en oeuvre pour gagner une jeune fille au fiancé céleste reassemblent par plus

d'un côté à ceux qu'emploie un séducteur pour faire le siège de la vertu: dans les deux cas, il s'agit d'entamer une volonté, de briser le 'non' d'une conscience qui se croit libre" (344). [The means put into play to win a girl over to the celestial fiancé resemble in many ways those that a seducer uses to win over the seat of virtue: in both cases, it's a question of undermining a will, of shattering the "no" of a conscience that thinks itself free.]

15. Dominique Jullien spatializes the convent as a uterine space that has been unnaturally deprived of its reproductive function (namely, the man who should inseminate it), which thus induces hysteria in the nuns:

> D'une manière plus essentielle, il est le lieu uterin, à la fois le lieu où ne vivent que des femmes, et la figure de l'organe de l'enfantement. Au couvent, l'uterus se trouve artificiellement privé de sa raison d'être biologique, privé de l'homme, qui, en lui permettant d'accomplir sa fonction reproductive, l'inscrit dans la chaîne des générations, c'est-à-dire dans l'ordre généalogique et temporel. Dans le couvent l'homme n'a pas sa place, si bien que le chaos regne." (146) [In a more essential manner, it is the uterine space, at once the space where only women live and the figure of the organ of birth. In the convent, the uterus is artificially deprived of its biological purpose; it is deprived of men who, in allowing it to accomplish its reproductive function, inscribe it in the chain of generations, in the genealogical and temporal order. In the convent the man has no place, and thus chaos rules.]

I argue the contrary: that *La Religieuse* suspends the question of the reproductive capacity of women as its opening premise and seeks to document feminine sexuality beyond and apart from the uterus.

16. Bernini's statue, *St. Theresa in Ecstacy*, is an emblematic image of the female mystic, in the throes of ecstasy, made visible to a male audience. The statue's placement within a larger grouping of statuary is infrequently noted. As Theresa swoons, her head thrown back, she is observed not only by Cupid bearing his arrow into her body, but also by an audience of male ecclesiastics. In Lacan's view, the female mystic knows nothing about her pleasure. Also see Toril Moi's reading of Luce Irigaray's essay "La Mystérique": "under patriarchy," Moi writes, "mysticism (like hysteria a few centuries later) offers women a real if limited possibility of discovering some aspects of a pleasure that might be specific to their libidinal drives" (136).

17. Philip Stewart's computer cataloging of the body parts in *La Religieuse* is a technological response that the novel seems already to anticipate, as it lists and relists the limited anatomy of the nun visible in her habit.

WORKS CITED

Bender, John. "Prison Reform and the Sentence of Narration in *The Vicar of Wakefield*." *The New Eighteenth Century: Theory, Politics, and English Literature.* Ed. Felicity Nussbaum and Laura Brown. New York: Methuen, 1987. 168–88.

Darnton, Robert. *The Forbidden Best-Sellers of Pre-Revolutionary France.* New York: Norton, 1995.

Diderot, Denis. *Memoirs of a Nun.* Trans. Francis Birrell. London: Elek, 1959.

———. *La Religieuse.* Intro. Roland Desné. Garnier-Flammarion, 1968.

DiPiero, Thomas. *Dangerous Truths and Criminal Passions: The Evolution of the French Novel, 1569–1791.* Stanford: Stanford UP, 1992.

Durand, Beatrice. "Diderot and the Nun: Portrait of the Artist as a Transvestite." *Men Writing the Feminine: Literature, Theory, and the Question of Genders.* Ed. Thais E. Morgan. Albany: State University of New York, 1994. 89–106.

Durham, A. Carolyn. "The Contradictory Becomes Coherent: *La Religieuse* and *Paul et Virginie*." *The Eighteenth Century: Theory and Interpretation* 23 (1982): 219–37.

Fauchery, Pierre. *La Destinée féminine dans le roman européen du dix-huitième siècle, 1713–1807: Essai du gynécomythie romanesque.* Paris: Armand Collin, 1972.

Foucault, Michel. *The Archaeology of Knowledge.* Trans. A. M. Sheridan Smith. New York: Harper and Row, 1972.

———. *Discipline and Punish. The Birth of the Prison.* Trans. Alan Sheridan. New York: Vintage, 1979.

Furbank, P. N. *Diderot: A Critical Biography.* New York: Knopf, 1992.

Hayes, Julie. "Retrospection and Contradiction in Diderot's *La Religieuse*." *Romanic Review* 77.3 (1986): 233–42.

Irigaray, Luce. *This Sex Which Is Not One.* Trans. Catherine Porter with Carolyn Burke. Ithaca: Cornell UP, 1985.

Jullien, Dominique. "Locus hystericus: L'Image du couvent dans *La Religieuse* de Diderot." *French Forum* 15.2 (1990): 133–48.

Lacan, Jacques. "God and the *Jouissance* of The Woman." *Feminine Sexuality: Jacques Lacan and the école freudienne.* Ed. and trans. Juliet Mitchell and Jacqueline Rose. New York: Norton, 1982. 137–48.

Levi-Strauss, Claude. *The Elementary Structures of Kinship.* Trans. James Harle Bell and John Richard von Sturmer. Boston: Beacon, 1969.

May, Georges. *Diderot and La Religieuse: Etude historique et littéraire.* Paris: Presses Universitaires de France, 1954.

Moi, Toril. *Sexual/Textual Politics: Feminist Literary Theory.* London: Methuen, 1985.

Rex, Walter E. "Secrets from Suzanne: The Tangled Motives of *La Religieuse*." *The Eighteenth Century: Theory and Interpretation* 24.3 (1983): 185–98.

Rubin, Gayle. "The Traffic in Women: Notes on the 'Political Economy' of Sex." *Toward an Anthropology of Women.* Ed. Rayna Reiter. New York: Monthly Review, 1975. 157–210.

Saint-Amand, Pierre. "Reproducing Motherhood: Diderot's *La Religieuse*." *Literature and Psychology* 34 (1989): 27–43.

Sedgwick, Eve Kosofsky. "Privilege of Unknowing." *Genders* (1988): 102–24.

Stewart, Philip. "Body Language in *La Religieuse*." *Studies in French Fiction.* Ed. Robert Gibson. London: Grant and Cutler, 1989. 307–20.

Thompson, Roger. *Unfit for Modest Ears: A Study of Pornographic, Obscene, and Bawdy Works Written or Published in England in the Second Half of the Seventeenth Century.* Totowa, N.J.: Rowman and Littlefield, 1979.

Todd, Janet. *Female Friendship in Literature.* New York: Columbia UP, 1980.

Undank, Jack. "Diderot's 'Unnatural Acts': Lessons from the Convent." *French Forum* 121 (1986): 151–67.

The Magdalen Charity for the Reform of Prostitutes

A Foucauldian Moment

Robert Bataille

In the first volume of his *History of Sexuality*, Michel Foucault has this to say about the eighteenth century: "Toward the beginning of the eighteenth century, there emerged a political, economic, and technical excitement to talk about sex. And not so much in the form of a general theory of sexuality as in the form of analysis, stocktaking, classification and specification. . . . [I]t called for management procedures; it had to be taken charge of by analytical discourses. In the eighteenth century, sex became a 'police' matter" (4). What was actually meant in the eighteenth century by the term *police* was something different than our modern usage. As Donna T. Andrews notes, *police* had a broader meaning than it does today and referred to the "maintenance of a civil order, a civilized society, and a refining process. Police was the practical, consensual expression of a society's social arrangements, mores, and beliefs" (6). But such maintenance, it may be argued, could be sustained only by the administrative discipline and control, by the regulating machinery, that Foucault speaks of in *Discipline and Punish* (73–78).

In London in the middle of the eighteenth century, one important site of such policing of sexuality—its reform and control—was the Magdalen House. Established in order to reform prostitutes and wayward girls[1] and turn them into useful servants, productive workers, and, ultimately, into wives and mothers, the Magdalen House may be seen as a product of the politics of identity, of those political and economic forces that converged to transform the illicit female body and its sexuality into a form that would accommodate the needs of the state. In attempting to demonstrate how an institution like the Magdalen House operated in the service of hegemonic class and gender interests, this essay first examines the reasons why this reformation was attempted and then analyzes the methods employed to discipline the female subjects.

David Owen has pointed out in his *English Philanthropy* that by the end of the seventeenth century a charitable tradition, somewhat decentralized, had already been established in England whereby an individual of means left funds to his or her community to establish almshouses or grammar schools for the poor (2). Furthermore, Owen notes that in the eighteenth century, it was private charity that had to cope with the evils of the new urban industrial society (4), and in order for it to do so successfully, the proposers of such a charity had to develop distinctively modern techniques employing some key features of corporate structures. One of these features was the development of the joint stock venture, in which a group of donor-investors would pool money to establish the charity on a firm financial footing. This precise step was undertaken by Jonas Hanway, Robert Dingley, and others who were involved in the initial efforts to establish the Magdalen House.

Such a charitable venture was often marketed to the prospective donors and the general public, in Paul Langford's view, by appealing to the practical commercial benefits to be gained by a specific charity (144–45). Langford argues that to be successful these new sorts of charitable activities and organizations required the practices of something akin to the modern discourse of public relations and propaganda (483). Certainly Jonas Hanway's propaganda campaign on behalf of the Magdalen House fits Langford's notion of how the midcentury philanthropist had to act somewhat like an "entrepreneur of charity," using market strategies to sell his product (485). And just as certainly the formation of the house highlights those political and economic forces that tended to legitimize specific social and personal characteristics, here those particularly associated with the transformation of the illicit female subjects into those more desired by hegemonic forces, that is, into the domestic servant or the domesticated wife. The actual functioning of the house, as dramatized in its rules and regulations, attempted to discipline its female subjects and to inculcate a kind of training, so that once the women were released they could play one of the useful roles as defined by the paternal economic and political forces that were in fact part of the supporting ideological-cum-financial structure of the house in the first place. The Magdalen House, once established, serves as an example of what Foucault calls in *Discipline and Punish* the "disciplinary space." His remark that "the rigors of the industrial period long retained a religious air" (149) is fully dramatized in both the rigorous temporal and spatial conceptions of Hanway's charity.

The establishment of the Magdalen charity was first publicly urged by Hanway, a tireless reformer,[2] in a pamphlet entitled *Letter to Robert Dingley*, published early in 1758; the plan was refined in another pamphlet, *A Plan for Establishing a Charity-House*, that came out later in the spring of the same year. In proposing the charity, houses of which had been long established on the continent,[3] Hanway urged that such an institution was needed for Britain's economic survival, but his initial appeals in the *Plan* are couched in religious idiom and argument: "Of the whole race of *Adam* there are surely none who stand in greater need of these helps, than these unhappy women. I appeal to every dispassionate mind, if there can be greater objects of commiseration, than poor thoughtless girls, hurried into ruin by temptations, to which they are sometimes exposed, against their *intentions*" (Hanway, *Plan* xiii). In his earlier *Letter to Dingley*, however, Hanway had stressed motives for forming such a charity that revealed the hegemonic political and economic power behind his intentions. In addressing Dingley, Hanway had urged that such an institution was needed for Britain's economic survival; a major portion of his argument here was focused on his concern with the relationship between England's ability to make war, the need for more soldiers and sailors, and the desirability of having married military personnel. Hanway hoped that the reformed prostitutes would then become the wives of military men and thus would help achieve these political and economic ends: married military personnel will not only fight more effectively but also contribute to the needed population increase, hence in turn creating more soldiers and sailors: all this might be possible, Hanway tells Dingley, if only good wives might be (re)constructed from deserted girls and reformed prostitutes. Such reconstruction was also carried out by later Magdalen institutions: as Linda Mahood has recently shown, the nineteenth-century Scottish Magdalen societies "never ceased to promote the virtues of domesticity for women"[4] but were more concerned to return inmates to their families rather than to prepare them to become wives of soldiers and sailors.

Hanway's concerns with the relationship between economics, warfare, and illicit sexuality were not untypical of social and political thinkers who supported eighteenth-century charities. As Donna T. Andrews has pointed out, because of the number of wars during the midcentury—the War of Jenkins's Ear (1739–1741), the War of the Austrian Succession (1739–1748), the Seven Years' War (1756–1763)—and the resulting loss of military manpower, philanthropists worried about the nation's ability to protect and defend itself. Furthermore, it was observed that many soldiers and sailors did not marry and thus when they engaged in illicit sexual relations, they contributed to the rise in debauched women and the spread of venereal disease; all of these tendencies mitigated against the establishment of stable families and thus the successful procreation and rearing of children (Andrews 54–57).

Andrews further notes that, in addition to their concern for the relationship between prostitution and the nation's self-defense capabilities, all of these institutions proposed to link commerce to charity in some fashion, and that the overcoming of poverty through such charities was a central concern of certain economists. These economic thinkers, whom she labels "political arithmeticians," were concerned more with overcoming general poverty rather than with the specific reform of prostitutes and other individuals and felt that the "promotion of the nation's wealth, power, and virtue, and not the accumulation of riches or the improvement of living standards, was the great end of economic . . . activity" (22–23). Andrews goes on to note that despite the deployment of religious idiom in the arguments of such economists, they were fundamentally practical in their outlook (23).

Jonas Hanway clearly understood all the interrelationships between charity, economics, and military strength, for the first charity he was centrally involved with, the Marine Society, was predicated on the navy's need for a steady supply of young recruits. Founded in 1756, the Marine Society accepted young male volunteers, gave them some training and, most importantly, provided them with an adequate supply of proper clothing. As James Taylor observes (69–70), part of the immediate propaganda in favor of the society's formation in the first place was the inadequate state of preparedness of the British Navy at the outbreak of the Seven Years' War. The need of the state for boys and young men was a part of Hanway's marketing strategy in 1756, and a similarly practical appeal in the *Letter to Dingley* introduced the campaign for the Magdalen House two years later.

Yet perhaps feeling that he had been somewhat too practical, and that the economic and political motives in the *Letter to Dingley* had been presented too harshly and needed to be softened, Hanway in the *Plan* does not make such economic-political arguments so explicitly. He does never-theless address them. Suggesting first that religious motives should take precedence over economic and political ones, Hanway then urges practical reasons to the politicians: "But these politicians should remember, that was there nothing more in view than political prudence, with regard to the increase of the species, and the good order of the state, there is utmost reason to check the progress of this baneful vice. As matrimony is the surest method of augmenting the number of people, and the truest ce-ment of civil society, it is surely no small object to *discourage whoredom,* though we know we cannot *suppress* it" (*Plan* xvii–xviii). But Hanway and his associates did not plan to incarcerate their subjects involuntarily. Rather, as it is pointed out in the general introduction to this volume, the majority of innovative political thinkers in the eighteenth century resisted traditional notions of the individual subjected to the state and instead pro-posed a structure of mutuality. Hanway in fact proposes that his charity accept only those females who voluntarily offer themselves; he explains this break with traditional coercive institutions as follows:

> As to a *coercive* law to accomplish a reformation in this great point; per-haps we might be driven, more or less *forcibly*, from an abandoned profligacy, to a serious habit of life; but I question much if it would an-swer in the present case. There are many inconveniences which free-born subjects will submit to, of their own choice, that the notion of *law* would render insupportable. If reason and religion have any power over the *mind*, I will be bold to pronounce, that the intended good work, so far as it is extended, *may* be accomplished, without the authority of the civil magistrate. (*Plan* xx)

Near the end of the prefatory section of the *Plan*, which introduces the main text describing the house and its rules, Hanway briefly touches on the end of the charity; the final products—the transformed females—will be rendered "useful to the community, and happy in themselves; which may restore them to the arms of their afflicted parents, and render them a comfort to their relations and friends" (*Plan* xxvi). This sentimental tableau seems illustrative of the domestic ideal constructed, as Nancy Armstrong and Leonard Tennenhouse argue, by the eighteenth-century novel, conduct book, and other elements of the discourse aimed at female readers. Both that discourse and the goals of Hanway's charity were aimed at creating a "form of power exercised through constant super-vision and the regulation of desire, thus preparing the cultural ground in which capitalism could rapidly flourish" (Armstrong and Tennenhouse,

11–12). The key difference here of course is that such power operated opaquely and indirectly with regard to the novel, whereas in Hanway's charity all was clear and explicit. Constant supervision was to become a touchstone of Hanway's method.

One is thus struck with the general tenor of Hanway's means and goals, and his proposal not only appears to illustrate key principles in Foucault's *History of Sexuality* but also to exemplify his contention in *Discipline and Punish* that the eighteenth century saw the growth of state control and a more immediate effort to "adjust the mechanisms of power that frame the everyday lives of individuals" (*Discipline* 77). Although Foucault studies prisons rather than charities, a good deal of what he says about developments in penal techniques seems to be confirmed by Hanway's pamphlets that spawned the Magdalen Charity and outlined its rules and methods of operation.[5] The relevance of Foucault's analysis here is clear, despite the fact that Hanway and his friends among the London merchants and noblemen who eagerly supported with funds the formation of the house created a private rather than a state enterprise. The very rules governing the charity, particularly its deployment of spatial and temporal regulation in the daily operation of the house itself, strongly resemble Foucauldian ideas concerning the rise of the penitentiary. And it was to be through the implementation of these rules that the wayward female body was to become transformed into a disciplined, serviceable vessel devoted to domestic regularity and order.

The rules and regulations that Hanway suggests as appropriate structures for the moral discipline and reconstructions of the young female residents of the house correspond very closely to those new penal techniques outlined by Foucault in his chapter "Generalized Punishment," a sample of which follows:

> Shift the object and change the scale. Define new tactics in order to reach a target that is now more subtle but also more widely spread in the social body. Find new techniques for adjusting punishment to it and for adapting its effects. Lay down new principles for regularizing, refining, universalizing the art of punishment. Homogenize its application. Reduce its economic and political cost by increasing its effectiveness and by multiplying its circuits. In short, constitute a new economy and a new technology of the power to punish: these are no doubt the essential *raisons d'etre* of penal reforms in the eighteenth century. (*Discipline* 89)

Foucault of course does not speak here specifically of the punishment and reform of prostitutes, but surely the system he exposes and the one Hanway proposes are similar enough. Hanway was certainly interested in reducing the political and economic costs of his reformation through training the young women under the regimen of the house to employ their needles to produce marketable goods that could in turn be sold to defray the cost of their own maintenance. A greater economic issue, however, is to be found in the gain to the navy and to the country at large, which benefits he speaks of in the letter to Robert Dingley that expresses the former's hope that the interest of Britain will be served by his plan to provide good wives for sailors from the ranks of these reformed prostitutes. Such unions would themselves produce more soldiers and sailors. In addition, Hanway stresses what Foucault calls the necessity of finding "new techniques for adjusting punishment" to the "social body" and in generally shifting the object of punishment from the body to the soul or perhaps more accurately of reforming the soul through attention to the body. Hanway writes:

> Lawgivers and magistrates have at all times supposed, that the fear of death or confinement; of compulsive labor, or corporeal correction, would either awe the wicked, and prevent iniquity; or that the actual suffering of these severities, would reform all gross enormities. But it is a fact too well known, that the abuse of houses of correction is carried to that pitch, with us, as to render them houses of corruption, not of reformation.
>
> What then is to be done, but, with a true gallantry of spirit, to endevor [*sic*] these unhappy women from slavery, disease and misery; from being vicious in themselves, and the cause of vice in others? Let us try a different kind of treatment, such as will at once render them useful to the community, and happy in themselves. (*Plan* xxv–xxvi)

Here is the rebellion against the existing conceptions of the individual subjected to the state and its institutions that DiPiero and Gill rightly point to in their introduction. Yet it is difficult to decide just how much of Hanway's scheme was actually new. If, as Sherill Cohen has recently argued, even well before the early modern period women's institutions "anticipated many later developments in the creation of institutions" and that for women "western patriarchal society has long been a 'panoptic regime,' with females being watched" (5–6),[6] then perhaps the degree of innovation in Hanway's *techne* is problematic.

Nevertheless, one is struck with Hanway's conceptual detail. In his *Letter to Dingley*, dated 18 February 1758, Hanway spoke of the function of spatial arrangement in the discipline of the Magdalen House itself. He recommended that the repentants pursue their reformation, particularly in the learning of a trade: "in the manufacture scheme, young sinners to be separated from old ones, and those who are in danger of going astray, be received, and distinguished from both" (15). Here in concrete terms is the assignment of the individual to a disciplinary space similar to that Foucault associates with the ordering of academic space in schools and colleges (*Discipline* 146–49). The function of such ordering is, as Foucault notes, the transformation of "confused, useless, or dangerous multitudes into ordered multiplicities" (148), which seems precisely Hanway's aim: he wishes to separate the newly admitted women, who may be rebellious, from the now docile veterans, and thus make the reformatory process more efficient and more likely to succeed.

In the *Plan*, his second pamphlet, Hanway also attempted to account for differences in caste and class, enforcing that difference with the spatial conception of the "Ward," the regulation of which is suggested by the following rules:

> 1. There shall be a superiority or preference of wards, according to the appearance, deportment, and the education of the persons admitted.
> 2. A ward shall be allotted for new admitted persons, where they shall remain for a month before they are classed in the other wards. . . .
> *A levelling scheme will as ill serve the vicious as the virtuous; and one might as well put a gentleman of birth and education to the plow-tail, because he had been a rake . . . as a girl bred up with any sort of delicacy to a wash-tub. (20)

That the class structure of the larger society should be replicated in the first rule of the Magdalen House ward should not surprise, but the second rule is more interesting insofar as it exemplifies what Foucault has called the "art of distributions." "Discipline proceeds," he writes in *Discipline and Punish*, "from the distribution of individuals in space" (141) and goes on to articulate several rules governing that deployment of space, yoking enclosure to partitioning: "But the principle of 'enclosure' is neither constant, nor indispensable, nor sufficient in disciplinary machinery. This machinery works space in a much more flexible and detailed way. It does this first of all on the principle of elementary location or *partitioning*" (143). That such distribution was necessary to the efficient functioning of the house and hence to the efficient reformation of the female body Hanway was well aware. He explains the necessity of spatial separation of the newly admitted as follows: "The better to guard against the irregularities which may arise, before any trial is made of the temper and sincerity of the party; upon the first admission, they shall be kept for a month in a ward assigned for this purpose, and not associate with those settled in their mind and manners, till they give proof of their acquiescence to what they have subscribed" (*Plan* 19). In a footnote, Hanway makes clear that this partitioning of the newly admitted penitents is undertaken so that those who are unruly may be dealt with "without blowing up the coals of discontent among others." Or as Foucault puts it, partitioning makes it possible to "be able at each moment to supervise the conduct of each individual, to assess it, to judge it, to calculate its qualities or merits" (*Discipline* 143).

Not long after the time that Hanway was proposing the establishment of the Magdalen Charity with careful attention to the spatial dimension of the repentants' relationships, other British reformers, as John Bender has pointed out,[7] were concerned with the architecture of the new prison. Speaking of developments after the 1760s, Bender notes that "prison interiors would shortly be reshaped into a powerful expository system, while horrific facades continued as mandatory exhibits . . . [of] the power of confinement to alter the spirit through material representation" (21). Hanway was of course not interested in "horrific facades," but he was very much aware of interiors as a powerful expository method for the purpose of character (re)formation. At the same time he wished to prevent class interaction, as we have seen: there was to be no liminality in the Magdalen community to threaten social distinctions or encourage recidivism as there had been in the old prison.

Foucault's "new principles for regularizing, refining, [and] universalizing the art of punishing" are certainly present in Hanway's construction, even though he does not aim at punishing but reforming his subjects. The regularizing and regulating microtechniques—part of the "new technology of power" Foucault describes—are to be found in the rules Hanway sets out in the *Plan:* indeed, the general section of "Rules and Regulations" runs for forty pages and contains thirty-five subsections, nearly all of which contain sets of rules. As we have looked briefly at spatial considerations in the wards of the house, it may be useful now to examine how the ordering of the Magdalens' time, seen in subsections XXVI through XXVIII, was typical of the house's regulating functions:

XXV. HOURS OF DEVOTION
1. A bell shall be rung to call them to prayers, soon after they are up, before they begin to work.
2. The prayers to be used shall be agreed to by the Committee, and care taken that they be uttered properly, and by no means become irksome by being too long.

3. Their evening prayers shall be soon after they have done work.

XXVII. HOURS OF REST

  1. From the Lady-day to Michaelmas they shall rise at six o'clock, and from Michaelmas to Lady-day at seven, except when the weather is very severe, the Matron shall then be directed to allow them half an hour, or an hour extraordinary.

  2. They shall go to bed at ten every night, and no fire or candle shall be allowed in the wards after that time, except in the sick ward, for which water candlesticks and other necessaries shall be provided.

XXVIII. HOURS OF WORK

  1. They shall work an hour before breakfast, and being allowed a competent time, till within half an hour of dinner.

  2. They shall be allowed an hour and an half for dinner and repose from work, and then work till night, according to the nature of their work and the season of the year. (*Plan* 28)

But who was to oversee the processes of this spatial and temporal discipline? In *Discipline and Punish*, Foucault speaks of the "disciplinary gaze,"[8] of how "surveillance" was to be managed, and here he describes this problem as pertaining not just to prisons but also to workshops and to factories. In Hanway's institution, which as we have already suggested contained elements of both factory and prison, surveillance was carried out through hierarchical segmentation. The process was similar to that surveillance order Foucault describes as occurring in the early modern French school: that is, supervisors were selected from among the students themselves whose responsibilities included surveillance functions (*Discipline* 175–77). Similarly, Hanway provided for a matron to be the immediate supervisor of the house: in his words, she "directs the Oeconomy thereof" (*Account* 127)[9] and was aided by an assistant matron who, we are told, "constantly attends with the women, and reports to the matron their behavior" (129). Needed was "intense, continuous supervision" (*Discipline* 174), as Foucault describes the requirements of the new prisons and factories, and such a process could perhaps best be carried out in the Magdalen House by using the female inmates themselves. All of the women are housed in wards and in each ward one of the inhabitants is "appointed to *preside*, and be accountable for the conduct and behaviour of the rest" (*Account* 132). Those capable of instruction—presumably in addition to surveillance—of the other inmates "shall be properly rewarded" (135), thus exemplifying Foucault's observation that surveillance was "integrated into the teaching relationship" (*Discipline* 175).

All these specific microtechniques of the Magdalen House when taken together may be said to constitute the industrialization of charity; these rules and regulations illustrate quite succinctly Foucault's notion of the "development, in the classical period, of a new technique for taking charge of the time of individual existences" (*Discipline* 28). But there is more here than a simple taking charge—there is also the reformation of the female subjects; it is that goal that all the technique is aimed at. What must be achieved for the self and for the state is a transformation of what Linda Mahood calls "'dangerous' female sexualities" (3) into what Foucault calls "docile bodies" (*Discipline* 135 and *passim*).

But how does one know that such transformations, such reformations, can actually be constructed? How can one be assured of the success of such processes? If we recall for a moment the analogies that David Owen and Paul Langford drew between the promotion and operation of eighteenth-century charities and corporate stock companies, then perhaps it is not surprising to discover that the products—the reformed prostitutes—produced by the Magdalen House needed further scrutiny in order to provide proofs to the stockholders that the house indeed "worked." Part of that assurance was provided in Hanway's 1761 *Account* through the publication in that report of letters of support mostly from both current and former inmates who had either expressed content at being in the institution or had already departed and gone on to lead productive and moral lives. As befitting an institution that shares characteristics both of a business and a religious retreat, the house received and had reprinted these letters of testimony from eleven young women who responded most positively to their Magdalen training and reported varying degrees of success in their current stations in life. One writer talks of her recent legacy, which she had given to her mother in recompense for the grief her previous ill conduct had caused; she claims that because of the charity's kind care, she was happily employed and did not herself require the money. Another, a current inmate, writes to her friend Betsy and in an appeal more practical than spiritual admonishes her to seek admission to the house: "You never will be so happy again as long as you live; Consider what a comfortable life we live here, every thing provided for us, and the best of provision" (xviii). There are even letters from the women's relatives, who express gratitude to the institution: one brother writes to the governors and matron of the house, thanking them for having been the "beneficent instrument of preserving a Sister of mine from eternal ruin" (xxv). These testimonials amounting almost to a kind of commercial propaganda for the house no doubt helped to allay whatever fears investors in the charity may have had about the efficacy of the disciplinary regimen.

Additional steps were taken to preserve the good effects of the Magdalen House upon their former subjects. The "Rules" provided each woman upon discharge from the house with assistance in finding employment; this placement service, reinforcing the commercial analogy, no doubt served to make certain that at least initially each former inmate was given some chance to maintain her newly found virtue. As a further inducement to good behavior, any woman after one entire year in service and upon the recommendation of her master or mistress would be eligible to receive a monetary reward. Additional bounties were provided by the governors to those young women who followed a trade or who married.

Such were the processes developed by the Magdalen House to produce a reformed prostitute, to create from that illicit body a docile and ordered being, one who might be marketed as a product fit for domesticity either as a wife or as a worker and who would, in fulfilling this domestic agenda, be also a contributor to the power and prosperity of the British Empire. To what extent we can speak of its success is problematic. Hanway himself certainly thought, as his biographer John Hutchins noted (115–19), that at least in 1761 the charity had proved itself. By that year, Hanway could say that of the nearly three hundred women helped, twenty-seven had been reconciled to parents and another eighty-two placed in secure domestic situations as servants. Only forty-one of these young women failed to reform. This figure needs to be weighted, however, against Vern L. Bullough's contention that as time went on, those reformed by the charity were more likely to have been girls seduced by lovers who had then abandoned them, rather than hardened prostitutes (71).[10] Yet if we return to our Foucauldian framework, the entire discourse surrounding the house, including the various proposals for its establishment and later on the reports of its progress and success, may be said to exemplify what Foucault calls "local centers" of "power-knowledge." The formation of this center revised the language of reform to conform to new economic interests, established the notion of reconstruction (re-formation) as a viable enterprise, and in the process refigured the bodies of wayward girls into the forms of productive servants and wives.

NOTES

1. "Girls" is Jonas Hanway's term and would seem to be appropriate, given that many of the prostitutes of London were in fact under the age of eighteen; the "Rules" section of Hanway's *Plan* stipulated that the Magdalen House would receive young

women and that no one over thirty years of age would be considered for admission (see *Plan* 17). Modern scholarship on the London Magdalen House is not extensive: Vern L. Bullough mentions the house briefly. For Stanley Nash's view of the house, see note 5, below.

2. Hanway was perhaps best known in his time as a major force behind the formation of the Marine Society in 1756; its function was to recruit and outfit men and boys for the British navy. For the most recent full treatment of Hanway and his life, see James Stephen Taylor.

3. See Victor Saxer, especially 249–50, for how Saint Mary Magdalen became in the sixteenth century the saint for communities of repentant sisters.

4. See her chapter, "The Domestication of 'fallen' Women," especially 92–94. Mahood's concerns overlap mine but are far from identical; her interest in Foucault is centered in his *History of Sexuality*; mine lies more in *Discipline and Punish*.

5. Stanley Nash (617–28) also cites Foucault's relevance here and notes how some of the house's features anticipate the prison reforms of the 1770s and 1780s as proposed by Hanway and John Howard. Nash's study is valuable, but he does not undertake the kind of specific analysis I attempt here and sometimes misstates the situation of the house in 1758 by conflating its rules with those of the 1820s.

6. Later in his study, Cohen touches upon Hanway and his house but does not consider Hanway's program in any detail (130–31).

7. For the role that Jonas Hanway was to play in prison reform, see Michael Ignatieff.

8. See, for example, the section "The means of correct training" (172–77).

9. Some changes in the rules had formulated between Hanway's original *Plan* and this progress report appearing three years after the house had begun its operation, but the differences are not substantial.

10. Stanley Nash (623) is also skeptical of the house's claims of success but admits that there is not enough evidence to decide the issue.

WORKS CITED

Andrews, Donna T. *Philanthropy and Police: London Charity in the Eighteenth Century.* Princeton: Princeton UP, 1989.

Armstrong, Nancy, and Leonard Tennenhouse. "Introduction." *The Ideology of Conduct, Essays in Literature and the History of Sexuality.* Ed. Armstrong and Tennenhouse. New York: Methuen, 1987. 1–24.

Bender, John. *Imagining the Penitentiary: Fiction and the Architecture of Mind in Eighteenth-Century England.* Chicago: U of Chicago P, 1987.

Bullough, Vern L. "Prostitution and Reform in Eighteenth Century England." *Unauthorized Sexual Behavior During the Enlightenment.* Ed. Robert Purks Maccubbin. [Special edition of *Eighteenth-Century Life* 9.3 (1985): 61–74.]

Cohen, Sherill. *The Evolution of Women's Asylums since 1500.* New York: Oxford UP, 1992.

Foucault, Michel. *Discipline and Punish. The Birth of the Prison.* Trans. Alan Sheridan. New York: Vintage, 1979.

———. *The History of Sexuality. Volume 1: An Introduction.* Trans. Robert Hurley. New York: Vintage, 1990.

Hanway, Jonas. *An Account of the Rise, Progress, and Present State of the Magdalen Charity.* London: William Faden, 1761.

———. *Letter to Robert Dingley.* London, 1758.

———. *A Plan for Establishing a Charity-House.* London, 1758.

Ignatieff, Michael. *A Just Measure of Pain: The Penitentiary in the Industrial Revolution, 1750–1850.* New York: Pantheon, 1978.

Langford, Paul. *A Polite and Commercial People: England 1727–1783.* Oxford: Oxford UP, 1989.

Mahood, Linda. *The Magdalenes: Prostitution in the Nineteenth Century.* London: Routledge, 1990.

Nash, Stanley. "Prostitution and Charity: The Magdalen Hospital, A Case Study." *Journal of Social History* 17 (1984): 617–28.

Owen, David. *English Philanthropy, 1660–1960.* Cambridge: Belknap, 1964.

Saxer, Victor. *Le Culte de Marie Madelain en occident.* Auxerre: Publications de la Société des Fouilles Archéologiques et des Monuments Historiques de l'Yonne, 1959.

Taylor, James Stephen. *Jonas Hanway, Founder of the Marine Society.* London: Scholar, 1985.

Beckford's Pæderasty

George E. Haggerty

What was the exact business, how, when,
& by whom, & with whom discovered?
Who passive & who active?
  —Pembroke Papers

Beckford is a Professor of Pæderasty
  —Hester Lynch Thrale, Thraliana

On 27 November 1784, the following notice appeared in the pages of London's *Morning Herald:* "The rumour concerning a *Grammatical mistake of Mr. B——* and the *Hon. Mr. C——*, in regard to the genders, we hope for the honour of Nature originates in *Calumny!*—For, however depraved the being must be, who can propagate such reports without foundation, we must wish such a being exists, in preference to characters, who, regardless of Divine, Natural and Human Law, sink themselves below the lowest class of brutes in the most *preposterous* rites" (Chapman 185). Anyone reading this newspaper report, it seems, would have known that the unnamed gender transgressors were the enormously rich William Beckford and his aristocratic cousin William Courtenay.[1] The occasion for the remarks had come to be known as the Powderham Affair, and private accounts of it had been circulating for some time. Beckford and Courtenay had been caught in compromising circumstances of some kind, and Courtenay's uncle, Lord Loughborough, chief justice of the court of common pleas, was determined to ruin Beckford.[2] The appearance of this announcement, however, set the scandal on new, openly public, terms. These remarks in the *Morning Herald*, which Brian Fothergill suggests were planted by Loughborough, plunged the twenty-five-year-old Beckford into a disgrace that was to haunt him until his death sixty years later. Coming as it does, however, midway between the molly house raids and executions of the 1720s and the Vere Street arrests of 1810, the Beckford scandal offers interesting insight into the history of sexuality and the codification of sexual identities.[3]

This first newspaper account begins to explain this process. It is surely significant that perceived irregularity in gender roles is labeled a "Grammatical Mistake." Grammar, in this reading, becomes the figure of hegemonic control, and it is control exercised most effectively at the level of language. Alain de Lille's twelfth-century *The Complaint of Nature* had made a similar claim: the "Man [who] is made woman . . . both predicate and subject, he becomes likewise of two declensions, he pushes the laws of grammar too far." Gregory W. Bredbeck claims that "De Lille's readers must 'read' sodomy, and hence sodomy becomes a part of who they are as readers. Obviously *The Complaint of Nature* . . . ascribe[s] a subjective potentiality to the rhetoric of homoeroticism" (146–48).[4] By 1784, the naturalization of grammar is such that a "grammatical mistake" of this kind challenges the "honour of Nature." The passage from the *Morning Herald* also ascribes a subjective potentiality, but it does so by means of an inscription that renders subjectivity itself a grammatical impossibility. The "characters" who would be the subjects of this report, its "beings," are here rendered the object of a dependent prepositional phrase. Grammar works, in other words, to marginalize and control that which it finds threatening. But it needs that threat in order to justify, as it were, its exclusionary system. By inscribing gender as a grammatical system without a subject, moreover, this writer suggests ways in which sexuality itself is inscribed. In cultural terms, subjectivity is only possible when a sentence is already passed: this sentence posits a being that could not, should not exist, but that by the very articulation of this "rumour" can and does. Sexual identity, sexuality itself, then, emerges from this cultural attempt to inscribe subjectivity in its own likeness. Beckford's "Grammatical mistake" becomes the sign of sexual difference.

George E. Haggerty

Significantly, the report fails to distinguish between the two "characters" involved. One would imagine that if Beckford alone were the object of the attack, it would emphasize his relation to the much younger William Courtenay (who had reached seventeen by the time of the scandal).[5] If it were not articulated as pæderasty as such, at least some mention of sexual victimization might be expected. But not here: Mr. B. and the Hon. Mr. C. are both involved in "*preposterous* rites": here the language of religion, devotions contrary to nature, gives their activity a status that can render it threatening to social order. For however sunk below the lowest class of brutes, these "*preposterous* rites" threaten, by their inversion of the natural order, the very terms by which a society constructs it own identity. Because "Law" determines what is "Natural," these characters are placed outside of nature. In practical terms, however, nature comes to mean merely polite society. As one writer from Italy asked, "Is Beckford at Fonthill, and is he chassé or still received in company?" (Herbert 274; qtd. in Fothergill 173).

A week later, another popular strain is introduced, and the "scene" of transgression is reinterpreted: "If anything could heighten the detestable scene lately acted in *Wiltshire*, by a pair of fashionable *male lovers*, the ocular demonstration of their infamy, to the young and beautiful wife of one of the monsters, must certainly have effected it (*Morning Herald*; qtd. in Chapman 185).[6] The laws of grammar work similarly here, and not only are the "lovers" relegated again to a prepositional position, but also the scene of their "infamy" is exactly what is not represented. The point of this piece, of course, is to evoke an image of male lovemaking and place it squarely in the public imagination. Margaret Beckford becomes a kind of conduit of voyeuristic pleasure for the reader of the *Morning Herald*, and the "ocular demonstration" that is described invites a range of fantastic recreations of the "detestable scene." More effective, perhaps, than grammar, the visual evocation of the "male lovers" fixes them in all their monstrosity in the imagination of anyone reading this passage. At the same time, however, "a pair of fashionable *male lovers*" is hardly the expression of monstrosity that contemporary accounts of sodomy would lead one to expect. In fact, it articulates the possibility of a male relation in a way that is rare in the eighteenth century, suggesting in its turn of phrase something more like our own configuration of relational possibilities. Of course, it may be possible that the writer, by coining this expression, was attempting to register horror, but what he or she does register is something like difference—the difference that the description of two men as lovers continues to make today.

Beckford met his cousin William Courtenay at Powderham Castle, the home of Beckford's aristocratic Courtenay relatives, when he was on a tour of England in the summer of 1779. Beckford was eighteen years old and Courtenay eleven. His attachment to the boy quickly became an intense romantic obsession that his closest friends seemed to know about and (perhaps) encourage. To Alexander Cozens, for instance, the drawing master who might himself have introduced young Beckford to exoticized desires, Beckford wrote at Christmas 1779 that he had been walking by moonlight: "I was so charmed with the novelty of the prospect that setting the cold at defiance, I walked to and fro on the platform for several minutes, fancying the fictions of romance realized, and almost imagining myself surrounded by some wondrous misty barrier no *prophane* could penetrate. How I wished for my dear Wm. to share with me this imaginary contentment" (Melville 77). All the elements of Beckford's sexual sensibility are implied in his few remarks to Cozens: the nervous anxiety, almost irritability, the romantic fictions, the imaginative isolation, the mist, the barrier between life and death, and, of course, William. These elements are so worked and reworked over the next five years— some throughout his entire life—that they begin to have an identificatory quality quite unlike that of any simple report of sodomitical behavior.

Just after Christmas, 1779, he writes to Cozens again:

> My cares have been a little while suspended—for I have been listening these several Evenings to plaintive Sicilian Airs. You can hardly believe what a melancholy has of late possessed me. My ideas of Happiness are at length very simple, for they consist alone in a secure retirement with the one I love. . . . Never could I have believed myself so entirely subdued—by whom you solely are acquainted. I wonder at myself every instant and only wish you was here to be surprized at me—One moment I am for flying into . . . the next . . . my Cheeks glow and I determine to remain immured in my Cell. Is it possible that a few Weeks' absence can have produced such effects—can have rendered me so miserable—Am I not the strangest of Beings? (Melville 77–78)

The exuberance of youthful infatuation becomes more like misery when emotion gives way to desire. What seems at first a pose—the Sicilian Airs, the melancholy, the "retirement with the one I love"—becomes an almost hysterical torment of frustrated desire. Beckford uses the vocabulary of dis-ease to emphasize the depth of his overheated emotion. The blood rushes to his cheeks in an anatomical redirection that calls to mind the reactions of "female" sensibility. This sensibility combines with the misery of the monkish "Cell" to color potentially "unnatural" desires with an exotic glow that resists the label of criminality. Beckford celebrates his own misery as a way of validating the feelings he has already been forced to question. In doing so, he attempts to defy the cultural conventions that would turn him against himself. This may be the gloomy sensibility of the exoticized man of feeling, but it begins to suggest the makings of a sexual "identity."

As a result of such careful probings of his own sexual makeup, Beckford became for his generation, in Byron's phrase, the "Apostle of Pæderasty," and his novel, *Vathek* (1786), a primer of man-boy love. Hester Lynch Thrale Piozzi announced that she found Beckford's "favourite propensity" in the "luscious descriptions of [the young boy] Gulchenrouz" when she read *Vathek* a few years after publication. She returned to this idea some years later, when complaining of the "luscious fondness" with which Richard Cumberland describes the *"personal Charms"* of the heroes in his novel *Henry* (1795); "The same is to be observed in Vathek," she says, "but then Beckford is a Professor of Pæderasty" (Thrale 2: 799 n. 969). Apostle of Pæderasty and Professor of Pæderasty are close enough—although the difference between a religious and an academic metaphor is hardly negligible; if Mrs. Piozzi's comment rings with the astuteness of a cultural critic, then Byron's shimmers with the excitement of a devotee—to suggest that a sexual role was being established for Beckford. This role seems to approximate our own notion of the pæderast. It seems, in other words, that Beckford played a significant role in the popular evocation of a sexual identity distinct from the various sodomitical labels that were current at the time. Beckford's unique blend of erotic desire and almost sickly sensibility makes pæderasty newly available as an explanatory label for male sexuality. Beckford creates his own sexuality in a series of letters that are astonishing in their directness and devastating in their implications. From this material and from the accounts of his life that were circulated in the popular press and in private accounts of his "scandalous" behavior, I hope to show how a sexual identity is articulated and why the public recognition of this articulation is both swift and unequivocal. In his open display of this particular sexual transgression, Beckford threatened to expose the very foundations of culture. The scandal surrounding his pæderasty is culture's response to his "eccentricity." In the language of Beckford's love, however, it is possible to hear a shift in the emphases of male-male desire.[7]

The *OED* defines *pæderasty* as "unnatural connexion with a boy; sodomy," and it defines *pæderast* as "sodomite." The elision between pæderasty and sodomy, which the *OED* reports and reproduces, is inherent in the trans-

lation of the Greek: boy-lover in the original becomes an "unnatural connexion" or even an activity. But unlike *sodomy* and *sodomite, pæderasty* and
pæderast imply no activity, natural or unnatural. The words speak of love.
Boy-love, if you will. And while this love is often erotic and at times explicitly physical, the term pæderast is not necessarily associated with behavior. It represents a relation that is nonetheless powerful and, some
would argue, pervasive in Western culture. Feminist and cultural critics
have argued that pæderasty is the structural basis of western civilization
and that it goes a long way toward explaining the inherent misogyny of
our culture.[8] David Halperin has taught us to understand Greek
pæderasty, moreover, not as some cozy classical prelude to "domestic part-
nership" but rather as a carefully hierarchized system of male relations
that both regulated desire and determined sexual positioning (Halperin
20–24, 54–71, and *passim;* also, Dover 16–17, 49–54, 73–109). When
Halperin says, for instance, that in Greek terms there is nothing problematical "about a desire on the part of males to obtain sexual pleasure
from contact with males—so long as that desire respects the proper phallocentric protocols (which . . . identify 'masculinity' with an insertive sexual role)," the distance from late twentieth-century sexual assumptions is
clear. There is little question of seeing classical pæderasty as anything
even approximating our own notions of mutual same-sex desire.

  Greek love, however, has often been idealized or sentimentalized, and a
sentimental reading of the Greeks was implicit in the first articulations
of sexual liberation—particularly for male homosexuals—in the late
nineteenth century.[9] This emotional understanding of pæderastic love
was to a certain extent implicit in the Greek original: platonic love itself
involves the idealization that leads to an extravagantly poetic expression
of the beauties of the object of desire, the boy, to the extent that the boy
himself becomes lost in the effusion of language articulating his attractions.[10]

  If this emotional pæderasty existed in early modern England, as a rich
range of sources suggests that it did, then by the time of the Restoration,
the tendency at least in aristocratic circles was either to condemn it as
sodomitical or condone it as no different structurally from other exercises
of male privilege, or both.[11] The male libertine, for whom a boy could
serve as a sexual partner as readily as a woman, offers a useful example of
how this system of simultaneous celebration and censure could work.
John Wilmot, Earl of Rochester, has helpfully memorialized this possibility in a number of poems. In a poem about impotence, for instance, the
poet insists on his earlier sexual achievements: "The *Dart* of love," he says,

through ev'ry *Cunt*, reacht ev'ry *Heart*.
Stiffly resolv'd, twould carelessly invade,
Woman or *Man*, nor ought its fury staid,
Where e're it peirce'd, a *Cunt* it found or made.
("The Imperfect Enjoyment," lines 37–43 [*Poems* 31])

Few would see this as a source for "homosexual" or even homoerotic be-havior.[12] What is interesting here, however, is the libertine ability to "make a cunt" in any place of choice. Like Halperin's Greek love, libertine love seems to be more about power than it is about desire. "Cunt-making," after all, is a process of subordination, a process, by the way, that depends on a functioning organ alone. The libertine can take pride in his ability as he takes pride in the position his penis guarantees him. Of course, the anxiety about the ability of that organ to function is an anxiety about the construction of masculinity itself. As the increasingly hysterical tone of the poem suggests, male subjectivity itself is threatened when the penis is flaccid: if it can't make cunts, it might as well become one.

In another poem, "The Disabled *Debauchee*," an aging rake, in the midst of recounting tales of past conquest, gives in to a moment of nostalgia:

Nor shall our *Love-fits Cloris* be forgot,
When the well-look'd *Link-Boy*, strove t'enjoy,
And the best Kiss, was the deciding *Lot*,
Whether the *Boy* fuck'd you, or I the *Boy*.
(lines 37–40 [*Poems* 99])

Again, the power dynamic seems what is most important here, and we would not want to make any claims about Rochester's "sexuality" on the basis of this kind of remark. And just as "cunt" in the previous passage was not clearly defined by gender, so "*Boy*" in this is not clearly defined by age. "*Boy*" defines social and sexual position more than it represents a sign of cross-generational desire. But surely that is not surprising when every sexual relation, as these poems suggest, is so rigidly hierarchical as to insist on power relations before any kind of desire can be articulated.[18] This is not even the kind of homosocial bonding that Sedgwick describes so effectively in *Between Men*. This is a sexuality of every "Man" for him-self, a libertinism, as Harold Weber argues, that observes "a strict erotic demarcation between the male object of desire and the desiring male sub-ject" (115; see also Trumbach, "The Birth of the Queen").

Pæderasty, then, is not a pretty picture, either in classical Greece or in eighteenth-century England.[14] Throughout the eighteenth century, pæderasty often seems interchangeable with sodomy, even if the former retains its association with boys. The term is less common than sodomy throughout the century, however, and it is not registered in the public imagination as a capital offense, as sodomy is. At times it retains its original meaning, as in Swift's use of the term in *A Tale of a Tub*, and at others it is at least culturally specific, as in specific references to the ancient world in Hume and Gibbon.[15] Whenever the word is used, it is either associated automatically with master-pupil relations in school (as Swift's use suggests), or it is a slightly fancier way of talking about the act of sodomy.[16] What seems clear, however, is that throughout the eighteenth century there was no cult of pæderasty, either in the popular imagination or in fact, as distinct from the sodomitical subcultures that were regularly harassed and persecuted.

The case of William Beckford, however, illustrates the limits of the sodomitical model. The Beckford scandal not only resulted in de facto exile and lifelong ostracism for the talented writer and musician but also a new and different understanding of male-male desire. For all the harm that came to Beckford and his paramour William Courtenay, I would claim that we can discover in this case the originary conception, in Beckford's writing, in the press, and in the popular response to his situation, of a particular kind of male homosexual sensibility. I do not mean that Beckford and Courtenay understood themselves in any way out of keeping with the grotesque way their culture saw them. I do think, however, that Beckford articulated his feelings for Courtenay in such a way that he opened a space, as it were, in which a man could identify his feelings for another male, in terms that suggest the recognition of a sexual identity. The particular combination of intelligence, self-indulgence, narcissism, sensibility, and descriptive power that was Beckford's gives his pæderasty a special place in the history of sexualities. For whatever Beckford is in his own and in the popular imagination, he is not a sodomite. This distinction is more than semantic.

By the time of his twenty-first birthday, in 1781, Beckford had had various emotional attachments with sensitive women within his larger family circle and with adolescent or preadolescent boys both within his family and without. The length he goes to express the emotional intensity of all these affairs suggests that he is making up for their lack of actual physical involvement. What is particularly striking, even at this early stage, is the degree to which his female lovers become a part of his pæderastic enterprise. Again and again throughout these early affairs, Beckford uses a woman to bring him closer to the boy he loves. In letters that I quote below, Charlotte Courtenay, Courtenay's aunt, Louisa, the wife of his cousin Peter Beckford, and the Contessa d'Orsini-Rosenberg each fill this role. Other women seem to have been somehow entangled in his love as well. The impression is one of an emotional bond that included acceptance of his "strange wayward passion."[17] Beckford seems to have needed a female friend to devote herself to him at the same time that she made herself an intermediary with the boy. As Fothergill said about the situation at Powderham, where Charlotte Courtenay was clearly devoted to Beckford and where Courtenay was quickly capturing his heart: "to be in love with the nephew and not to be unaware of the admiration of the aunt was a situation very much to Beckford's taste" (70). What these letters demonstrate is that this was more than an arrangement of practical or emotional convenience for Beckford: the female figure, like Halperin's Diotoma, is necessary to the erotic attachment to the boy: she allows it, she encourages it, she creates a space through which the man can reach out to the boy.[18]

In one letter, for instance, he writes to Courtenay's Aunt Charlotte, later to become the wife of Beckford's tormentor, Lord Loughborough, asking her to intercede with the boy, who has not responded to his letters:

Surely he [Courtenay] will never find any other Being so formed by nature for his companion as myself. Of all the human creatures male or female with which I have been acquainted in various countries and at different periods he is the only one that seems to have been cast in my mold.

When I first began to know him the pleasing delusion would often suggest itself of our having been friends in some other existence. You know he was never so happy as when reclined by my side listening to my wild musick or the strange stories which sprang up in my fancy for his amusement. Those were the most delightful hours of my existence. (Chapman 81–82; see also, Fothergill 98–99)

This letter goes on to tell of shared musical moments and of a friendship on which he depends for life itself. Beckford uses a vocabulary understood as erotic in the eighteenth century: "wild music" and "strange stories" could hardly be considered innocent, nor would the image of the younger and older boy "reclined" together be anything but provocative. Fothergill calls these comments "reckless," but they can only be understood as reckless if Beckford did not mean them actively to imply an intimacy outside of the bounds of social respectability. But he could hardly mean anything else: "How often has my sleep been disturbed by his imaginary cries, how frequently have I seen him approach me, pale and trembling as I lay dozing at Caserta lulled by my dear Lady Hamilton's musick and bathed in tears. . . . If anything could reconcile me to death it twould be the promise of mingling our last breaths together and sharing the same grave" (Fothergill 99). Far from hiding his feelings, or exposing them unwittingly, Beckford seems to threaten the boy's aunt with his own increasingly urgent desire. That he writes this way to a woman who has exposed her own deep feelings for him is more than reckless: it seems on the one hand an elaborate courtship ritual that all his women friends have been subjected to; and it seems on the other an excuse for spelling out the details of his attachment to the boy in heightened emotional detail. The presence of the woman, in other words, allows Beckford to write out his passion in terms that defy convention and create a new vocabulary for male-male desire at the same time that they mimic conventional sexual transgression. Beckford needs to write about his love because it has been silenced elsewhere, everywhere. Beckford takes the crime not to be mentioned among Christians and gives it all the emotional superstructure of "romantic friendship," and in doing so he liberates himself, as it were, from the silences that surround him.[19]

At the same time, even at this early stage, his "romantic friendship" seems to have taken on a quality that embodies the threat of social opprobrium within it. For all the poetic liberation it embodies, internalized self-hatred seems increasingly to haunt Beckford's pæderasty. Beckford's ever-more perfumed sensibility begins to seem lethal: desire implies death, brings the threat of death, becomes almost a desire for death—as Beckford's culture had taught him all too well. I resist the obvious implication of a Freudian death instinct, here and later, not because I do not see such a function in representations of desire in the eighteenth century but because Beckford's articulation of the attractions of death is never less than conscious.

In a letter to the Contessa d'Orsini-Rosenberg, the wealthy widow who befriended him in Venice and was witness to his emotional attachments to various young men, Beckford writes out the details of his love for Courtenay in a way that confirms the physical expression of their love at the same time that it dramatizes the specific dimensions of his fear:[20]

From the theater, I take him to my bed. Nature, Virtue, Glory all *disappear*—entirely lost, confused, destroyed. O, heavens, that I could die in these kisses and plunge my soul with his into the happiness or the pain which must never end. Must I live in fear of a moment which must separate us again. Do not be surprised if I desire death with eagerness.

Hurry, compose some sweet potion which will put all three of us to sleep, which will close our eyes without anguish, which will steal our souls away and deliver them imperceptively to the flowered fields of some other existence. . . .

Surely there is no hell for me in the other world because I am damned on earth. Do you know of a state more frightening than this which I suffer—spied upon by a thousand Arguses without hearts and without ears, constrained to abandon the unique hope that reconciles me to life, menaced at each instant, accused of the ruin of a being I adore in whom all human affections are concentrated to a point. Such is my present situation, such are the Demons that Destiny has set on my trail.[21]

Beckford, at twenty-two, has effected a link between sensibility and erotic activity that will not be fully realized until the end of the nineteenth century. To say that he is ahead of his time is only to confess that we have not understood the implications of his love for Courtenay. Pæderastic love is not idealized here. Happiness and pain are interchangeable partly because Beckford only finds happiness in pain and partly because he knows that his love brings with it the social condemnation he fears. He asks for death as both a way of preserving their moment of happiness and a way of escaping the torment of a world that persecutes what it does not understand. At the same time, he seems to want to disembody his affection and translate it into a sensuously spiritual realm. The "other existence" that he desires is as much an escape from life, from the implications of the physical, as it is a life away from the spying Arguses. It almost seems as if it would be an escape into life, into a life in which their love would be possible precisely because it would be an impossibility. If this sounds paradoxical, it is no more so than Beckford's desire itself. The "unique hope" that "reconciles [him] to life" is the hope that Courtenay will offer him a way out of this dilemma; but of course that is precisely what Courtenay can never do. That Beckford could imagine that Courtenay could be anything but a victim, either of himself or of his society, is a measure of his delusion. Beckford lives in his emotion, but at the same time, that emotion embodies the fear of desire, the "Demons" that come to torment him from within as well as without. The sympathetic contessa can compose the potion that will effect this transformation because she can sympathize, she can understand, she can give their love a place that exists outside of time and consequently outside of desire as well as fate. It is a place, of course, that Beckford never found.

A little over a year later, he writes to Courtenay in terms that dramatize this complicated emotional stance even more vividly. The boy had
scribbled a postscript to a letter written by the ever-devoted Louisa, his
cousin Peter's wife, who was by now almost desperate in her love for
Beckford. I quote this letter at length because it seems to me to tell the
whole story of Beckford's pæderasty:

> I read your letter with a beating heart, my dearest Willy, and kissed it
> a thousand times. It is needless for me to repeat that I am miserable
> without you. You know I can scarcely be said to live in your absence. No
> words can express my feelings when I saw the Afft. lines you wrote in
> our dear Louisa's letter. At this moment I am ready to cry with joy. Do
> not forget me my own William. Do not forget the happy hours we have
> passed together. Your poor Mother loved you not better than I do. At
> any time I would sacrifice every drop of blood in my veins to do you
> good, or spare you a moment's misery. I shall never enjoy peace again
> till I know whether I am to be with you when I return. I am certain
> your Father is set against us, and will do all in his power as well as your
> cruel Aunt to keep us asunder; but it will be your fault, if you intirely
> abandon me. What have we done, Wm., to be treated with such se-
> verity! I often dream after a solitary ramble on the dreary plains near
> Rome, that I am sitting with you in a meadow at Ford on a summer's
> evening, my arm thrown round your neck. I seem to see the wilds be-
> yond the House and the Cattle winding slowly among them. I even
> fancy, I hear your voice singing one of the tunes I composed when I was
> in Devonshire. Whilst thus engaged and giving way to a languid mel-
> ancholy tenderness, two snakes start from the hedge and twine round
> us. I see your face turn pale and your limbs tremble. I seem to press you
> closely in my arms. We both feel the cold writhing of the snakes in our
> bosoms, both join our lips for the last time and both expire. . . . Louisa
> can tell you that this is not the first time such horrid dreams have
> haunted me. If I might interpret my vision, . . . and . . . are the Snakes,
> who under the appearance of prudence and affection would creep into
> our bosoms and sting our vitals. Why cannot we be friends in peace? Is
> there any crime in loving each other as we do? You will hardly be able
> to read this letter: it is blotted with my tears. My William, my own dear
> Friend, write to me for God's sake: put all your confidence in Louisa
> who loves us both. (Chapman 135–36; dated Rome July 1st, 1782)

This letter exposes the nature of this love affair in dazzling detail. At first,
this account heightens the difference that I have articulated between "sod-

omy" and Beckford's male version of "romantic friendship." Moving, as it does, from the excitement of anticipation ("a beating heart") through misery and lifelessness, to exuberant feelings and tears of joy—all in the first few sentences—the letter comes alive with a high-pitched emotionalism that begins to suggest what Beckford's "pæderasty" has come to mean. A simple "do not forget me" becomes "your poor mother loved you not better than I do"; Courtenay's mother (recently deceased) was Beckford's friend, of course, and Beckford seems quite ready to invoke the female component of his affection even if the female, as in this case, is deceased. A Freudian reading of this attempt to express love for a boy by means of an appeal to his dead mother might suggest that Beckford was rewriting Courtenay's family romance with himself in the maternal position, perfectly reasonable if Beckford's intention was to construct a subjectivity receptive to his "maternal" love. But Beckford also knows that a mother's love can be as brutalizing and devastating as any antagonistic force—his own mother had hardly begun her openly antagonistic campaign against him, nor had her violent affection for her son brought him anything but heartache—and he may have meant the maternal analogy as a threat. Both are implicit in his ready transition from mother to martyr, and his perfunctory willingness to "sacrifice every drop of blood" stops just short of making himself the victim of Courtenay's innocence.

Once Beckford mentions the boy's father, however, undisguised recrimination and threat follow fast upon one another, and the letter quickly turns from a love letter to a death threat. The love itself implies this hideous denouement, the letter suggests, and the boy is made to seem responsible for whatever effect paternal disapproval will finally have—"it will be your fault if you intirely abandon me"—and his pathetic "What have we done"—as if the twelve-year-old could answer that question better than he—smacks either of total innocence or total disingenuousness. What begins then as the tale of music on a summer's evening and is so calculatingly disfigured as a hideous nightmare suggests not just the threat that Beckford is sending to his young cousin but also his own deepest sense of what their affection means. The boys embrace as they are "giving way to a languid melancholy tenderness" only to find that they feel "the cold writhing of the Snakes in our bosoms." Of course, the snakes represent Courtenay's father and his aunt, but they also represent the destructive power of desire to corrupt the pure love that Beckford constantly tries to articulate when talking to the boy. It is as if he is saying that the destruction of their love is present in its very constitution; that he cannot put his arm around the boy without the snakes intruding, winding in their entrails, and finally destroying them. Beckford seems unclear as to whether it is the world outside or the world within that is most destructive.

"Why cannot we be friends in peace? Is there any crime in loving each other as we do?" The answer to Beckford's question is of course both yes and no. There is no crime in their love, or in any other that is as deeply mutual as this seems to have been. But it is a crime to defy cultural dictates in this way, as Beckford knows. By loving the boy as he does, Beckford condemns them both to a life of ignominy and shame. What Beckford has done, however, is subtly to have leveled the criminal accusation at the boy who returns his love. Courtenay is blamed here as blatantly as he will be later on. For after all, Beckford seems to say, he causes the desire that threatens to destroy them both. At Powderham that threat was fulfilled.[22]

When the scandal first broke, Beckford thought of fleeing, but if he did start to leave the country he got no farther than Dover. He sat out the vilification of his name at home in Fonthill. That is what makes the following notice so surprising.

> Mr. —— of ——, &c. &C. is certainly gone post haste to *Italy!*
> Master ——, the eldest, indeed the only son of Lord ——, has left Westminster School, and accompanies Mr. ——!
> Dr. M—— D—— was the gentleman who was unlucky enough to detect the late nasty flagitious business.
> Florence is the place of destination fixed on for the eccentric travellers.
> (*Public Advertiser*, 1 December 1784; correction of Chapman 185)

The hints at actual scandal are more suggestive here, and the tone of public outrage has achieved something of its vocabulary of exclusion: the terms, that is, that will keep Beckford out of polite society for sixty years. That such a scandal would place Beckford and Courtenay in Italy is of course no surprise in the eighteenth century. Italy had already been called the "*Mother* and *Nurse* of *Sodomy*" (in *Satan's Harvest Home*) and even Beckford's friend, Sir William Hamilton, received from his nephew the following account of what had happened at Fonthill: "his promised honours will be withheld; he probably will be obliged to vacate his seat, and retire to Italy to make up the loss which Italy has sustained by Lord Tilney's death, unless he aspires to the office of G. Chamberlain to the K[ing] of P[russia]" (Trumbach, *Satan's Harvest Home* 51).[23] Both accounts assume that Beckford has fled, or that he has been sent away ("the destination fixed on for . . ."), and that there are witnesses to a "late nasty flagitious business." Neither assumption is correct, but each remains useful in the years to come. The term "eccentric travellers," however, hints again at a space—however distant from the center—for two such men to occupy. Of course it is a euphemism, but is the very choice that suggests a kind of public recognition even in public censure.[24]

In the "episodes" of *Vathek*, which were never published in his lifetime, Beckford articulates a tale of pæderasty that is both elegant in its expression and chilling in its implication. In "The Story of Prince Alasi and the Princess Firouzkah," as Brian Fothergill notes, Beckford reworks his portrayal of innocent youth.[25] In this story a young boy, Firouz, becomes the obsession of Prince Alasi and leads him into a nefarious world of desire and recrimination. Notwithstanding an opportune change in the boy's gender—Firouz reveals himself later as the Princess Firouzkah—Beckford's issues are not far from the surface. Fothergill makes an almost too easy connection between Firouz and Courtenay, but it seems fair to say that in the character of Firouz Beckford was looking for ways to explain the failure of his own pæderastic attachments (Fothergill 142). When Firouz first appears Alasi says: "At last . . . Heaven has hearkened to my dearest wish. It has sent me the true heart's-friend I should never have found in my court; it has sent him to me adorned with all the charms of innocence—charms that will be followed, at a maturer age, by those good qualities that make of friendship man's highest blessing." Soon, however, that "innocence" proves to be corrupt and corrupting. Firouz's last act of villainy is his revelation of himself as a woman: no treachery in the story seems greater than this. "What irresistible power compels me to love you," Alasi asks the boy Firouz (Beckford, *Episodes* 5, 13).

Compulsive love of a boy inherently wicked is a not quite fitting epitaph to the affair with William Courtenay. Nor was Beckford's love of Courtenay as beneficent as that expressed in this moral tale. Still, the tale is suggestive. The ideal transition from love-object to friend that is celebrated in this passage eluded Beckford.[26] Firouz's ability to change gender suggests how little control one's love can ever exert on another. The search for a "true heart's-friend" may never be more than illusory. Beckford found in his own sexuality a quality that he did not understand, that he did not trust, and that he knew would destroy him. But he also knew that this was who he was. He grappled throughout his life with a sexual instinct that made him a criminal in his own desire. By acknowledging it in his writing, however, he gives it an identity, a sexual identity, that defies "grammatical" convention. With Beckford, the pæderast becomes a part of speech.

The Pembroke Papers are quoted in Trumbach, and also in Fothergill (173). Lord Pembroke was writing to England at the time of the Powderham scandal; interestingly, his knowledge of the situation led him to no conclusions about sexual roles.

1. William Beckford was born in 1760 to one of England's wealthiest families. His father was alderman and lord mayor of London; his mother a strict Calvinist who did her best, especially after his father died when he was ten years old, to form a young gentleman who would rise to political prominence as his father had. Beckford early on showed tendencies of which his mother disapproved: his devotion to music, his fascination with "oriental" tales, and his love of young boys. William Courtenay, born in 1768, was the son and heir of the second Viscount Courtenay; the youngest of thirteen children, and the only boy, he was known in the family as "Kitty."

2. It is impossible to say what "really" happened at Powderham. There is little reason to think that Beckford and Courtenay were exposed in some dramatic way: Beckford himself protested that he was innocent of any wrongdoing, and he nursed a grievance against Loughborough throughout his entire life. Loughborough may only have had Beckford's letters to Courtenay. But then, what more did he need to exercise complete control over his eccentric victim? For details of the Powderham scandal, see Fothergill 163–75.

3. To prosecute Beckford, Loughborough would have needed at least an eyewitness, which, in spite of the lurid accounts that emerged from Powderham, he seems not to have had; and he would have needed Courtenay's willingness to hand over letters and to participate in the prosecution. Records of eighteenth-century sodomy trials, such as they are, suggest no precedent for prosecuting a person of Beckford's class or social status. Some of these trials are reprinted in Trumbach, ed., *Select Trials at the Sessions-House in the Old Bailey* 2: 362–65, 367–69; and in Trumbach, ed., *Sodomy Trials*; see also Bray 81–114; and Trumbach, "London's Sodomites."

4. See de Lille, *Complaint of Nature* 3; see also, de Lille, *Plaint of Nature* 68.

5. Fourteen was the age of consent for males at the time; see Trumbach, "Sodomitical Assaults" 410.

6. For a similar argument against sodomy, see *Satan's Harvest Home* 50–55.

7. The pæderasty of *Vathek*, obvious to readers such as Hester Piozzi, is so suffused with the twilight glow of Beckford's emotion as to defy late twentieth-century notions of child abuse and victimization. It is centered on the figure of Gulchenrouz, the only central character who escapes damnation in the novel, and he does so by remaining within "the pure happiness of childhood" in which love remains unsullied by the promptings of desire. See Haggerty.

8. See, for instance, MacCannell, and Gallop. MacCannell develops Gallop's argument about the relation between pedagogy and pæderasty from the time of Plato.

9. As early as 1831, Arthur Hallam wrote his prizewinning essay on Greek love, which parallels arguments made even earlier by Percy Bysshe Shelley; see Dellamora 16–17, 24–25.

10. For a discussion of the language and imagery of Greek love, see Dover 39–59.

11. For an instance of Renaissance pæderasty, see Barnfield.

12. The most complete classification of male-male sexual possibilities in the eighteenth century is that found in Rousseau; for Rousseau's account of Beckford, see 144.

13. It was not only court libertines who felt this way. Trumbach alludes to the 1761 court martial in which "Charles Ferret testified that when he was awakened by the noise of the sexual exertion of Henry Newton on Thomas Finney's body, '[I] put my left hand up and got hold of both his stones fast, the other part was in the body of the boy, I asked him what he had got there, he said cunt'" (Trumbach, "Sodomitical Assaults" 415); see also Gilbert 74–75. Gilbert also explains that, "In spite of the supposed legal difficulties of proving buggery in the courts, a high percentage of purported sodomites are convicted and executed. While proof of penetration rules protected some men on trial for this offense, the navy still managed to hang more than half the men brought to trial for buggery between 1749 and 1806" (86).

14. Pæderasty, of course, was implicit in accounts of male-male erotic attraction that centered on the figure of Ganymede; see, for instance, Saslow; for a discussion of the "cultural translation" of the myth, see Barkin 8, 21–24, 29–36, 56–59. See also Bredbeck 3–23; Bredbeck explains Renaissance distinctions among the terms Ganymede, catamite, and ingle, see 16–18.

15. In *A Tale of a Tub* (1704), Swift mentions that his academy will include a "large *Pederastick* school with *French* and *Italian* masters" (41); see also Gibbon 4: 233. Hume says that "Solon's law forbid pæderasty to slaves, as being an act of too great dignity for such mean persons" (2: 292, n.).

16. Cannon's *Ancient and Modern Pæderasty Investigated* is the text one would wish to turn to in this context, but it is unfortunately lost.

17. Beckford uses this phrase in a reverie written to Courtenay but never sent; see Chapman 55.

18. David Halperin tries to argue the role that femininity might play in the definition of male-male desire, and Kaja Silverman, too, talks about the "place of femininity in male homosexuality." See Halperin 113–51; Silverman 339, also 339–88.

19. On "romantic friendship," Mavor; see also Todd 1–6.

20. Not all of Beckford's women friends were as supportive as these. Beckford's experience in Venice was a source of serious concern to his patroness, Lady Hamilton, wife of Sir William Hamilton, envoy to Naples. Beckford could say to her, typically: "I can venture expressing to you all my wayward thoughts—can murmur—can even weep in your company" (Melville 98; see also, Fothergill 93); her response was clear: "Take courage. You have taken the first steps, continue to resist, and every day you will find the struggle less—the *important* struggle—what is it for? no less than *honour, reputation*, and all that an honest and noble soul holds dear, while infamy, *eternal infamy* (my Soul freezes when I write the word) attends the giving way to the soft alluring of a criminal passion" (qtd. from the *Hamilton Papers*, Chapman 78). It is important to remember that even at the time of the scandal, Beckford's wife was present. It is perhaps because she *was* present that the scandal ever occurred. Perhaps the presence of his wife who supported and loved him and who, if she was like any of the other women to whom he was attached, knew about his devotion to William, gave him permission, as it were, to pursue the boy during their visit there. Whatever is true, she remained faithful to him till her death a few years later.

21. Written in December 1781, in French; quoted in Alexander 263–66 (my translation).

22. There is ample evidence that Beckford was less charmed with the sixteen-year-old William Courtenay than he had been with the "luscious" youth of twelve or

thirteen. He wrote letters complaining of the boy's effeminacy, his interest in fashion, and his lack of attention in matters artistic or musical. After the crisis, Beckford blamed Courtenay for all that occurred.

23. Hamilton quoted in Fothergill 173, from *Hamilton Papers* 1: 95, letter 133; both characters were notorious for sexual "eccentricity."

24. Courtenay may have left Westminster School, but he did not accompany Beckford anywhere, nor were the two ever really close again. He went on to succeed his father as third Viscount Courtenay and later ninth earl of Devon, and himself became notorious as a homosexual who was nearly prosecuted for his behavior. When convinced that a "jury of his peers" would not condone his activities, he "wept like a child and was willingly taken abroad on a vessel . . . and passed there under a false name" (qtd. in Fothergill 178, from *Farington Diary* 6: 273). He died in exile in 1835. Few critics or biographers have shown much interest in the later career of Courtenay, but some have gone so far as to blame him for Beckford's downfall. One biographer, for instance, says that "in apportioning blame it is only fair to Beckford to remember that the life of Courtenay (afterwards Earl of Devon) ended, years after he and Beckford had drifted apart, in shame and moral catastrophe" (Oliver 196 n).

25. On both *Vathek* and "The Story of Prince Alasi and the Princess Firouzkah," see Fothergill 128–34, 142–43.

26. For an account of Beckford's later love affair with Gregorio Franchi, which was uniquely satisfying, see Fothergill 199–200; see also, Norton 221–31.

WORKS CITED

Alexander, Boyd. *England's Wealthiest Son.* London: Centaur, 1962.

Barkin, Leonard. *Transuming Passion: Ganymede and the Erotics of Humanism.* Stanford: Stanford UP, 1991.

Barnfield, Richard. *The Affectionate Shepheard, Containing the Complaint of Daphnis for the loue of Ganimede.* London, 1594.

Beckford, William. *The Episodes of Vathek.* Trans. Sir Frank T. Marzial. London: Chapman and Dodd, n.d.

———. *Vathek.* 1786. Ed. Roger Lonsdale. Oxford: Oxford UP, 1983.

Bray, Alan. *Homosexuality in Renaissance England.* London: Gay Men's P, 1982.

Bredbeck, Gregory W. *Sodomy and Interpretation: Marlowe to Milton.* Ithaca: Cornell UP, 1991.

Chapman, Guy. *Beckford.* London: Jonathan Cape, 1940.

Dellamora, Richard. *Masculine Desire: The Sexual Politics of Victorian Aestheticism.* Chapel Hill: U of North Carolina P, 1990.

Dover, K. J. *Greek Homosexuality.* Cambridge: Harvard UP, 1978.

Fothergill, Brian. *Beckford at Fonthill.* London: Faber, 1979.

Gallop, Jane. "The Immoral Teachers." *Yale French Studies* 63 (1982): 117–28.

Gibbon, Edward. *The History of the Decline and Fall of the Roman Empire.* Ed. J. B. Bury. 4 vols. London: Methuen, 1900.

Gilbert, Arthur N. "Buggery in the British Navy." *Journal of Social History* 10 (1976): 74–75.

Haggerty, George E. "Literature and Homosexuality in the Later Eighteenth Century: Walpole, Beckford, and Lewis." *Studies in the Novel* 18 (1986): 341–52.

Halperin, David M. "Why Is Diotima a Woman?" *One Hundred Years of Homosexuality and Other Essays on Greek Love.* New York: Routledge, 1990. 113–51.

Herbert, Lord. *Pembroke Papers.* 1780–1794. London, 1950.

Hume, David. *Essays: Moral, Political, and Literary.* Ed. T. H. Green and T. H. Grose. 2 vols. London: Longmans, 1875.

Lille, Alain de. *The Complaint of Nature.* [*De Planctu Naturae,* c. 1165.] Trans. Douglas M. Moffat. New York: H. Holt, 1908.

———. *Plaint of Nature.* Trans. James J. Sheridan. Toronto: Pontifical Institute of Medieval Studies, 1981.

MacCannell, Juliet Flower. "Resistance to Sexual Theory." *Theory/Pedagogy/Politics: Texts for Change.* Ed. Donald Morton and Mas'ud Zavarzadeh. Urbana: U of Illinois P, 1991. 64–89.

Mavor, Elizabeth. *The Ladies of Llangollen.* Harmondsworth: Penguin, 1974.

Melville, Lewis. *The Life and Letters of William Beckford.* London: Heinemann, 1910.

Norton, Rictor. *Mother Clap's Molly House: The Gay Subculture in England 1700–1830.* London: Gay Men's P, 1992.

Oliver, John W. *The Life of William Beckford.* London: Oxford UP, 1932.

Rochester, John Wilmot, earl of. *Poems.* Ed. Keith Walker. Oxford: Basil Blackwell, 1984.

Rousseau, G. S. "The Pursuit of Homosexuality in the Eighteenth Century: 'Utterly Confused Category' and/or Rich Repository?" *'Tis Nature's Fault: Unauthorized Sexuality During the Enlightenment.* Ed. Robert Purks Maccubbin. Cambridge: Cambridge UP, 1987. 132–68.

Saslow, James. *Ganymede in the Renaissance: Homosexuality in Art and Society.* New Haven: Yale UP, 1986.

Sedgwick, Eve Kosofsky. *Between Men: English Literature and Male Homosocial Desire.* New York: Columbia UP, 1985.

Silverman, Kaja. *Male Subjectivity at the Margins.* New York: Routledge, 1992.

Swift, Jonathan. *A Tale of a Tub.* Ed. A. C. Guthkeltch and D. Nichol Smith. 2d ed. Oxford: Clarendon, 1958.

Thrale, Hester Lynch. *Thraliana, The Diary of Mrs. Hester Lynch Thrale (Later Mrs. Piozzi), 1776–1809.* Ed. Katharine C. Balderston. 2d ed. 2 vols. Oxford: Clarendon, 1951.

Todd, Janet. *Women's Friendship in Literature.* New York: Columbia UP, 1980.

Trumbach, Randolph. "The Birth of the Queen: Sodomy and the Emergence of Gender Equality in Modern Culture, 1660–1750." *Hidden from History: Reclaiming the Gay and Lesbian Past.* Ed. Martin Bauml Duberman, Martha Vicinus, and George Chauncey Jr. New York: New American Library, 1989. 129–40.

———. "London's Sodomites: Homosexual Behavior and Western Culture in the Eighteenth Century." *Journal of Social History* 2 (1977): 1–33.

———, ed. *Satan's Harvest Home.* 1749. *Hell Upon Earth and Satan's Harvest Home.* New York: Garland, 1985.

————, ed. *Select Trials at the Sessions House in the Old Bailey.* 2 vols. New York: Garland, 1985.

————. "Sodomitical Assaults, Gender Role, and Sexual Development in Eighteenth-Century London." *The Pursuit of Sodomy: Male Homosexuality in Renaissance and Enlightenment Europe.* Ed. Kent Gerard and Gert Hekma. New York: Harrington Park P, 1989. 407–32.

————, ed. *Sodomy Trials: Seven Documents.* New York: Garland, 1986.

Weber, Harold. "'Drudging in Fair Aurelia's Womb': Constructing Homosexual Economies in Rochester's Poetry." *The Eighteenth Century: Theory and Interpretation* 33 (1992): 99–117.

Shifting Ground

Sade, Same-Sex Desire, and the
One-, Two-, and Three-Sex Models

William F. Edmiston

Thomas Laqueur recently hypothesized a transition from a one-sex conceptual model of the human body, which is evidenced in the medical literature of classical antiquity, to a two-sex model, which came into being during the Enlightenment. In the one-sex model, the male body was the standard, while the female body was an inverted, imperfect and subordinate form of that standard. Laqueur proposes that in pre-Enlightenment texts, sex (the body) must be understood to be secondary, while "gender—what we would take to be a cultural category—was primary or 'real.'" As long as the one-sex model dominated Western civilization, gender was a cultural and social form of behavior that was ascribed according to biological organs: "To be a man or a woman was to hold a social rank, a place in society, to assume a cultural role, not to be organically one or the other of two incommensurable sexes. Sex before the seventeenth century, in other words, was still a sociological and not an ontological category" (Laqueur 8). Laqueur agrees with Michel Foucault, Randolph Trumbach, and others that human sexual nature began to change in or around the eighteenth century (although he differs from Foucault in that the latter would see one episteme decisively replacing another). The two-sex model began to emerge during the late eighteenth century at a time of great transformation in biological science: medical discoveries and new theories of reproduction seemed to point toward anatomical difference, toward the existence of two incommensurable and fully differentiated sexes. According to Laqueur, however, the establishment of two sexes was not the consequence of scientific discovery but rather that of an epistemological and sociopolitical change, which was in turn confirmed by medical advances: "Sexual difference no more followed from anatomy after the scientific revolution than it did in the world of one sex," but rather from new cultural imperatives of interpretation (163). In this new two-sex conception, invented and made possible by an epistemic shift that had less to do with science than with the politics of gender, biological difference became the new foundation for behavioral differentiation between genders.

Laqueur's study mentions the phenomenon of same-sex desire in the one-sex model to explain the problematics of gender transitivity. In homosexual relations, the active male and the passive female were not perceived as threatening to the social order of the classical world, whereas the sexual behaviors of the passive male and the active female were deemed unnatural because they embodied culturally unacceptable reversals of power and prestige (Laqueur 53). In his subsequent discussion of the two-sex model, however, same-sex desire is ignored, and it is here that we must turn to Trumbach. Trumbach disagrees with Laqueur on sex—in the older paradigm of early modern Europe there were *three* sexes (man, woman, hermaphrodite)—but agrees that there were only two genders.[1] Before 1700 many European men married women and had sexual relations with teenage boys. Same-sex relations did not violate the gender code unless they also involved a transgression of the patriarchal code; that is, when adult men allowed themselves to be penetrated. What changed in the eighteenth century, according to Trumbach, was that the bisexual model disappeared and the paradigm of two genders founded upon two biological sexes began to predominate. A third, illegitimate gender arose from the notion of gender transitivity: adult men desiring other males were likely to "transform" themselves into females by speaking and dressing as women. Such desire was taken to be the result of corruption of an individual's mind and not the structure of his/her body. Trumbach's third gender involves a combination of male and female characteristics, and these are behavioral rather than biological (Trumbach, "London's Sapphists" 112–14; "Sex, Gender" 90–93).

It is tempting to juxtapose Trumbach's third-gender theory with the emergence of a third-sex model in the nineteenth century. The notion of a third sex began to be employed to designate an attraction—perhaps innate—to one's own sex, as opposed to the "opposite" sex. David Greenberg notes that the phrase "third sex" is attested in English as early as 1722 and used to refer to an androgynous and bisexual person without suggesting that this condition was congenital.[2] In the nineteenth century both the notion and the phrase began to show up in French fiction. In Balzac's *Le Père Goriot* (1834), the Maison-Vauquer is advertised as a "pension bourgeoise des deux sexes et autres" [middle-class boarding-house for both sexes and others] (Balzac 2: 849).[3] In *Splendeurs et misères des courtisanes* (1839–1847), Balzac uses the term to convey to his readers no more than a vague idea of the elusive nature of the homosexual, by recounting the visit of Lord Durham to one of the prisons of Paris:

> Le directeur, après avoir montré toute la prison . . . désigna du doigt un local, en faisant un geste de dégoût.
>   — Je ne mène pas là Votre Seigneurie, dit-il, car c'est le quartier des *tantes*. . . .
>   — Hao! fit lord Durham, et qu'est-ce?
>   — C'est le troisième sexe, milord. (Balzac 5: 1055)
>   [The director, after having shown the whole prison . . . pointed to a certain locality with a gesture of disgust.
>   "I shall not take Your Lordship there," he said, "because that is where the *queens* are kept. . . ."
>   "Hao!" said Lord Durham. "And what are they?"
>   "They are the third sex, my Lord."]

In Gautier's *Mademoiselle de Maupin* (1835), the androgynous heroine readily admits that she does not fit the conventional categories: "En vérité, ni l'un ni l'autre de ces deux sexes n'est le mien . . . je suis d'un troisième sexe à part qui n'a pas encore de nom"; [In truth, neither one nor the other of the two sexes is mine . . . I am of a third and separate sex which does not yet have a name] (Gautier 352).[4] The term *third sex* was later reintroduced in Germany by Karl Heinrich Ulrichs, who coined the term *Uranians* to describe the congenital condition of cross-sex identification. The "third sex" theory of homosexuality influenced the growing psychiatric literature on sexual problems in the nineteenth century, and it also contributed to the German homosexual liberation movement, led by Magnus Hirschfeld (Greenberg 408–10). Hirschfeld, as John Fout explains, "in our own contemporary terms, adopted an essentialist position, arguing that homosexuality was deeply rooted in a biological imperative" (269). Hirschfeld argued that a third sex existed, "and it was to be found somewhere between the two dominant genders. Individuals of this third sex, he believed, should be understood to be homosexuals. Though they might have the physical body of one gender, their personality often manifested behavioral characteristics and sexual desires of the opposite" (Fout 269–70). Hirschfeld took his notion of a third sex to great lengths: members of this sex were not only products of an inborn hereditary condition, but they actually exhibited "visible" physical differences, which tended to further prove that same-sex desire was wholly an innate rather than an acquired condition (Fout 271). According to Jeffrey Weeks, nineteenth-century sexologists often differentiated between the "inverts," who were inherently and perhaps congenitally homosexual and who often displayed stereotyped "effeminate" characteristics, and the "perverts," libertines who behaved in a homosexual way from lust (Weeks 59).

In the late twentieth century many gay-oriented studies have attempted an adjudication of the debate between essentialist and social constructionist views of homosexuality. For the essentialists, homosexual desire is a transcultural, transhistorical state of being that is and has always been intrinsic in certain individuals. Social constructionists, who do not deny these rather self-evident facts, believe in addition that consciousness of both homo- and heterosexual categories is a modern and culturally specific reality. Foucault, for example, locates in the nineteenth century a shift in European thought from viewing homosexual behavior as a matter of prohibited *acts* (in which anyone might engage) to viewing it as a function of stable definitions of *identity*, dependent upon personality even in the absence of sexual acts.[5] Eve Sedgwick redefines this shift as an intrusion into the "universalizing" discourse of sodomitic acts by a "minoritizing" understanding of sexual identity. While the universalizing concept implies bisexual potential, the minoritizing one is predicated on a third-sex model, suggesting a specifically gay identity and a conflation of sexual deviance with gender deviance, or same-sex desire with cross-gender behaviors (Sedgwick 89). Sedgwick rejects Foucault's view of the supersession of one model over another and posits instead the contemporaneous coexistence of different models of same-sex desire. Jonathan Dollimore concurs that the modern sense of sexual perversion as an identity, a congenital abnormality, displaced the older conception of perversion as a sinful and evil practice, yet he demonstrates that the newer, scientific conception still bore traces of the older, theological one (Dollimore 41).

These debates have led me to wonder what insights might be gleaned from the works of D.A.F. de Sade, who was writing during the turning point of all these conceptual models and who is surely the first writer in French literature to move beyond a plea for tolerance and to justify the issue of same-sex desire on theoretical grounds (Stockinger 181). If same-sex genital activity was seen as primarily a *social* transgression of gender, a form of (mis)behavior, before the Enlightenment, then we would expect Sade, as a defender of sodomy, to attack the social laws and mores that condemned it, and indeed he does. If same-sex desire came to be considered a *biological* deviation in the nineteenth century, then we might find markers of this newer, minoritizing model in his work.

We must first distinguish between homosexual desire and activity and the Sadean value of sodomy. Sodomy, says Jane Gallop, is the central Sadean libertine act inasmuch as the anus is a detour in relation to the "normal" central sexual goal: penetration of the vagina (75). Much of Sade's work describes sodomy as a form of behavior with many variations, all involving anal penetration. Most often we see men sodomizing women, but also, less frequently, men sodomizing men, and women "socratizing" men with various objects. Sodomy implies a substitution of the dichotomy active/passive for that of male/female, one that trifles with gender identity. The substitution of anus for vagina slips into that of male for female, and once we are exclusively in the world of males, the active/passive structure becomes a reversible one (Gallop 80).[6] Such substitutions, while prevalent in Sade's works, should not lead us to conclude, along with Marcel Hénaff, that homosexuality in Sade always blurs into a sodomitical bisexuality: "In fact, all his characters are indifferently hetero- or homosexual. For them the question does not even arise: they live in a sort of indifference toward sexual difference, a difference which disappears precisely in the sodomitical desire by which bodies become equal through anal identity" (Hénaff 148). Hénaff's remarks are certainly true of many of Sade's characters, but there are nonetheless a few who admit to preference for one sex over the other. Many are bisexual, but a few are not "indifferently" so. At the other extreme, we should not allow these exceptions to become the dominant exponents of Sade's thought, as did Simone de Beauvoir. In her famous essay, "Must We Burn Sade?" Beauvoir conflates sodomy with homosexual activity: "There is no perversion of which [Sade] speaks so often and with so much satisfaction, and even impassioned vehemence." This is true, perhaps, of sodomy, but certainly not of homosexual intercourse. In an attempt to prove that Sade was a "sodomite" (by which she seems to mean "homosexual"), Beauvoir adds to her list of biographical elements "the enormous importance which Sade accords to this 'fantasy' in his writings, and the passion with which he advocates it" (23). Aside from her confusion of sodomy and homosexuality, Beauvoir seems to be striving to bolster her belief in Sade's homosexuality with quantitative textual proof. While Sade may be the first writer in French to defend homoerotic desire, one can hardly speak of the "enormous importance" of the latter in his works.[7] Similarly, it is difficult to agree with Lucienne Frappier-Mazur when she states that Sade's texts "repeatedly and force-fully proclaim the 'superiority' of sodomy between men" (137). They do so, indeed, on occasion, but such is hardly their dominant discourse. It is my contention that Sade's critics have been either too quick to dismiss his homosexual discourse, or too quick to exaggerate its importance.

Sade's work contains both a plethora and a paucity of homosexual references. A plethora, compared to earlier eighteenth-century French fiction, in which homosexual desires or acts are rarely mentioned (Diderot's *La Religieuse* being a notable exception); a plethora as well, in that Sade's characters rarely find homosexual acts repugnant: they usually engage willingly and gleefully in the whole gamut of sexual activity.[8] A paucity, nonetheless, in that there are very few Sadean creations who desire others of their own sex exclusively, as we shall see. Sodomy is sometimes viewed as a taste, sometimes as a philosophy or principle, but it is always defined as counter-generality and is synonymous with the eighteenth-century term *antiphysical*. The aspect of counter-generality, desire transgressing a law, seems to be generally more crucial for Sade than that of same-sex desire, but on occasion the definition of sodomy is more limited. We look first at Sade's most developed philosophical defense of homosexual activity, and then at several Sadean characters who manifest special interest in their own sex.

The pamphlet entitled "Français, encore un effort si vous voulez être républicains" [Frenchmen, one more effort if you wish to be republicans] forms an important section of *La Philosophie dans le boudoir*. It contains a four-page defense of "sodomy" and "pæderasty" that is primarily concerned with same-sex desire in males (Sade 3: 509–13). The author of the pamphlet begins and ends his defense with a plea for civil tolerance of "this weakness of some men." Adopting first a mock-orthodox attitude, he poses a rhetorical question about the need to censure the "monstrous deviations" that drew divine punishment down upon the cities of the plain. The author subsequently expresses scornful reproach for his barbarous ancestors, who ordered the execution of sodomites, as well as sorrow for individual victims, whose only crime was to have different tastes. Next he voices an optimistic confidence that such executions will occur no more, convinced as he is that the enlightened wisdom of legislators will ensure that henceforth "such an error cannot be criminal." Sodomy is no longer a crime in France in 1795, nor is it a crime ontologically: Nature has not given man the possibility of offending her laws. What she inspires must therefore be respected by all men. Using an empirical, existential argument, the author defends this taste by demonstrating that Nature places no importance on bodily fluids or their destination, does not distinguish between "pure" and "defiled" parts of the body, and is oblivious to the loss of semen since she permits it in dreams and in male orgasms during sex with pregnant women. Nature does not permit us to outrage her laws: front or back, girl or boy, all tastes come from Nature.

To defend homosexual "tastes" by stating that all sexual inclinations come from Nature, however, does little to explain the "origin" of same-sex desire, that is, the contemporary conception of it as a social phenomenon or as a biological dictate. An empirical and nonhierarchical view of Nature does not differentiate between behavioral and biological "sources" of homosexuality: whether such tastes are innate or acquired, they are part of Nature because they exist. This concept of Nature is thus indifferent to sexuality. It is only in the teleological conception of Nature that such a distinction assumes importance. If Nature has laws and ends, and if the origin of same-sex desire is biological, then Nature consecrates that desire and tends toward it, regardless of society's approbation. Nature is thus in favor of pleasure and against procreation, at least on a part-time basis. If same-sex desire is a universal potential and a behavioral choice, then each society must decide if it is to be encouraged or forbidden, with a view toward its own welfare. The author of the pamphlet at first leans toward biology. The penchant for sodomy, he says, is the result of "organisation"—the eighteenth-century word for genetic configuration—which is beyond our control. Even children can have this taste, and those who do are never corrected. Most of the discussion is devoted to examples aimed at proving that same-sex desire has existed at all times and in all cultures, from the harems of Algiers to the natives of America. Curiously, the energetic justifications are punctuated with a cascade of demonstratives specifying the identity of same-sex desire. The lexical items chosen reveal the point of view of a majority viewing a minority, a norm categorizing an other and thus creating an alterity not shared by author and implied reader. One feels today, says the author, that "such an error" cannot be criminal, and he goes on to defend "this taste," "this depravity," "this debauchery," and most often, "this vice." There is no danger in "all these manias," and one who is inclined to "these afflictions" cannot be deemed guilty by our wise legislators, no more than those whom Nature has created deformed. Despite the plea for tolerance, the author's language normalizes, hierarchizes, and excludes.[9]

There are definite markers of a minoritizing discourse here, one that points toward Foucault's notion of a nineteenth-century categorization and medicalization of a modern species, the homosexual, and perhaps to a new way of viewing a third sex with a unique "organisation" for which only Nature is responsible. But there is another discursive force—perhaps an older one—at work in these pages, between the pamphlet's initial and final pleas for tolerance of sexual difference. The author not only demonstrates the transhistorical and transcultural existence of "this taste," but he also affirms its social utility, and the recognition thereof by various cultures.[10] The multitude of examples of men loving men or boys, from all times and all cultures, seems at first blush to be an attempt to demonstrate the universality of homosexual desire and to suggest an innate quality. In fact, however, same-sex desire appears to be less an identity decreed by Nature and more a form of voluntary behavior that was approved and even encouraged in certain societies. In many cultures, says the author, women are regularly scorned except for purposes of procreation. This "vice" is more frequent in republics because of men's habit of living together. The ancient Greeks, according to the pamphlet, believed it necessary to a warrior people and *introduced* it into their republic. To become attached to women was considered by the Greeks to be a weakness, whereas the love of boys was thought to be entirely compatible with military service and indeed to foster courage and patriotism. The Romans praised love between men and found this "vice" to be useful in a republic, and even sanctified it through religion, as did Mohammed in the Koran. The author seems slightly less sure about the social utility of lesbianism, yet he affirms that the Greeks supported "this freakish notion" because it prevented women from meddling in public affairs. Not only is there no danger in "all these manias," but they can serve a useful purpose by strengthening the military and the republic. Sexual *behavior* can thus be deployed in service to the state. Moreover, the pamphlet states that sodomy can be the result of a natural satiation with other sexual practices, which again suggests behaviorism and voluntarism rather than a stable identity. Such a universalizing discourse is predicated not on the conceptual third-sex model but on one of bisexual potential in all men and women, in whom homosexual desire can be politically mobilized for the general welfare. At the end of his discussion the author returns to "organisation," the biological source of "these miseries," but ultimately the argument contains very little that points to an identity based on innate characteristics. Homosexual desire comes from Nature; it can be observed in children and in the inhabitants of an unspoiled America. But it is also a form of behavior in which anyone can indulge and which many societies have sanctioned. The most minoritizing feature of the pamphlet is the vocabulary used to express its message: the discourse retains the (perhaps inevitable) marginalizing language throughout.

Sade's fictional characters who experience same-sex desire can tell us more than the pamphlet's abstract expositions—sometimes literally, since they are allowed to speak about their passions. One of Sade's biographers, Geoffrey Gorer, adopts a severely minoritizing point of view of these characters and of same-sex desire in Sade's writings as well:

> Natural homosexuality is—as opposed to that suggested by satiety— a rare phenomenon; I do not think there are more than five male homosexuals in the whole of [Sade's] thickly peopled works; of these, two are *almost* exclusively pathics [by which Gorer surely means "almost exclusively homosexual"]. He states categorically that all vary in their secondary sexual characteristics from more normal males as well as in their voice and character [by which Gorer means that several of Sade's characters and narrators state as much]. (183)

We can only speculate about which characters Gorer has in mind when he speaks of "five male homosexuals," but it is true that Sadean characters who are "exclusively" or "almost exclusively" homosexual are extremely rare. Homosexual sodomy is more often a mere variant of—and a diversion from—heterosexual sodomy. The four libertines of *Les 120 Journées de Sodome* appear at first to represent the kind of same-sex desire that is a diversion for sated tastes. At the first of their five weekly suppers, the one devoted exclusively to the pleasures of sodomy, only males are invited. The four libertines are regularly sodomized by sixteen young men, while sixteen younger boys are always on hand to "remplir l'office de femmes" [fulfill the duty of women] (13: 4). The other weekly suppers, however, are all devoted to sexual pleasures with women, so that the libertines seem to demonstrate a bisexual potential. It is only a bit later in the text that we learn that the Bishop and Durcet have a special fondness for being sodomized and that they lean toward a preference for men.

Is it true, as Gorer states, that the penchant for same-sex desire in Sade's characters is linked to behavioral and even physiological differences from more "normal" men? Certainly, countless Sadean characters, male and female, indulge and revel in homosexual acts (albeit not exclusively) while bearing no remarkable physical differences from those who do not.

Yet there does seem to be an attempt, on occasion, to link men who enjoy being sodomized to feminine physical traits and forms of behavior. Durcet, a rather extreme example, is described as follows in *Les 120 Journées de Sodome:* "Durcet est âgé de cinquante-trois ans, il est petit, court, gros, fort épais, une figure agréable et fraîche, la peau très blanche, tout le corps, et principalement les hanches et les fesses, absolument comme une femme; son cul est frais, gras, ferme et potelé, mais excessivement ouvert par l'habitude de la sodomie; son vit est extraordinairement petit . . . il a de la gorge comme une femme" (13: 19); [Durcet is fifty-three years old, he is small, short, fat, very thickset, with a pleasant and fresh face; he has very white skin, and his whole body, especially his hips and buttocks, are absolutely like a woman's; his butt is fresh, fat, firm and chubby, but excessively agape, due to the habit of sodomy; his penis is extraordinarily small . . . he has breasts like a woman].

The description of this character seems to be an overwrought exaggeration, a caricature of an individual whose physiology can be readily identified with neither sex and who therefore suggests the existence of a third one. Durcet's same-sex desire is not only equated with cross-gender behavior—his effeminacy and his desire to be penetrated—but it is also identified and associated with a grotesque amalgam of masculine and feminine physical characteristics. Does the anatomical reinforce the behavioral, or—"due to the habit of sodomy"—vice versa? Indeed, this is not clear. Other characters, such as Dolmancé in *La Philosophie dans le boudoir,* and Bressac in *Justine,* are described as physically different from other men, which might imply a correlation between their sexual orientation and their anatomical composition. These descriptions are perhaps markers of a newer, minoritizing model.

At the beginning of *La Philosophie dans le boudoir,* the Chevalier de Mirvel describes Dolmancé to his sister as follows:

Dolmancé . . . est grand, d'une fort belle figure, des yeux très vifs et très spirituels, mais quelque chose d'un peu dur et d'un peu méchant se peint malgré lui dans ses traits; il a les plus belles dents du monde, un peu de mollesse dans la taille et dans la tournure, par l'habitude, sans doute, qu'il a de prendre si souvent des airs féminins; il est d'une élégance extrême, une jolie voix, des talents, et principalement beaucoup de philosophie dans l'esprit. (3: 372)

[Dolmancé . . . is tall, with a very beautiful face, very lively and intelligent eyes, but something a bit harsh and a bit wicked may be seen in his features; he has the world's most beautiful teeth, a bit of effeminacy in his figure and form, probably from the habit he has of taking on feminine airs so often; he is extremely elegant, he has a pretty voice, talents, and especially much philosophy in his mind.]

Here it appears that the feminine traits of Dolmancé's body are attributed to his effeminate behavior, to his transgression of gender. Madame de Saint-Ange understands this and is not interested in these physical details (especially since she has seen Dolmancé before). She cares not about his body but about his "tastes." Her brother assures her that Dolmancé prefers men: "[L]es délices de Sodome lui sont aussi chers comme agent que comme patient; il n'aime que les hommes dans ses plaisirs, et si quelquefois, néanmoins, il consent à essayer les femmes, ce n'est qu'aux conditions qu'elles seront assez complaisantes pour changer de sexe avec lui" (3: 373); [The delights of Sodom are as dear to him in the active as in the passive role; he likes only men in his pleasures, and if however he sometimes consents to try women, it is only on condition that they be obliging enough to change sexes with him].

The biological has been shaped by the behavioral: Dolmancé has *become* something because he *behaves* like that something.[11] Dolmancé may be viewed as a paradigm for Foucault's epistemic shift. He performs sodomitic acts with men, and he therefore assumes a homosexual identity— almost. But not quite, in the modern sense of the term. It is true that he praises the passive role in sodomy and the transgression of gender: "On a souvent mis en question laquelle de ces deux façons de commettre la sodomie était la plus voluptueuse: c'est assurément la passive, puisqu'on jouit à la fois de la sensation du devant et de celle du derrière; il est si doux de changer de sexe, si délicieux de contrefaire la putain, de se livrer à un homme qui nous traite comme une femme, d'appeler cet homme son amant, de s'avouer sa maîtresse" (3: 431); [One has often questioned which of these two ways of committing sodomy was the most pleasurable: it is undoubtedly the passive way, since one enjoys sensation from the front and from the rear at the same time; it is so sweet to change sexes, so delightful to counterfeit a whore, to surrender oneself to a man who treats us like a woman, to call this man our lover, to admit to being his mistress]. When Dolmancé says "to change sexes" he means "to change genders," to exchange social and especially sexual behaviors with the female sex. While he makes his preference quite clear, his joyful willingness to engage in sexual acts with both female characters undermines any attempt to ascribe an exclusive homosexual identity to him. He is surely "almost exclusively homosexual."

Of all Sade's fictional creations, it is Bressac who seems to be exclusively homosexual in the modern sense of the term. The reader of *Justine* first encounters Bressac and his servant Jasmin locked in a passionate act of anal penetration, in which the master is the passive partner: "Deux tendres et légitimes époux se caresseraient avec moins d'ardeur" (3:104); [Two tender and legitimate spouses could not caress one another more passionately]. The lovers then discover, much to Bressac's annoyance, that a woman, Thérèse/Justine, has been witness to what he calls "our mysteries" (3:104). There is a mysteriousness, a secrecy, an otherness to their pleasure that Justine cannot understand. Nonetheless, she soon falls in love with the handsome young nobleman, whom she describes as physically somewhat effeminate: "M. de Bressac réunissait aux charmes de la jeunesse la figure la plus séduisante; si sa taille ou ses traits avaient quelques défauts, c'était parce qu'ils se rapprochaient un peu trop de cette nonchalance, de cette mollesse qui n'appartient qu'aux femmes; il semblait qu'en lui prêtant les attributs de ce sexe, la nature lui en eût également inspiré les goûts. . . . Quelle âme, cependant, était enveloppée sous ces appas féminins!" (3: 109); [Monsieur de Bressac had both the charms of youth and the most attractive face; if his figure or his features had a few flaws, it was because they were too similar to that listlessness, that softness which belongs only to women; it seemed that Nature, in lending him the attributes of the female sex, had also inspired in him the tastes of that sex. . . . Yet what a soul was wrapped up in those feminine charms!].

This portrait seems to be a reversal, a mirror image of that of Dolmancé: this time, the behavioral is shaped by the biological. Not only is Bressac different from other men in appearance, but the narrator leaves no doubt about his gender: the young master is "always a woman" in his sexual pleasures, and although he has the necessary equipment to "become a man in his turn," he has no desire to do so (3:104). The terms *woman* and *man* refer to gender, a social construct based on behavior, which in turn is based on a biological distinction. Bressac behaves in certain ways because he is biologically different from other men. Like Dolmancé, Bressac is stimulated by the confusion of gender roles, and he praises the reunion of male and female pleasures to be found in playing the whore to a man. He responds to Justine's tears by stressing his otherness: "Ah! Thérèse . . . si tu connaissais les charmes de cette fantaisie, si tu pouvais comprendre ce qu'on éprouve à la douce illusion de n'être plus qu'une femme! . . . Ah! qu'il est doux d'y réussir, Thérèse, qu'il est délicieux d'être la catin de tous ceux qui veulent de vous. . . . Oh! non, non, Thérèse, tu ne comprends pas ce qu'est ce plaisir pour une tête organisée comme la mienne" (3: 111); [Ah! Thérèse . . . if only you knew the charms of this penchant, if only you could understand what one experiences in the sweet illusion of being only a woman! . . . Ah! how sweet it is to succeed, Thérèse, how delicious it is to be the whore of all those who desire you. . . . Oh! no, no, Thérèse, you do not understand what this pleasure is to a head organized like mine].

Bressac makes no attempt to justify his sexual conduct on the basis of its naturalness, its social utility, or its universality. On the contrary, he points only to the intense pleasure he derives from it, he and others who are "organized" in similar fashion. Bressac testifies to a gender difference based on biology. He assures Justine that he is anatomically different from normal men, having different erogenous zones: "Ne t'imagine pas, Thérèse, que nous soyons faits comme les autres hommes; c'est une construction toute différente, et cette membrane chatouilleuse qui tapisse chez vous le temple de Vénus, le ciel en nous créant en orna les autels où nos Céladons sacrifient: nous sommes aussi certainement femmes là, que vous l'êtes au sanctuaire de la génération" (3: 111–12); [Do not imagine, Thérèse, that we are made like other men; it is a completely different construction, and that sensitive membrane that lines your temple of Venus, heaven, upon creating us, used it to adorn the altars where our lovers make sacrifice: we are as certainly women there, as you are in the sanctuary of reproduction].

On both psychological and physiological grounds, Bressac considers himself to be other than normal. In *La Nouvelle Justine* (an expanded version of the novel), Bressac makes an interesting differentiation between sexual identity and sexual acts, by demonstrating awareness of a distinction between himself and men who perform homosexual acts but who are nonetheless heterosexual. Bressac proposes to Justine that she assist him in his pursuit of such men: "Parmi les jeunes gens que je débauche, Justine, il en est quelques-uns qui ne se livrent à moi que par complaisance; ceux-là auraient besoin de voir à nu les traits d'une jeune fille" (6: 176); [Among the young men whom I debauch, Justine, there are some who agree to have sex with me only to oblige me; these men would need to see a young girl's naked charms]. Bressac knows that men can perform sodomitic acts without sharing his sexual penchants. He can sometimes enjoy such men only after they first use a woman to excite them, for they are "normal" while he admits to being "other." He knows the difference between universal bisexual potential and exclusive same-sex desire in a minority, and he defines himself by the latter. More than any Sadean character, he seems to be conscious of what later generations will call a homosexual identity.

Many of Sade's critics have noted the universalizing discourse about same-sex sodomy that is abundant in his work. Roland Barthes, for example, speaks of the "rule of reciprocity," by which "everyone can be either sodomist or sodomized, agent and patient, subject and object" (30). In the works of Sade, says Barthes, there are only classes of actions, not groups of individuals, and sexual preference never serves to identify a subject. Barthes's statement is largely true. As we have seen, however, there are markers of a minoritizing discourse in Sade's writing, one that differentiates and excludes from the norm those who are attracted exclusively or primarily to others of the same sex. Physical differences are not always indicative of this minority. Sade's novels contain numerous characters who transgress gender without manifesting any physiological abnormalities, yet Durcet—at the opposite end of the spectrum—is extremely different from most men in his physical features. The characters Dolmancé and Bressac present two opposing and contradictory logics. Dolmancé performs sodomitic acts, which influence his behavior and appearance. Because he behaves like a homosexual, he becomes one. Bressac, on the other hand, has been created by Nature as a homosexual, so he plays the part. Since he has a homosexual identity, he behaves accordingly. Both enjoy changing gender, playing the woman to the men who desire them.

Literary critics as well as historians have noted a shift in conceptualization, in the eighteenth century, from a behavioral view of sex toward an emerging recognition of sexual identity. D. A. Coward hypothesizes that the eighteenth century's relative lack of interest in homosexuality was perhaps due to the fact that divisions between genders were less clearly drawn than in our own times (250). Over the course of the century, as Michel Rey explains, the older term *sodomite*, rich in biblical overtones, disappeared and was replaced by the more learned term *pederast*, used to designate a type of individual without making reference to any specific act (145). According to Foucault, the sodomite had been one who engaged in aberrant behavior, whereas the homosexual would come to be identified as a nineteenth-century species (*History of Sexuality* 43). Texts of the nineteenth century will increasingly refer to a third sex, a new sexual identity that will be baptized as *gay* in the late twentieth century. In most Western societies today the term *gay* denotes a sexual identity that is recognized and marginalized (although there is still much debate over whether this identity is psychologically formed or genetically ascribed). It is far from certain that such an identity existed in early modern Europe. Even if same-sex desire is a transhistorical and transcultural phenomenon, most scholars agree that the recognition of individuals who experience that desire as a distinct group is a relatively modern one.[12] Sexual identity is, to a large extent, discursive and representational, as Foucault asserts. The determinants for identity were still in flux at the end of the eighteenth century, and the difference between doing and being had not yet crystallized into a stable network of features.

The works of Sade do not offer proof of this Foucauldian shift, but they do bear witness to a late eighteenth-century coexistence of at least two discourses concerning same-sex desire, with no evidence of strong dominance of one over the other. The two logics coexist, overlap, and contradict, just as contradictory discourses on sexuality coexist in our own time. More important is the contribution of Sade's texts to a politics of identity. His narrators and fictional characters attempt to justify same-sex desire in both models: it is defended as a natural and biologically determined identity, and elsewhere it is described as a "taste," an inclination forged from certain behaviors that can be mobilized for political reasons other than reproduction. Sade's texts make a forceful appeal for valorization of this form of sexual desire, like all others, in the new republic. Moreover, Sade certainly posited one of the first third-sex models of sexual desire to be found in Western literature. His work must be a starting point for anyone wishing to examine the great shift in thinking and writing about sexuality that began to take place during the Enlightenment.

NOTES

1. Hermaphrodites, says Trumbach, were classified as biologically deviant. They "were obliged to permanently choose one gender or the other for themselves and then to take sexual partners only from the remaining opposite gender. If hermaphrodites moved back and forth in their gender, their sexual relations could then be stigmatized as the crime of sodomy" ("London's Sapphists" 113). Foucault agrees on this point: "Changes of option, not the anatomical mixture of the sexes, were what gave rise to most of the condemnations of hermaphrodites in the records that survive in France for the period of the Middle Ages and the Renaissance" (*Herculine Barbin* viii).

2. Greenberg notes further that the phrase "third sex" was used in nineteenth-century America to denounce feminists and to impugn the virility of political opponents (407 n. 45).

3. All translations from French are mine except those noted in the works cited.

4. I am indebted to Aron and Kempf (144) for the reference to *Splendeurs et misères des courtisanes*, and to Greenberg (406) for the reference to *Mademoiselle de Maupin*.

5. Foucault's position is succinctly summarized by Sedgwick (83). Many participants in the debate take a position somewhere between these two poles. Greenberg states that a few Renaissance authors wrote of sexual orientation as a relatively stable

trait, and he points to an "incipient group consciousness" in early modern Europe (408). Weeks believes that "lesbian and gay identities are both constructed and essential, constructed in the sense that they are historically moulded . . . essential in the particular sense that they are necessary and in the end inescapable" (98). For a thorough yet brief treatment of the debate, see Edward Stein. Stein regrets that the social constructionist-essentialist debate is often conflated with that of source ("nature/nurture") and with that of free will ("voluntarism/determinism") (327).

6. Frappier-Mazur sees sodomy in Sade as the basis for the negation of sexual difference, and particularly for the eradication of the feminine reproductive role (133). Hénaff says essentially the same thing: "The differences of masculine and feminine are annulled in the identity of the anus" (263).

7. One can only wonder about Beauvoir's justification for the following statement: "We must not, of course, attribute to Sade the opinions held by the confirmed homosexuals of his novels, but the argument put into the mouth of the Bishop in *The 120 Days of Sodom* is close enough to his heart to be considered as a confession" (24).

8. It is surely this willingness to discuss and defend homosexual tastes, so innovative in French literature, that has led critics to overemphasize the homosexual element in Sade's writings and even to conclude that Sade himself must have been *essentially* homosexual.

9. One might argue that it is impossible to speak about any difference, any "other," without using marginalizing language. I would agree, and this statement supports my point that Sade's text does tend, on one hand, to marginalize same-sex desire, to view it as a difference that must be defended and tolerated as a minority. Women are marginalized in the pamphlet through the use of pronouns ("they" versus "we"). They, too, are viewed as an other, but less generously and with less compassion.

10. Examples are drawn from the Gauls, Persians, Turks, Africans, and Americans, as well as the ancient Greeks and Romans.

11. This determination of sexual identity by sexual behavior had already been postulated in the influential work of Samuel Tissot: "Tissot's awful warnings in the eighteenth century about the disastrous effects of masturbation had already marked a crucial transition; what you did was now more than an infringement of divine law; it determined what sort of person you were" (Weeks 70).

12. For an opposing view see John Boswell.

WORKS CITED

Aron, Jean-Paul, and Roger Kempf. "Triumphs and Tribulations of the Homosexual Discourse." *Homosexualities and French Literature: Cultural Contexts/Critical Texts.* Ed. George Stambolian and Elaine Marks. Ithaca: Cornell UP, 1979. 141–57.

Balzac, Honore de. *La Comédie humaine.* Ed. Marcel Bouteron. 10 vols. Paris: Gallimard, 1935–1959.

Barthes, Roland. *Sade, Fourier, Loyola.* Trans. Richard Miller. Berkeley and Los Angeles: U of California P, 1976.

Beauvoir, Simone de. "Must We Burn Sade?" Trans. Annette Michelson. *The 120 Days of Sodom and Other Writings.* Trans. Austryn Wainhouse and Richard Seaver. New York: Grove Weidenfeld, 1966. 3–64.

Boswell, John. *Christianity, Social Tolerance, and Homosexuality: Gay People in Western Europe from the Beginning of the Christian Era to the Fourteenth Century.* Chicago: U of Chicago P, 1980.

Coward, D. A. "Attitudes to Homosexuality in Eighteenth-Century France." *Journal of European Studies* 10 (1980): 231–55.

Dollimore, Jonathan. *Sexual Dissidence: Augustine to Wilde, Freud to Foucault.* Oxford: Clarendon, 1991.

Foucault, Michel. *Herculine Barbin.* Trans. Richard McDougall. New York: Pantheon, 1980.

———. *The History of Sexuality. Volume 1: An Introduction.* Trans. Robert Hurley. New York: Vintage, 1990.

Fout, John C. "Sexual Politics in Wilhelmine Germany: The Male Gender Crisis, Moral Purity, and Homophobia." *Forbidden History: The State, Society, and the Regulation of Sexuality in Modern Europe.* Ed. John C. Fout. Chicago: U of Chicago P, 1992. 259–92.

Frappier-Mazur, Lucienne. "The Social Body: Disorder and Ritual in Sade's Story of Juliette." *Eroticism and the Body Politic.* Ed. Lynn Hunt. Baltimore: Johns Hopkins UP, 1991. 131–43.

Gallop, Jane. *Intersections: A Reading of Sade with Bataille, Blanchot, and Klossowski.* Lincoln: U of Nebraska P, 1981.

Gautier, Théophile. *Mademoiselle de Maupin.* Ed. Adolphe Boschot. Paris: Garnier, 1966.

Gorer, Geoffrey. *The Life and Ideas of the Marquis de Sade.* New York: Norton, 1962. Westport, Conn.: Greenwood, 1978.

Greenberg, David F. *The Construction of Homosexuality.* Chicago: U of Chicago P, 1988.

Hénaff, Marcel. *Sade: L'Invention du corps libertin.* Paris: Presses Universitaires de France, 1978.

Laqueur, Thomas. *Making Sex: Body and Gender from the Greeks to Freud.* Cambridge: Harvard UP, 1990.

Rey, Michel. "Police and Sodomy in Eighteenth-Century Paris: From Sin to Disorder." *Journal of Homosexuality* 16 (1988): 129–46.

Sade, D. A. F., marquis de. *Oeuvres complètes.* Ed. Gilbert Lely. 16 vols. Paris: Cercle du Livre Précieux, 1966–1967.

Sedgwick, Eve Kosofsky. *Epistemology of the Closet.* Berkeley and Los Angeles: U of California P, 1990.

Stein, Edward. "The Essentials of Constructionism and the Construction of Essentialism." *Forms of Desire: Sexual Orientation and the Social Constructionist Controversy.* Ed. Edward Stein. New York: Garland, 1990. 325–53.

Stockinger, Jacob. "Homosexuality and the French Enlightenment." *Homosexualities and French Literature: Cultural Contexts/Critical Texts.* Ed. George Stambolian and Elaine Marks. Ithaca: Cornell UP, 1979. 161–85.

Trumbach, Randolph. "London's Sapphists: From Three Sexes to Four Genders in the Making of Modern Culture." *Body Guards: The Cultural Politics of Gender Ambiguity.* Ed. Julia Epstein and Kristina Straub. New York: Routledge, 1991. 112–41.

———. "Sex, Gender, and Sexual Identity in Modern Culture: Male Sodomy and Female Prostitution in Enlightenment London." *Forbidden History: The State, Society, and the Regulation of Sexuality in Modern Europe.* Ed. John C. Fout. Chicago: U of Chicago P, 1992. 89–106.

Weeks, Jeffrey. *Against Nature: Essays on History, Sexuality, and Identity.* London: Rivers Oram, 1991.

3
Another Subject

Englishness "A'muck"
De Quincey's *Confessions*

Rajani Sudan

"Nothing is more revolting to English feelings," writes De Quincey in the preface to his autobiographical *Confessions of an English Opium Eater*, "than the spectacle of a human being obtruding upon our notice his moral ulcers and scars, and tearing away that 'decent drapery' which time, or the indulgence to human frailty, may have drawn over them." No, he insists, such "acts of gratuitous self-humiliation" have no part in English representation; for *that* one must "look to French literature, or that part of German, which is tainted with the spurious and defective sensibility of the French" (1). The lurid spectacle of the human body is a metaphor for autobiography here, and De Quincey's own project of self-representation (which he has so propitiously assumed) is almost immediately called into question because, according to De Quincey's own assessment, it depends on a defective French genre: the confession. Confessional discourse—at least, as it is written by Rousseau, with whose *Confessions* De Quincey seems to take issue—represents the ulcer on the body of culture, and De Quincey's quandary is to justify the difference between the "defective sensibility of the French" and his own deeply flawed life. Recognizing this problem, De Quincey continues: "I here present you, courteous reader, with the record of . . . my . . . life. . . . I trust that it will prove . . . useful and instructive. In *that* hope it is, that I have drawn it up: and *that* must be my apology for breaking through that delicate and honourable reserve which . . . restrains us from the public exposure of our own errors and infirmities" (29). De Quincey presents his *Confessions* as a text that is both "useful" in its exposure of personal error and "instructive" in its endeavor to distinguish itself from the French texts De Quincey identifies as erroneous.

De Quincey's *Confessions* illustrates how the construction of national identity, represented by his notion of Englishness, is dependent on his representations of the foreign, particularly of France, but more problematically of the "Orient." De Quincey uses these various representations as both apology and excuse for the production of his confessional narrative, while firmly maintaining his place as a representative of England and as an advocate of English feeling. Because his text doesn't break through the "delicate and honourable reserve" constituting English feeling and English propriety, it is "useful and instructive" and somehow more authentic, especially in relation to a "spurious" and scandalous French confessional. France is the site for the "defective" text, and equally defective codes of propriety and sexuality, that are responsible for turning autobiography into the shameless exhibitionism displayed by Rousseau. De Quincey is very careful to distinguish his project from those of "demireps, adventurers, or swindlers" and is quite anxious over the "propriety of allowing this . . . to come before the public eye" (29). If we are to believe De Quincey, Rousseau's document represents only the unfortunate cultural tendency of the French to disguise, however transparently, shameful secrets about sexual excess between textual sheets masquerading as confessional autobiography. According to De Quincey's estimation, self-representation is an index for cultural representation; it stands to reason, then, that his *Confessions* is an exhumed history of imperialism. Under the cover story of De Quincey's confessions to drug addiction lies the dirty secret of English cultural imperialism.[1]

The "great central organ, the stomach" is the excuse for De Quincey's first experiment with opium, and, appropriately, the afflicted sociopolitical body, with its attendant "moral ulcers and scars," becomes the first excuse for De Quincey's *Confessions*. Although ostensibly written in order to instruct the reader on the effects of opium upon the body, the *Confessions* function more significantly as a representation of the body of English culture, or Englishness. Just as De Quincey's body functions as a justification for indulging both in opium and in confessional discourse, so De

Quincey's textual self-portrait—his inscribed "body"—becomes a meta-phor for English intellectualism and culture. Clearly embedded in this self-representation are many issues problematizing De Quincey's politics of identity. De Quincey's account of his life is the account of his flaw: his recovery consists of producing a written representation of himself that appropriates the genre of Rousseau's "spurious and defective" confessional in order to expose his own error of indulging in an excess of opium. De Quincey unfolds a moral hierarchy determined by xenophobia in his proj-ect. His self-representation is an attempt to represent Englishness to the English at the expense of the French. Hence the privileged place "English feelings" occupy in this address to the reader and his own English anxi-eties regarding the "propriety of allowing this, or any part of my narra-tive, to come before the public eye" (1).

De Quincey, however, also writes his *Confessions* during a period of his literal recovery from his addiction to opium. Thus opium constitutes an-other excuse for his narrative, one that ostensibly forms its "center," use-ful in its provision of a medical documentary of addiction as well as an excuse for justifying the cultural difference between an *Englishman* and "any Turk . . . that ever entered the paradise of opium-eaters" (78). Opium simultaneously represents De Quincey's physical and psychical illness and well-being but also functions in another, more integral, way that connects personal history and cultural and national identity. As a form of exotic property or spoil, opium conjures up an image of the "Orient" that De Quincey commandeers to make his own, not unlike the way in which his putative claims to mastery of the confessional genre mark, for him, the cultural eminence of England over France.

Opium, the central excuse for De Quincey's narrative, is an Oriental spoil or product that De Quincey makes his own; his narrative, therefore, is produced not only at the expense of the French but via a commodifica-tion of the Orient. De Quincey's attempts at representing English pro-priety depend on the appropriation of a foreign product, and his attempts at representing himself depend on, so to speak, the appropriation and in-corporation of the other, figured by an opium-eating Malay. John Barrell suggests in his illuminating book *The Infection of Thomas De Quincey* that examining the "self" in relation to the "other" always invokes more than one "other," and he posits an intermediary other: "this/that/the other." He argues: "there is a 'this,' and there is something hostile to it, something which lies, almost invariably, to the east; but there is an East beyond that East, where something lurks which is equally threatening to both, and which enables or obliges them to reconcile their differences" (10–11).

What Barrell's unfixed category of a hostile other cannot account for is how a discrete English identity can be produced not only by its difference from a foreign other—or series of foreign others—but also by its use of the transgressive and somewhat slippery figure of the feminine as a way of regulating and confirming difference. My own distinctions of "otherings" are more in line with the terms Gayatri Spivak suggests in "The Rani of Sirmur": the "self-consolidating other" and "absolute other," for, as she argues, the process of identity making seems to involve a consolidation of the self. The term "self-consolidating other," however, is even more slippery in its propensity to consolidate than what I suggest to be the intermediary term: gender (128–51).

While the adoption of the French confessional genre suggests xenophobic appropriation, the incorporation of opium reveals a related, but in this case more directly imperialist, appropriation. De Quincey's representation of the foreign demonstrates the proximity of xenophobia and imperialism. Even while discussing his addiction, he establishes clear differences between, on the one hand, defective French sensibilities and opiated Turkish torpor and, on the other, the decency of English reserve and the purity of English morals. De Quincey questions whether any "Turk . . . can have had half the pleasure [he] had" in his consumption of opium, but hastily goes on to add that he "honour[s] the Barbarians too much by supposing them capable of any pleasures approaching the intellectual one of an Englishman" in the context of opium eating (45). In addition to the chauvinistic association of intellectuality and Englishness, and sensuality and the Oriental, this passage anxiously insists on De Quincey's capacity for intellectual apprehension as his mark of distinction from the undifferentiated mass of opium eaters. His eventual failure to distinguish himself from "the Opium-eater" as monstrous type and cliche tellingly demonstrates his questionable status in scholarly society: he is "an unworthy member of that indefinite body called *gentlemen*" (85). Toward the end of his narrative, he refers to himself in the third person as "the opium eater," and his efforts at establishing nice distinctions between himself and the "Barbarian" disintegrate because "opium had long ceased to found its empire on spells of pleasure; it was solely by the tortures connected with the attempt to abjure it, that it kept its hold" (114). Doomed to borrow from others, De Quincey rehearses Continental discourse—the French confessional—and engages "intellectually" with the Orient only through the exchange of opium. His dreams and fantasies about the Orient are produced through opium. De Quincey's dependence on the other both for a sense of himself and for a sense of alienation becomes increasingly untenable.

De Quincey's attempts at recovering himself within his autobiographical project, made by means of adopting foreign discourse, raises further, more troubling problems in representing and reconfirming the hegemony of an English self in relation to foreign others. There are many "others" that occupy or invade this text—the Malays, the prostitutes, strangers, opium. De Quincey creates these others by inscribing their difference from himself and, therefore, difference from Englishness. The frontiers of the foreign are thus outlined not merely by national boundaries, but by what can and cannot be included within his self-representation.[2]

Writing becomes a process of exhuming a repressed history and bringing it to the public eye, a process that De Quincey claims to regard with extreme aversion: "All this I feel so forcibly, and so nervously am I alive to reproach of this tendency, that I have for many months hesitated . . . to come before the public eye, until after my death" (1). De Quincey publishes these confessions anyway: the need to expose this repressed history quite obviously comes before issues of propriety. What is more pressing for De Quincey is to create for himself a distinct individuality while at the same time maintaining his place in the less distinct cultural category of Englishness. The force that propels De Quincey's confessional narrative strikingly resembles that which enables the process of coming out of the closet. At the same time that he confesses to his drug addiction, he appeals to a kind of male acceptance into both the dubious company of opium eaters and the more conventionally sanctioned fellowship of English intellectuals. Gender operates as a way of negotiating his identity. His acceptance by women, established by relationships of power in the text with the young women in Wales for whom he writes love letters, or the prostitute Ann, whose social position is below his own, functions as a way of negotiating his desires for acceptance into more masculine groups.[3] The desire for male fellowship, prefaced in the introduction to his *Confessions* as a desire to "claim fellowship with the great family of man," manifests itself elsewhere in his desire to be included within peculiarly English institutions. The most important institution is the academy, and De Quincey reveals a constant urge to announce his position as a classicist.[4] De Quincey's desire to belong to an established group is matched by his equally compelling desire to confess his "otherness" from such groups. These conflicting desires prefigure a central division in De Quincey's writing: the reality of his life of literary toil and the fantasy of his other pastoral life. Together, they operate as the mechanism for self-representation.

Several parts of the *Confessions* describe in detail the faces of others whom De Quincey places in relation to himself: that of Ann, the prostitute, that of the Malay, a prominent character in his Oriental dreams, and that of the English servant girl, whose contrast with the Malay's face sustains De Quincey's desire to impose national identities. De Quincey's descriptions of his own face, however, remain oddly indistinct, despite his anxiety to offer the reader a detailed self-representation. In a moment when he "forces" himself to draw a picture of his face for the edification of his readers, he defers to the reader, claiming that if "the public (into whose private ear I am confidentially whispering my confessions, and not into any painter's) should chanced to have framed some agreeable picture for itself of the Opium-eater's exterior . . . why should I barbarously tear from it so pleasing a delusion—pleasing both to the public and to me? No: paint me, if at all, according to your fancy" (61). The faces of foreign and feminine others, functioning in different ways as "self-consolidating" and "absolute" others, in this text occupy the double place of familiarity and unfamiliarity: their place is defined by De Quincey's notions of the border between the familiar and the foreign, of self and others.

His story of the Malay who wanders around the Lake District illustrates the facing-off of the foreign and the familiar, in which encounter De Quincey's own position gets reinscribed in a sublimely ridiculous moment:

> One day a Malay knocked at my door. What business a Malay could have to transact amongst English mountains, I cannot conjecture: but possibly he was on his road to a sea-port about forty miles distant. The servant who opened the door to him was a young girl born and bred amongst the mountains. . . . a more striking picture there could not be imagined, than the beautiful English face of the girl, and its exquisite fairness, together with her erect and independent attitude, contrasted with the sallow and bilious skin of the Malay, enamelled or veneered with mahogany, by marine air, his small fierce restless eyes, thin lips, slavish gestures and adorations. (55–56)

What is striking about this moment is the obsessive reproduction of the moral hierarchy that establishes racial difference. The English servant girl's demeanor is described in terms that are simultaneously physical and moral: "attitude" connects "erect" with "independent" while the Malay's "gestures" are "slavish," reminding us that the ultimate foreign commodity is the slave.[5] This picture is inscribed by De Quincey's own construction of the other and by the more general imperialist ideology that underwrites cultural production in this period. In this passage the face becomes the place where such an ideology is marked. The servant girl's face is not as clearly defined as the Malay's face; what makes it beautiful is what makes it English—that vague yet thoroughly recognizable quality— its "exquisite fairness." The description of the Malay, on the other hand, is much more detailed. It depends on the language of art: language that turns him into an appropriatable object, like an Oriental artifact—his face is "enamelled or veneered," his skin is "mahogany." The juxtaposition of these two faces reconfirms racial and therefore moral difference.

De Quincey keeps his own face out of this picture in order to maintain a marginal presence as both spectator and director of this scenario. The double position he occupies, at once self-effacing and self-imposing, illustrates the ambivalence with which De Quincey engages in self-representation as a continual process of drawing and erasing. It is curious and perhaps symptomatic of De Quincey's pathology that he can only recover or save face, so to speak, in the form of a deliberately mendacious self-representation. Called by the servant girl to talk to the Malay, and conscious of his reputation among his neighbors as a great scholar, De Quincey saves face by replying to the Malay with a few lines from the *Iliad*, Greece being geographically closest to the Malay's country of origin, or so De Quincey conjectures, confident in the fact that "the Malay had no means of betraying the secret," that is, both the "secret" of De Quincey's intellectual inadequacy—he can't speak Malay—and the "secret" of De Quincey's "murder" of the Malay (57).

The means by which De Quincey secures his secrets confirms the moral and racial superiority of his master language, English; it matters not if De Quincey's mastery of other languages is inadequate when only the master language has access to power, even if the articulation of mastery is illusory. Together with his knowledge of foreign languages, although not Malay, De Quincey's education positions him as other, or at least distinct from the other opium eaters he tends to group together in an uneducated mass; he matches his otherness against the Malay's exoticism in the guise of his "art." De Quincey reconfirms his Englishness by using the culturally sanctioned practice of displaying his knowledge of Greek as a mark of an exclusive and upper-class English education. Imperialist power as it is represented here rests on linguistic power, the institutionalization of Greek—a process that signifies the superiority of English imperial might by its appropriation of ancient Greek, and the cultural necessity for face saving, that together produce their own anxieties in the form of persecutory dreams.[6] "This incident I have digressed to mention because this Malay (partly from the picturesque exhibition he assisted to frame, partly from the anxiety I connected with his image for some days) fastened afterwards upon my dreams, and brought other Malays with him worse than himself, that ran 'a'muck' at me, and led me into a world of troubles" (57–58). What is also connected with De Quincey's anxiety and persecution, however, is not merely the fact that his face or reputation is dependent on a lie but that a literal exchange of faces occurs in this scene. De Quincey offers the Malay enough opium to "kill three dragoons and their horses" and, after watching the Malay "bolt the whole," cannot "think of violating the laws of hospitality, by having him seized and drenched with an emetic, thus frightening him into a notion that we were going to sacrifice him to some English idol" (57). Instead, De Quincey sacrifices the Malay to his obedient adherence to the English social code. That sacrifice itself stages as a sort of murder—even as the passage stresses, albeit humorously, the Malay's un-European and indeed nonhuman invulnerability to a potent drug—the gesture whereby De Quincey exchanges or saves his own face by the literal effacement of the Malay's face through murder.

In his essay "On Murder As Considered One of the Fine Arts," De Quincey suggests rewriting conventional aesthetic to include the celebration of the flaw, of imperfection, and of transgression. His aestheticization of murder complicates his responsibility for the Malay's figurative and possibly actual murder: on the one hand, he confesses to guilt for this murder, on the other, such a murder functions more like a staged tableau than a crime. Issues of reality and fantasy, especially as they are problematized by British notions of the Orient, come into play in the context of the tableau the Malay and the servant girl represent.[7] De Quincey suggests: "We dry up our tears, and have the satisfaction, perhaps, to discover that a transaction, which, morally considered, was shocking, and without a leg to stand upon, when tried by the principles of Taste, turns out to be a very meritorious performance" ("On Murder" 19).

De Quincey stages the Malay's intrusion upon an English scene in terms of Western-created notions of exoticism. His very clothes cloak his "real" identity, he wears "Asiatic dress," his turban "confounds" the English servant girl who answers his knock. De Quincey reacts to this tableau: "the group presented itself, arranged as it were by accident, though not very elaborate, took hold of my fancy and my eye in a way none of the statuesque attitudes exhibited in the ballets at the Opera House, though so

ostentatiously complex, had ever done" (56). Such a "meritorious performance" is accomplished without any overt dramatic machinery, yet its very
suggestion of staginess, figured in part by the girl's innocence of anything Oriental, is inscribed in the language of art and fantasy. The girl, De
Quincey writes, "gave me to understand that there was some sort of
demon below, whom she clearly imagined that my art could exorcise from
the house" (56). The scene of the Malay's murder is equally staged; the
boundary between representation and reality is effaced by De Quincey's
aesthetic, and the real possibility for the Malay's murder is registered in
several ways.

One of these ways is the mechanism of displacement. Earlier in the
Confessions De Quincey describes another account of murder:

> There had been some time before a murder committed on or near
> Hounslow-heath. I think I cannot be mistaken when I say that the
> name of the murdered person was *Steele*, and that he was the owner of
> a lavender plantation in that neighborhood. Every step of my progress
> was bringing me nearer to the heath: and it naturally occurred to me
> that I and the accursed murderer, if he were that night abroad, might
> at every instant be unconsciously approaching each other through the
> darkness. (29)

The "unconscious approach" is effected in the text, where the separate
identities of De Quincey and a murderer come together in the incident
of the Malay's "murder," and "unconsciously" De Quincey displaces his
possible guilt for the Malay's death onto the earlier figure of a reputed
murderer. The inverted chronology of this moment is established in the
beginning of his text where he suggests that "guilt and misery shrink,
by natural instinct, from public notice: they court privacy and solitude:
and, even in their choice of a grave, will sometimes sequester themselves
from the general population of the churchyard" (1). De Quincey stages
a burial of his guilt, which, in the course of his investigative confession,
is exhumed and recovered in a displaced narrative of dreams. The guilt
De Quincey claims to bury in this "choice of a grave"—that is, his
narrative—is one of the dominant subjects of his *Confessions*.

De Quincey's attempt at face saving, however, results in the loss or confusion of his identity. The threat the Malay poses is his ability to multiply
into a profusion of foreign faces: like the cultural stereotype of Oriental
races, the Malay is able to turn himself into frightening numbers or teem-
ing myriads of bodiless faces that threaten De Quincey's own inscribed
body. If De Quincey's written "face" represents the "face" of English

culture, and especially English culture in relation to other cultures, its ef(face)ment represents the loss of self-definition and, consequently, the loss of cultural definition. Thus De Quincey's anxiety over "other Malays" grows into a horror of them. The *Confessions* begin to lose their continuity as an autobiographical narrative in the second part and become more of a vehicle for repeating fragmentary, recurrent dreams and fantasies, and the Malay is recalled as a figure of terror. De Quincey writes, "the Malay has been a fearful enemy for months" and then continues self-consciously to conflate the Near, Middle, and Far East, and Africa, into a horrific image of the "Orient."

> I have often thought that if I were compelled to forego England, and to live in China, I should go mad. The cause of my horror lies deep. . . . Under the connecting feeling of tropical heat and vertical sun-lights, I brought together all creatures, birds, beasts, reptiles, all trees and plants, usages and appearances, that are found in all tropical regions, and assembled them together in China or Indostan. From kindred feelings, I soon brought Egypt and all her gods under the same law.[8] (72–73)

However strongly De Quincey establishes his difference from Oriental races, his xenophobic account of this dream/fantasy assumes another, more complicated form. The display of Occidental superiority is underwritten by a more fundamental anxiety about the contamination by the other. Imperialist appropriation—its "usages and appearances"—can only occur by controlling and maintaining cultural and racial difference, even if the effect of imperialism is that all otherness is regulated under one law, that of the empire. The possibility of the collapse of those differences produces in turn the necessity of reestablishing the exclusivity of Englishness. However, De Quincey's desires at this moment in the narrative don't necessarily fall into straightforward alignments of cultural identification. De Quincey describes the climax of his dream of Oriental horror as a form of collapsed difference. He ends with the following scene: "I was kissed, with cancerous kisses, by crocodiles; and laid, confounded with all unutterable slimy things, amongst reeds and Nilotic mud" (73). This horrific fantasy is complicated by something other than an anxiety of contamination by the other, namely by the paradoxical desire for such contamination, by an eroticized desire for submerging himself in what he finds horrific. This results, in part, from his position as an already contaminated being through his addiction, but it also suggests something else that complicates his relation to the Orient, and that is the generic issue of *eros*. His personal repressed erotic desires are written off as passing relations with the various women that populate his confessions, which results in the need to eroticize the exotic.[9] De Quincey's self-consciously inscribed position as an English author, however, prevents him from embedding himself too deeply in representations of the absolute other, and perhaps we can read the presence of erotic desire, embodied by the feminine, as the self-consolidating other whose task it is to merge with the self in order to present a united front against the absolute other. Even if his "sleep is still tumultuous" because of these horrific fantasies of crocodiles and such, he is able to see the "gates of Paradise" in ways similar to "our first parents when looking back from afar." He concludes his *Confessions* with a "tremendous line of Milton"—"With dreadful faces throng'd and fiery arms" (116). While this line gestures toward De Quincey's unhappy resolution of the adventures of an English opium eater, it still places his narrative within a firmly established English canonical history. His *Confessions* provides for him a legitimizing framework for exhuming a repressed history while simultaneously performing the task of absolution: his guilty pleasure in dabbling in the polluted exotic somehow gets projected onto his penitent confession to addiction.

Repression operates strongly in this text, however potent De Quincey's desire for exposure, and after indulging in the textual and sexual excess of revealing his Oriental dreams, De Quincey paints quite another pastoral picture to obscure the horror and desire of those dreams. The potential dissolution of his English ego that his indulgence in opium risks is again displaced into an imperialist context. De Quincey writes:

> I thought it was a Sunday morning in May, and that it was Easter-Sunday. . . . I was standing, as it seemed to me, at the door of my own cottage. Right before me lay the very scene which could really be commanded from that situation. . . . There were the same mountains . . . but the mountains were raised to more than Alpine height . . . in the green churchyard there were cattle tranquilly reposing upon the verdant graves, and particularly round the grave of a child whom I had tenderly loved . . . and immediately I saw upon the left a scene far different; but which yet the power of dreams had reconciled into harmony with the other. The scene was an Oriental one. . . . And at a vast distance were visible, as a stain upon the horizon, the domes and cupolas of a great city—an image or faint abstraction, caught perhaps in childhood from some picture of Jerusalem. And not a bow-shot from me, upon a stone,

and shaded by Judean palms, there sat a woman; and I looked; and it was—Ann! (75–76)

Before him is the sublime, on the left is the Orient. As in the earlier scene with the Malay, De Quincey turns away from the purely English representation—from the scene that can "really be commanded from that situation"—to seize upon the latter picture whose Orientalism functions as a backdrop for the English face of Ann. De Quincey again opts against the picture of reality, perhaps because his command of the situation of unquestionable authority is tenuous. He focuses instead on his pastoral fantasy of the other. The structure of this other picture and the language De Quincey uses to describe it are nonetheless strongly determined by an imperialist ethic based on appropriation and reconciliation of the foreign. Unable in his present contaminated condition to confront the "well-known scene" of Englishness, and also uneasy, because of his addiction, about his reception into the fellowship of Lake District poets represented in this context by the unnamed grave of Kate Wordsworth where he lingers, De Quincey eventually chooses an exotic scene over Kate Wordsworth's grave.

The power of his fantasy to reconcile the Occident with the Orient— here suggested by these opposite fantasies that present themselves to him concurrently—also implies that the power of Englishness over Orientalism has similar fantastic origins. Like a crusader, De Quincey has sought out the exotic in order to claim it as his own: he brings Jerusalem to the Lake District in the name of Christianity. The city—in this particular example, the picture of Jerusalem, but formerly "Oxford-street, stony-hearted stepmother" that "echoe[s] to the groans of innumerable hearts"—is cleansed of its former association with contamination and horror and becomes the site of the pastoral (67).[10] In the same way Ann's role as a former prostitute is recast into an idolatrous mold, as in *The Prelude* where Le Brun's Magdalene streams tears and becomes the representation of the English feminine for Wordsworth: "I kissed her lips (lips, Ann, that to me were not polluted), her eyes streaming tears" (76).[11] De Quincey's power to recover informs his appropriation of Ann: he wipes away her tears and makes her "more beautiful than she was." The kisses that he bestows on her, however, suspiciously repeat the earlier crocodile kisses and tears of Oriental horror. Ann and opium function as tokens of negotiation for issues of identity and otherness. Like foreign products, the prostitute is an object for sale, and as such she can never hope to maintain any sense of individual integrity but, rather, must depend on De Quincey for a voice. For example, a "brutal ruffian" has plundered what little property she owns, and De Quincey urges her to seek a magistrate where he "should speak on her behalf" (51). She is his figure of appropriation and recovery throughout the text and, more significantly, the picture he paints of himself in the frame of a fantasy. Ann's problematic position for De Quincey, as both an object of desire and an object of dread, parallels De Quincey's desire for opium and his dread of addiction to Oriental sensuality.

The Oriental dreams occur in a part of De Quincey's text entitled "The Pains of Opium," and it is during this last section that the text loses its formal integrity as an autobiographical narrative and becomes a series of dream fragments, fantasies, and journal entries. De Quincey writes: "For several reasons, I have not been able to compose the notes for this part of my narrative into any regular or connected shape" (62). The repetition of figures in dreams, of truncated images contrasting with myriads of faces, suggests De Quincey's incarceration by the unsuccessful recall of repressed desire: he is locked into a pattern of repetition. The disintegration of the text also suggests an escape from restrictive form, a sense that autobiography is no longer the issue and that repeating dreams is the only form of relieving repression, a method of relief that refers to the process of addiction.

Although the pressure I am placing on this reading of autobiography is in the interest of ideological interpretation, any investigation of the question of subjectivity can also usefully draw on psychoanalytic discourse to uncover and understand ideological formations. De Quincey's *Confessions* connects geographical entities and political formations to powerful cultural fantasies, and links all three to a politics of erotics. The "natural" right to European imperialism may be usefully addressed by psychoanalytical discourse.

In his essay on the uncanny, Freud describes his own experience of being drawn back to the red-light district, locating the "uncanny" in the foreign (Italian) city, in prostitutes, and in his own labyrinthine repetition as a wanderer, street-walker, and peripatetic. Freud writes,

> once as I was walking through the deserted street of a provincial town in Italy which was strange to me . . . I found myself in a quarter the character of which could not long remain in doubt. Nothing but painted women were to be seen at the windows. . . and I hastened to leave the narrow street. . . . But after having wandered about for a while without being directed, I suddenly found myself back in the same street, where my presence was now beginning to excite attention. I hurried away once more, but only to arrive yet a third time by devious paths in the same

place. Now, however, a feeling overcame me which I can only describe as uncanny. ("The Uncanny" 42)[12]

One is reminded not only of the various painted women to whom De Quincey has been attached—the copy of a Van Dyck portrait of a woman on which he fixes his parting kiss when leaving his uncle's house to wander through Wales, the picture of the prostitute Ann, which he also kisses—but of his curious, erotically excitable relation to their "contaminated" position. Like Freud, De Quincey engages in his own wandering in which he confronts various feminine figures—most notably Ann, whose image he tries later to repaint in his narrative: "Being myself at that time of necessity a peripatetic, or a walker of streets, I naturally fell in more frequently with those female peripatetics who are . . . called street-walkers."[13] De Quincey's connection with impure women is precedented by his contaminated position as an addict, and, like Freud, his contamination is both repressed and recalled by repetition.

However disintegrated the *Confessions* becomes, the ideology of imperialism is always closely linked to the production of fantasy. The Orient's relation to England is unequal in terms of morality and intellectual ability, and, as inferior, functions as the place where appropriation can occur. Contrary to this representation, the very image of the Orient created by the Western dominant culture is one of inaccessibility. Oriental mystery and fantasy cannot exist in any material reality, although its place in a psychical reality is another question. Freud repeats this ideology in "The Unconscious," where he claims that the origins of the unconscious level at which fantasy operates maintain the same racial difference and imperialist ethic that determine De Quincey's text:

On the one hand they [phantasies] are highly organised, free from self-contradiction, have made use of every acquisition of the system Cs. and would hardly be distinguished in our judgement from the formations of that system. On the other hand they are unconscious and are incapable of becoming conscious. Thus *qualitatively* they belong to the system Pcs., but *factually* to the Ucs. Their origin is what decides their fate. We may compare them with those human half-breeds who, taken all round, resemble white men, but betray their coloured descent by some striking feature or other, on account of which they are excluded from society and enjoy none of the privileges of white people. (138)

The metaphor occurring to Freud here is a function of a Eurocentric and racist point of view of nonwhite peoples as more instinctual, less in-

tellectual, having lower faculties. The anxiety of the inability to differentiate between unconscious impulses and a conscious process of thought
("our judgement") is allayed by the "unconscious" display of difference.
Although fantasies may pass as products of a system of judgment, they
"betray" their true descent by a "striking feature" of difference, here written as a difference between being qualitative and factual. Freud compares
the repression of unconscious impulses with the repression or exclusion
of nonwhites. Although I don't exactly mean to suggest that Freud establishes racial inferiority as a scientific fact, it is curious that this particular
metaphor emerges not only in Freud's discussion of the unconscious, in
which a largely imaginative notion is legitimated for the first time by the
language of science, but also in Laplanche and Pontalis's *The Language of
Psychoanalysis*, where this passage is quoted to illustrate their definition of
"phantasy."[14] The distinction between "imagination" and "perception" (reality) so carefully evoked in this definition—phantasies are purely illusory
products that cannot maintain any "real" coherence once the reality principle has been imposed—disintegrates in the very example chosen to
illustrate this mechanism.

Freud privileges the notion that the origins of the Orient are fantastic
and remain within the system of imagination and the unconscious (his distinction between qualitative and factual): the half-breeds are unconsciously
and instinctively read through their body in the same way that the feminine
is first and foremost read through her body in De Quincey's narrative. It
seems as if more than half a century later, the institution of psychoanalytic
discourse shoulders the "white man's burden," reestablishing in a new "scientific" context the "natural" conjunction of imperialism and the English
psyche. De Quincey, who cannot have known about these new scientific discourses, makes connections between his personal addiction to opium and
the language of xenophobia in a displaced narrative of eroticism. As
readers of De Quincey, we cannot *not* be aware that such a displacement,
read in conjunction with the discourse of psychoanalysis, represents a
larger, more powerful cultural addiction to fantasies about the Orient and
reproduces and repeats for a further posterity the system of national and
racial difference that defines, for the English, the order of things.

NOTES

    1. I want to make a distinction between the ways I use the names *England* and
Great Britain. This difference is between the geopolitical, imperialist identity of Great
Britain and the domestic, cultural identity of England. The former is an appellation
invented in 1707 with the Act of Union, which sought to link Scotland to England

and Wales; the latter is less obviously marked by a specific historical event. Despite the fact that Great Britain's national identity is established by forging other discrete nations, as Linda Colley puts it, English chauvinism persists in privileging the cultural authority of *England* or *Englishness*. Invoking the name *Great Britain* displays to the world at large an outward show of imperial force, while embedded in *England* is a domestic hierarchy practiced by English cultural imperialism, to use Edward Said's term. De Quincey is not unaware of this distinction. His descriptions of preliminary wanderings in Wales are attended by continual references to his class position and intellectuality, both of which protect him from the blemish of being mistakenly identified as Welsh.

2. Another way of thinking through the ways in which ideology speaks in De Quincey's text is to examine it in the context of Eve Sedgwick's suggestion about narrative and ideology in *Between Men:* "It is important that ideology in this sense . . . is always at least implicitly narrative and that, in order for the reweaving of ideology to be truly invisible, the narrative is necessarily chiasmic in structure: that is, that the subject of the beginning of the narrative is different from the subject at the end, and that the two subjects cross each other in a rhetorical figure that conceals their discontinuity" (14–15). In this model, the differences between subjects—opium, confession, self-portrait, cultural portrait—work together to reconstitute the ideological formulation of European hegemony.

3. De Quincey's relation to the Welsh women would also be an example of England's cultural imperialism in relation to other parts of Great Britain; the Welsh, though British, are distinctly un-English and, as such, perform the role of a "self-consolidating" other.

4. One could also read this claim for fellowship as a "homosocial moment," which Eve Kosofsky Sedgwick "invents" as a "strategy for making generalizations about, and marking historical differences in, the structure of men's relations with other men" (1–2). In this case De Quincey's bond to male academic institutions is cemented through his "trafficking" in his relations with women—the sisters in Wales and Ann the prostitute.

5. De Quincey's social hierarchy established on the grounds of a moral hierarchy position the Malay as inferior even to the lower English classes. The difference of "body" is illustrated in the absolutist terms Henry Louis Gates, Jr., identifies in "Talkin' That Talk" as terms that "*fix* culturally defined differences into transcendent 'natural' categories or essences" (402).

6. Linda Colley accounts for this English ambivalence toward the vast expansion of its empire by suggesting that, when "Britain's empire no longer pivoted on commerce but was sustained by force of arms like earlier empires, what guarantee could there be that it would not in turn decay and destroy the mother country in the process? The question nagged at a whole generation of British intellectuals, most profitably Edward Gibbon who made the decision to chronicle the decline and fall of the Roman empire just one year after the signing of the Treaty of Paris" (102). One can read De Quincey's version of this question as part of his Romantic anxiety about identity and authorship (an eighteenth-century concern) in terms of a more general cultural anxiety about the fear of contamination by the other that underwrites imperialist ideology.

7. I am indebted to Edward Said's work *Orientalism* in which he argues that the "Orient" and "orientalism" are products of Western cultural fantasy that employ racial difference as a way of guaranteeing discrete Occidental cultural identities, in this case British (1–28).

8. Much of this fantasy is ostensibly produced under the influence of opium; De Quincey uses opium—and its corresponding narrative genre of the confessional—to allow an articulation of a racist and imperialist imaginary, while excusing the autobiographical subject of moral blame, because he is under the influence of opium.

9. De Quincey's need to eroticize the foreign is another example of how the political and the erotic "necessarily obscure and misrepresent each other." Eve Sedgwick suggests that the primary space for ideological formation is in the shared boundary between the categories of political and sexual: that the "developmental fact that, as Freud among others has shown, even the naming of sexuality as such is always retroactive in relation to most of the sensations and emotions that constitute it, is *historically* important. What *counts* as the sexual is . . . variable and itself political" (15).

10. Linda Colley locates the myth of the New Jerusalem, as represented by Blake's *Jerusalem*, by recounting the importance of Protestantism in seventeenth-century England. She writes:

> When William Blake wrote [*Jerusalem*] in the early 1800s, he was employing for his own mystical and political purposes a set of images that had been at the centre of Protestant thought in Britain since the early seventeenth century. That they were a chosen people struggling towards the light, a bulwark against the depredations of the Antichrist, had proved as compelling an idea for English puritans, as it did for the Scottish Covenanters. Superimposing the language of the Bible on their own countryman's progress through life and towards redemption had seemed to these earlier generations of Protestants both natural and instructive, and in the eyes of many clergymen, this continued to be the case throughout the eighteenth century and long after. (30)

11. De Quincey's anxious relation to the Lake District poets and particularly to Wordsworth underwrites this image. "De Quincey's" cottage is in fact Wordsworth's Dove Cottage, and his choice of the Oriental picture over the Romantic sublime as his scene of recuperation, reproduced in the same image Wordsworth uses to describe *his* appropriation of the French Revolution as an eroticized picture of Le Brun's Magdalene in book 9 of *The Prelude*, seems at once an effort to incorporate Wordsworthian imagery—or pass it off as his own—as well as an attempt to establish poetic difference. De Quincey in fact alludes to Ann as "a Magdalene taken away, before injuries and cruelty had blotted out and transfigured her ingenuous nature, or the brutalities of ruffians had completed the ruin they had begun" (65), in much the same way that Wordsworth uses the figure of Le Brun's Magdalene to emblematize his disillusionment with the French Revolution.

12. Of course, the complication here is identifying the various hierarchies of cultural difference within a European context. Freud is German and is locating the uncanny and its erotic possibilities in an Italian city, which may suggest that a Teutonic sensibility corresponds with a British one against Franco-Latinate cultures.

13. In their study of the semiotics of the carnivalesque, Peter Stallybrass and Allon White argue that cultural categories of high and low, popular and aesthetic, are

reproduced in both the physical and the geographical body and depend on each other for discrete articulations. They map out some of the hierarchies of the body, the psyche, social formation, and geographical formation (e.g., the city) in "the terrain of literary and cultural history," particularly as they are manifested in a high-low opposition. De Quincey seems to be invoking these hierarchies in his self-conscious association of certain discourses with certain topographical locations.

14. Laplanche and Pontalis's project also deploys a process of the legitimization of psychoanalytic discourse by containing it within a lexicographical framework.

WORKS CITED

Barrell, John. *The Infection of Thomas De Quincey*. New Haven: Yale UP, 1991.
Colley, Linda. *Britons: Forging the Nation, 1707–1837*. New Haven: Yale UP, 1991.
De Quincey, Thomas. *Confessions of an English Opium Eater*. London: Penguin, 1971.
———. "On Murder As Considered One of the Fine Arts." *Selected Essays of Thomas De Quincey: Narrative and Imagination*. Edinburgh: Adam and Charles, 1888.
Freud, Sigmund. "The Uncanny." *Studies in Parapsychology*. New York: Macmillan, 1977.
———. "The Unconscious." *General Psychological Theory*. New York: Macmillan, 1963.
Gates, Henry Louis, Jr. *"Race," Writing, and Difference*. Chicago: U of Chicago P, 1985.
Laplanche, J., and J. B. Pontalis. *The Language of Psychoanalysis*. New York: Norton, 1973.
Said, Edward. *Culture and Imperialism*. New York: Vintage, 1993.
———. *Orientalism*. New York: Vintage, 1979.
Sedgwick, Eve Kosofsky. *Between Men: English Literature and Male Homosocial Desire*. New York: Columbia UP, 1985.
Spivak, Gayatri. "The Rani of Sirmur." *Europe and Its Others*. London: U of Essex P, 1985.
Stallybrass, Peter, and Allon White. *The Politics and Poetics of Transgression*. Ithaca: Cornell UP, 1986.
Wordsworth, William. *The Prelude*. New York: Norton, 1979.

The "French Threat" in Anti-Jacobin Novels of the 1790s

Nancy Johnson

In Jane West's novel *A Tale of the Times* (1799), when the young and impressionable Lady Monteith is seduced by the French-trained *philosophe* Edward Fitzosborne, they both pay dearly for their transgressions. Lady Monteith falls ill and dies; Fitzosborne commits suicide after learning that he has been sentenced to the guillotine. The severe punishments in West's novel are certainly meant to function didactically and define familial roles and social duty. Young women are taught to be cognizant of their domestic responsibilities (for example, marriage choices) and warned to beware the delusionary wiles of romantic strangers. Yet the retribution the couple is forced to pay also reveals a heightened fear of the potentially terrifying consequences of unbridled sexual behavior in a period of sociopolitical turmoil and transformation. The "French threat" in the Anti-Jacobin novel is embodied in the "French principles" that infiltrate moral structures and endanger the fabric of English culture. The "new philosophy," which is associated with revolutionary France in these narratives, thrives on families weakened by wayward individuals who are enticed by thoughts of self-determination and advancement. The ambition and vanity of characters like Monteith and Fitzosborne allow for the neglect of familial duties to such an extent that the entire community suffers from the loss of moral guidance and social cohesion. The borders of the English family, West warns, are in danger of invasion.

The fear voiced by Jane West was not an uncommon or excessive one in conservative British discourse of the 1790s. The anxiety over monitoring desire, containing passion, and impressing the importance of obedience and fidelity on the hearts and minds of young English men and women, as well as their parents, has a pervasive and resonant presence in the Anti-Jacobin novel. Although the legislation of desire is often cloaked in the language of Christian morality and frequently located in the domestic sphere, the need to restrict intimate behavior and protect the structure of the family betrays an attempt to control the acquisition and transmission of property, preserve the social and political authority of the already propertied, and maintain the laws that legitimate and protect the existing distribution of wealth. The behavior of West's misguided married woman and duplicitous seducer affects the entire nation. It threatens to undermine the security of Britain because it entertains alternative conceptualizations of property and makes assumptions about the parameters of ownership that are dependent on the recognition of individual rights. In the following discussion of five Anti-Jacobin novels, I argue that the "French threat" was actually an English threat derived from British reform movements and internal struggles. The focus on France, however, indicates a dread of infiltration, fueled not only by the instability of war but also by a fear that the British family—the cornerstone of social constructs—was in a perilously vulnerable state. Rather than secure the boundaries of the self for individual empowerment, which would actually hasten social changes, Anti-Jacobin novelists insisted that the borders of the English family be secured, because therein lay the preservation of economic order.

In the Anti-Jacobin novel, amoral behavior jeopardizes the "security of property," which Mary Wollstonecraft proclaims in her *Vindication of the Rights of Men* (1790) is the meaning of "English liberty" (24). Security of property was indeed at the core of the debate on natural and civil rights that dominated political dialogues at the end of the eighteenth century. It was at the heart of Edmund Burke's opposition to revolution in *Reflections on the Revolution in France* (1790), and it was a crucial point of debate in responses to *Reflections* by Mary Wollstonecraft, Sir James Mackintosh, and Thomas Paine. To acknowledge a person capable of controlling his or her own physical and emotional passions was to recognize an ownership of the self and a relationship to the "other" that had tremendous repercussions for social constructs. The danger was in the perceived potential of self-governance to empower the individual, extend political agency, and enable participation in a market economy and in the formation of a government based on the prototype of the contract. Twentieth-century analysis of subjectivity and contract theory has shown that status persists in the age of the contract and that the actualization of agency for marginalized segments of the population is severely limited; however, late eighteenth-century perceptions of self-governance and its impact on property gleaned the potential for radical change from the promise of the contract, particularly in the possibility of extended franchisement.[1]

The threat inherent in reconstituting the body politic rallied supporters of monarchical rule who campaigned against the most obvious forces of change. Consequently, the Anti-Jacobin text both defined and was defined by its self-proclaimed adversary—English Jacobinism. In conjunction with the periodical founded by George Canning in 1797, *The Anti-Jacobin; or Weekly Examiner*, the novels of Jane West, Elizabeth Hamilton, Charles Lloyd, Henry James Pye, and Isaac Disraeli, among others, comprised a discourse in opposition to reform movements within Britain.[2] William Godwin's rational anarchism was a favorite target, as was Mary Wollstonecraft's feminism and Thomas Paine's political theory. As advocates of natural rights and early supporters of the French Revolution, the "English Jacobins" were labeled as such by those antagonistic to the principles associated with the rights of man. The ideological stances of the English Jacobins were actually much closer to those of the moderate Girondists, as noted by Gary Kelly, and follow in the tradition of rights theorists such as Hobbes, Locke, and Rousseau. The association with radical Jacobin rule in France, however, provided a far more provocative touchstone for determining revolutionary sentiments (Kelly 7). In addition, by attributing the notion of individual natural rights to revolutionary France and the *philosophes*, rather than to the English Dissenting tradition, conservative rhetoric exacerbated xenophobic sentiments directed at France. Anti-Jacobinism had a particularly vivid and carnal example, in the violence of the French Revolution, of the inevitability of disaster when the course of nature is disobeyed and attempts are made at instituting democratic authority. But it also had a profound economic mission in trying to firm up and protect the boundaries of the British identity by distinguishing it from a universal or revolutionary one.

Jacobinism is boldly cited, in the prospectus to *The Anti-Jacobin*, as the culprit of subversive activities bent on destroying the family and thereby throwing into anarchy the source of defining social roles and the means of transferring property: "Of all these and the like principles,—in one word, of JACOBINISM in all its shapes, and in all its degrees, political and moral, public and private, whether as it openly threatens the subversion of States, or gradually saps the foundations of domestic happiness, We are avowed, determined, and irreconcilable enemies" (1: 7). While the "subversions of States" remained the primary interest of *The Anti-Jacobin*, the mention of "foundations of domestic happiness" concomitant with public affairs provides a key to a philosophical premise of the Anti-Jacobin novel, derived from classical patriarchal thought: that private affairs are of public concern because private obedience and domestic order are essential to public peace and the fostering of loyal subjecthood. The reciprocal support between devotion to a father and veneration of a king was thought to be necessary for the stability of the family, the most basic unit of society, and the community at large (Schochet 10–16). In the interest of preserving respect for the authority of the father and king and the intimate connection between the family and the state, fathers in the Anti-Jacobin novels tend to be exemplary figures or heart-wrenching victims. Elizabeth Hamilton, in her novel *Memoirs of Modern Philosophers* (1801), frequently satirizes William Godwin and his essay *Enquiry Concerning Political Justice* (1793) because of his insistence that the criterion for respect should be personal merit rather than familial affiliation (Godwin 168–77). Her attacks are then buttressed by the tale of a father, Captain Delmond, who never recovers from the loss of his wayward daughter, Julia— a young woman overcome by her passions and seduced by a "new philosopher." Though this father, in particular, was not always exemplary but rather served as a testimony to human imperfectibility (thereby reverencing God), his sole status as a father rendered him worthy of his daughter's obedience. As articulated by Sir Robert Filmer in his account of patriarchalism, compassion stirred for the father is sympathy inspired for the monarchy.

Proponents of the contract as the paradigm for political authority were, of course, regarded by Anti-Jacobins as a threat to inherited property, status, and civic power. Although conservative discourse often points to France as the source of instigation, the peril of reform actually came from internal struggles. Protestant Dissenters who advocated the recognition of inalienable rights, such as Thomas Paine, Dr. Richard Price, Dr. Joseph Priestley, and Dr. Andrew Kippis, did indeed threaten social constructs because they were supporting a fundamental change in the relationship of the individual to civil authority. But when Edmund Burke responded to Dr. Price's sermon, "A Discourse on the Love of Our Country,"[3] by charging Price with espousing French principles, he set about a strategy of focusing attention on foreign infiltration (very specifically, revolutionary France) and the foreboding picture of utter chaos in the abandonment of the social order marked by inherited status and monarchical rule. Burke envisioned law as an institution derived of experience and marked by historical continuity. To overturn, revolutionize, or radically reform law that is "immemorial" and beyond the complete comprehension of human reason, as J. G. A. Pocock interprets Burke's view, is to violate nature (Pocock 202–32). If this ancient law is broken and nature is "disobeyed," Burke warns, a state of chaos will ensue in which "the rebellious are outlawed, cast forth, and exiled, from this world of reason, and order, and peace, and virtue, and fruitful penitence, into the antagonist world of madness, discord, vice, confusion, and unavailing sorrow" (195).

In his sermon, Price passionately congratulates France on her rebellion against tyranny at the fall of the Bastille and clearly sees the French as heralding a new world order for Europe. This is done, however, only at the end of the sermon and in a congratulatory address drawn up by the Revolution Society at a later meeting in the London Tavern. The focus of Price's text is the development of a policy of individual rights that he regards as the legacy of the Glorious Revolution. Price considers it the business of Dissenters and other reformers to continue the work implied in the principles established by the English revolution—principles that begin to consider the extension of franchisement. The celebrated resolutions Price articulates were drawn from the Dissenting tradition; as recently as the previous year, 1788, the Revolution Society passed similar resolutions after listening to a sermon by the Reverend Dr. Andrew Kippis.[4] In addition to a call for the right of the English people to choose their own governors, cashier them for misconduct, and form their own government, the resolutions included an assertion of liberty of conscience in religious matters. The pronouncement of religious freedom was a direct reference to the penal laws that continued to restrict the Dissenters' access to public office. One of the benefits Protestant Dissenters realized from the Glorious Revolution was the right to worship, authorized by the Toleration Act of 1689, yet they did not enjoy the full spectrum of rights available to Anglicans. This was one of the pieces of unfinished business that Price insisted must be addressed. In his sermon, therefore, he encourages further attempts at repealing the Test and Corporation Acts.[5]

Although Burke had at one time courted the electoral support of Dissenters, he abstained from earlier votes on the Test and Corporation Acts and eventually opposed their repeal because he saw them as precursors to an outright attack on the Church of England (Cone 301–6). Fully cognizant that the dispute with Dissenters was an issue of British legislation, Burke, in his response to Dr. Price's sermon, turned his focus to France to exaggerate the danger of reform. The affiliation of Dissenters with the revolutionary turbulence of France appealed to British fears of French influence and invasion. Thus began a tradition in the rhetoric of Anti-Jacobinism of concentrating on the "French threat," whereas the real danger was in the growth of contract theory and the proclamation of rights from within Britain. Furthermore, Anti-Jacobin discourse ignores Price's claim that it was *English* principles derived from the Glorious Revolution that fueled the American and French Revolutions (Price 50). The marquis d'Argenson wrote of France in 1751 that "there is a philosophical wind blowing toward us from England in favor of free, anti-monarchical government . . . it is entering minds and one knows how opinion governs the world" (qtd. in Baker 208). Far from being the fallout of the French Revolution, the movement toward contract theory in Britain was a gradual one, and it was well under way by the time the Bastille fell and the dialogue of rights became a fevered public debate (Cone 301).

Though the real and imagined dangers posed by France in the 1790s ranged from military advancements to the export of citizen unrest, the "French Threat" in Anti-Jacobin novels was represented in terms of sexual license. The unleashing of desire was a particularly onerous threat because, if allowed to develop, it could undermine the foundation of social order and hinder the vehicle for the control and transmission of property: the family. In addition, it privileged a powerful, independent self that assumed a form of autonomous governance. This was an especially bold pronouncement for women that had implications for property rights and political participation not often (if ever) sanctioned by legislative bodies—certainly not by the Constituent Assembly in France when it excluded women from enfranchisement (Hufton 3–4). Nonetheless, given the assertion by Locke that the origin of property is located in the self, and the assumption by Rousseau and Paine, among others, that society is a covenant, the fear of French principles was, in large part, a fear of a new polity based on the rights of man. Liberty founded on agreement involved recognition of inalienable natural rights, which are not surrendered when entering into civil society, and this meant extending political agency to those who could claim self-governance. The effort to legislate desire was an attempt to bring the natural rights of individuals back into the fold of civil society where they would fall within the confines of law and, by that means, to limit the expansion of political authority.

The formidable menace of social upheaval is embodied in Anti-Jacobin novels in the figure of a rogue who is either French or has traveled to the Continent and there been initiated by French principles (Butler 117). Their villainy is in the seduction of a daughter or wife, or in the brain-washing of a vulnerable young Englishman. The cunning rake functions as both a metaphorical image for the insidious danger and beguiling power of the "new philosophy" (belief in the perfectibility of man and the potency of rational thought) and as a literal enemy to domestic order and economy. Representations of sexual aberration or illicit desire appear frequently in the iconography of the French Revolution to denounce the excesses of the monarchy or to signify the insidious and alluring dangers of the "goddesses" of equality, liberty, and reason (Hunt 42–43). Yet, in British Anti-Jacobin discourse, the association of licentiousness with the new philosophy was a deliberate attempt at presenting "English Jacobinism" as a menace to the British family and its central role in economic functions. The invasion of a foreign element into the business of the family endangered efforts to concentrate wealth that were regarded as essential to national security, such as the practice of primogeniture and the legal restrictions on married women's property. "The power of perpetuating our property in our families," Edmund Burke writes, "is one of the most valuable and interesting circumstances belonging to it, and that which tends the most to the perpetuation of society itself. It makes our weakness subservient to our virtue; it grafts benevolence even upon avarice. . . . The possessors of family wealth, and of the distinction which attends hereditary possession (as most concerned in it) are the natural securities for this transmission" (140–41).

The *philosophe* in the Anti-Jacobin novel insinuates himself into the British family, usually through sexual seduction, and destroys familial affection, jeopardizes property, and often brings about the death of a parent or guardian. The moral and political anxiety Anti-Jacobin writers felt about the breakdown of domestic structures is evidenced by the numerous illustrations they provide of the devastating physical, emotional, and financial consequences of unwieldy passions. In West's *A Tale of the Times*, Lady Monteith (née Geraldine Powerscourt) becomes aware only at the end of the narrative that her victimization is both political and personal. The language of politics blends with that of passion when she confesses that her "rebel heart, imperceptibly alienated from its lawful possessor, admitted an usurped claim" (West 3: 318). But in spite of her apparent repentance and acceptance of the civil authority of marriage over her unlawful passion, the affair leads to a question about the paternity of her son. Her personal transgression becomes a problem for the economics of the family and the state because it disrupts the system of inheritance. "Consider, of what importance to society the chastity of women is," remarked Samuel Johnson. "Upon that all the property in the world depends. We hang a thief for stealing a sheep; but the unchastity of a woman transfers sheep, and farm and all, from the right owner" (qtd. in Boswell 3: 340). When young Geraldine marries, she does so with her father's approval. But his reservation about the soundness of his daughter's marriage choice leads him to deviate from the usual management of familial property. Instead of following the custom of primogeniture, her father stipulates that his name and estate be bestowed on the second son or first daughter of her marriage. And instead of turning all of Geraldine's inherited property over to her husband's control, he agrees that two thousand pounds a year should be left to her discretion. The disastrous turn of the Monteiths' marriage justifies Sir William's precautions; yet it also necessitates a slight correction in the process of inheritance. Sir William eventually leaves his estate to Henry Powerhouse, a distant relation and onetime rival for Geraldine's hand. The virtuous behavior and financial responsibility demonstrated by Henry require a reward. Furthermore, a large estate, such as that of Powerscourt, must remain with someone who has nurtured a stable family and can ensure that the estate will remain intact.

Anti-Jacobin novelists pinpoint an overly indulgent concern with the self as perhaps the primary culprit behind the vulnerable condition of the British family. The individual, which is exalted in contract theory, is presented here as a disembedded, isolated self, replete with the anti-Christian vices of pride, vanity, greed, and ambition. These are the very weaknesses that leave Lady Monteith and her husband vulnerable to the advances of Edward Fitzosborne, the menacing outsider who espouses Jacobin principles. He identifies the Monteiths' failings and targets them in his systematic attempt to ease himself into the family, destroy the marriage, and perhaps acquire Lady Monteith's fortune. Lady Monteith's flaw, and one of the characteristics that enables her seduction, is her vanity and assumption of self-governance. Because Lady Monteith is working against "nature" in her attempts at autonomy, they are doomed to failure. By an error of judgment, she marries an alluring but superficial charmer (Lord Monteith) when she could have wed a quiet, honest man of humble means (Henry Powerhouse) whose exceptional virtues lay beneath the surface. She refuses to listen to parental advice and, because of her vanity, is unable to see beyond the cursory indications of character and temperament. Her independence proves to be faulty and her judgment, which we can see is repeatedly plagued by distorted vision, is inadequate. She errs because she assumes that she can forego the wisdom of experience and the lessons of history and live by the guidance of her own reason. In so doing, Lady Monteith starts down a path of blind vanity that ends in the death of the self that she tried to assert beyond its appropriate confines of family, community, and gender. Lady Monteith realizes her inability for self-governance only on her deathbed, after she has been seduced and sees the destruction of her family. In retrospect, she understands that wives must relinquish the desire for "rights" and turn the responsibility of their development and behavior over to their husbands. Speaking for all wives, she warns husbands that they should not "entirely depend upon the stability of our principles or the constancy of our attachments." They ought to "treat our foibles with generous lenity" and "make our faults conducive to our security" (West 3: 318–19). Her own tragic fate, she concludes, was borne of "a vain confidence in [her] own strength" (3: 329–30).

The messenger of French principles in West's novel, Edward Fitz-osborne, is an Englishman enthralled with the political developments of France who believes, early on, that his observation of events in France will make him a worthier "British legislator" (2: 97). Like Satan in Milton's *Paradise Lost*, Fitzosborne is intent on destroying the domestic happiness of which he is so jealous. His seduction is a sexual one, but he is credited with grander desires than the mere acquirement of a woman. His vices, which he shares with French *philosophes* and English Jacobins, are not driven by passion. They are dangerous because they are "systematic, the result of design, guided by method, sanctioned by sophistry, and originating from the covert war which he waged, not merely against the chastity, but also against the principles of his victims" (2: 153). He rejects Burke's notion of a cumulative history when he concludes that "the present age ha[s] more wisdom than all the preceding ones taken collectively" (3: 125) and appeals, instead, to "individual action" supported by inalienable natural rights. He eventually sets his sights on Lady Monteith's fortune, rather than the legislature, but never fails to remind us of the connection between radical politics and licentiousness, and hence, his own threat. "La Liberté," he announces, is "the handsomest courtesan in all Paris" (2: 100–101).

While the representation of "French principles" and the general support of classical patriarchal thought in West's novel betray an awareness of the politics of the domestic, the ideal family is presented as one whose boundaries are clearly defined and capable of standing firm against possible trespassers. The Evans family lives in an Austenian world of a small country rectory and offers its community wisdom rather than abstract reasoning, charity rather than universal benevolence, and forgiveness rather than righteousness or revenge.[6] They live by modest means and remain unplagued by the ambition, indulgences, and duplicity that destroy families of rank and fortune. The enclosure of their world provides the personal stability, the recognition of individual contributions and talents, and the moral well-being of society that "new philosophers" are seeking. But instead of looking toward France and alternative concepts of government (or more accurately, British reform movements), the Evanses look to their own traditions of Christian morality and the stability of gendered roles that maintain private and public peace. While Lady Monteith's family collapses, the virtuous Evans family is rewarded with the inheritance of Sir William Powerscourt when Lucy Evans marries Henry Powerhouse.

Ironically, the purity of Burke's system of inheritance as a paradigm for the transferal of all civic privileges is somewhat violated by this change of hands. Yet even Burke admits that adjustments have to be made to maintain the customs and practices that preserve our rights in the ancient constitution. Corrections are necessary to preserve the family and its crucial function as the vehicle for the transmission of property and rights. According to Burke, political rights are manifest in the economics of the family. Our liberty is an "entailed inheritance," bequeathed to us by our forefathers and intended to be transmitted to posterity. Our rights are "locked fast as in a sort of family settlement" and "grasped as in a kind of mortmain for ever." The state, finally, maintains "the image of a relation in blood; binding up the constitution of our country with our dearest domestic ties; adopting our fundamental laws into the bosom of our family affections" (Burke 119–20). Empowerment of a self-governing individual was seen as a direct and tangible threat to the family, and therefore the control of property, the accompanying franchisement, and the stability of law.

The containment of financial resources and authority by circumscribing the independent agency of the individual, particularly women, is a prevailing concern of Hamilton's novel, *Memoirs of Modern Philosophers*. Indulgence in one's personal imagination or intellect, at the expense of common sense and responsibility to family and friends, is a perilous extravagance of passion because it distorts reality and too often assumes a capacity for reason that supersedes moral instruction. As in *A Tale of the Times*, the danger of unchecked desire comes in the form of a French-trained Englishman, Alphonso Vallaton, who speaks the enticing but duplicitous language of English Jacobinism. Hamilton notes that her novel is a satire of the "New Philosophy" (xiii). Yet the comical confusions of love and courtship that flirt with issues of perception and judgment only lightly veil the very serious warning against the deceptively naive hopes of political reformers in Britain. The adventures of Bridgetina Botherim, who is a foolish and "bothersome" convert to the new philosophy, are entertaining and seemingly harmless. But the seduction of Julia Delmond, like that of Lady Monteith, ends in the destruction of her family and her own death. The seriousness of her error—the source of which is an indulgent, liberal upbringing—demonstrates the severe dangers posed by French principles. Like West, Hamilton warns of the need to bolster the British family against invasion by reformers.

One particular duty that Hamilton assigns to women is to reign in their imaginations (fed by romantic novels of female heroism, such as Richardson's *Clarissa*) and exercise their judgment. In contract theory, the ability to reason is associated with the capacity to enter into an agreement. In Anti-Jacobin texts, however, rationality is a component of social duty and a theoretical guarantee that each person will function in his or her familial role as an obedient daughter, commanding father, or faithful wife. Hamilton very carefully defines what she means by the exercise of reason, and it is clearly not the elevation of humanity to the level of God, as the doctrine of human perfectibility suggests. Dr. Orwell, a father in the novel who fulfills his role as social and familial caretaker, entreats women to act rationally and ignore those who "have made it their business to pervert that reason by turning it into a principle of revolt against the order of Providence" (Hamilton 1: 199). The reason of which he speaks is that necessitated by Christianity. Women must be educated and intelligent not for the purpose of reconstituting political authority but to perform their Christian duties. Presented in the text as a form of "feminism," Dr. Orwell's position on women echoes that of seventeenth-century discourses on the female sex. In their role as "helpmeet" to husbands and joint custodians of earthly dominions (based on the Adam and Eve paradigm), women could claim a form of domestic authority that allowed them to govern within the family;[7] however, Hamilton does not adapt this notion of female development to that of late eighteenth-century feminism, such as Wollstonecraft's, in which the authority of women is considered in relation to a separating public sphere.

As in West's novel, the unprotected family permits the infiltration of foreign influences. Julia Delmond's parents do not fulfill their social obligation to provide moral direction and an appropriate sense of humility to Julia. Only after Julia runs off with Vallaton does her father Captain Delmond realize that he "encouraged her to throw off the prejudices of religion ... and to consult the dictates of her mind instead of the morality of the gospel" (Hamilton 3: 53). As a result, Julia succumbs to the "bewildering mist" of imagination and fails to discern Vallaton's evil (2: 125). Examples of parents shirking their responsibilities comprise a cornerstone of Hamilton's argument that the British family is in a weakened state. But it is the *philosophes* who come under the harshest criticism for undermining the British family by denouncing marriage, encouraging infidelity, and ignoring the needs of immediate families while focusing on abstract philosophy. When Vallaton urges Julia to assert her "rights"—in particular, "the right of following your own inclination"—he acts as a subverter of filial obedience (2: 275). When Bridgetina embraces Godwinian anarchy and talks of going to live with the Hottentots, she does so in celebration of their sexual libertinism. Members of this primitive tribe, Bridgetina explains, "live together as long as harmony subsists between them; for should any difference arise, they make no scruple of separation, but part with as little ceremony as they meet; and each one, free to form other connections, seeks elsewhere a more agreeable partner" (1: 328).

The licentious rake of Hamilton's text, Alphonso Vallaton, is a clever hairdresser who has "risen" to the rank of philosopher by acquiring a few wily talents. Although he bears a French name, Vallaton was born in England, abandoned "in one of those subterraneous abodes, vulgarly denominated cellars, in a little alley of St. Giles" (Hamilton 1: 43), and then raised by a charitable Bloomsbury lady who was grateful to him for capturing her squirrel. Under the guise of social reform, he practices his artfulness for selfish gain and, in so doing, bolsters the Anti-Jacobin argument that the discourse of rights is a disguise for personal opportunism. Vallaton pilfers money from a fund he is to deliver to a friend's brother in Paris and borrows from Godwin an individual code of ethics to rationalize his theft: property, he argues, belongs to those who *need* it. Yet, once the omnipotent authority of civil society is broken, we see a proliferation of personal moral laws that destabilize the community and lead to violence and chaos—just as Burke prophesied. Vallaton's theft is only the seed of further crimes. He fabricates a note that identifies the brother as a counterrevolutionary, informs on him to a revolutionary council, and stands by silently as the old, innocent man is sent to the guillotine.

The antithesis to Vallaton's ambition is Mrs. Fielding's charity. In gestures meant to negate or at least sublimate the self, she promotes private benevolence and acknowledges the appropriate exclusion of women from the body politic. In regard to the poor, she admits that "there ought to be a reputable receptacle established for affording temporary shelter to those who are willing to eat the bread of honest industry. The government ought—but alas! I cannot dictate to the government. I have not the power to influence the makers of our laws. But cannot I do something towards the relief of a few of these unhappy individuals?" (Hamilton 3: 38). The strength of Mrs. Fielding's approach is not in her capacity to reform law; it is in her ability to protect the distribution of wealth by keeping tight control over her charitable giving. It is also in her proficiency at facilitating the return of Mr. Glib, the wayward revolutionary who has selfishly deserted his wife and children. By reuniting a family, Mrs. Fielding does far more for moral and economic security than she could as a political reformer. Julia Delmond echoes Mrs. Fielding's acceptance of a limited agency. On her deathbed, after a suicide attempt, Julia recognizes that she was "intoxicated" with French principles (3: 312–14), and she realizes that she has overstepped her own gendered boundaries by assuming not only an intellectual and physical self-determination, but a public authority as well. She concedes that "whether the unrelenting laws of society with regard to our sex are founded in injustice or otherwise, is not for me to determine. Happy are they who submit without reluctance to their authority!" (3: 322).

In Charles Lloyd's *Edmund Oliver* (1798), external authority is not an overwhelming force because the protagonist is male and is held less accountable to the economic pressures of moral behavior.[8] Still, it is Edmund Oliver's social duty to learn to discipline his emotions and practice self-control. If he does not, he will succumb to the disempowerment that one suffers under the influence of sexual allurement. Anti-Jacobinism in *Edmund Oliver* is also tempered with a romanticism that actually entertains thoughts of a redistribution of property when administered by the appropriate hands. But the novel still contains a tragic story of a fiery young woman, Gertrude Sinclair, who embraces "English Jacobinism" as well as the man who introduces her to its principles, Edward D'Oyley, a democrat of French descent. Gertrude is seduced by the glorious promise of new opportunities in a reformed society and by the Godwinian notion that familial affections are no more powerful and demand no more responsibility than any other forms of affection. What she does not realize, however, until she is already pregnant with Edward D'Oyley's child, is that he is married to an older, wealthy woman—a woman he married only for her money. His objections to marriage, it would seem, have less to do with new philosophy than the demands of his wife and laws against bigamy. In the end, French principles only lead Gertrude and Edward to chimerical hopes and tragic death: Edward dies in a duel and Gertrude commits suicide.

The primary Anti-Jacobin concern of Lloyd's text is that of controlling desire and curbing indulgence in emotional fervor. Extravagant attention paid to personal aspirations leads to a self-absorption that affects the stability of the home and the security of the community at large. Charles Maurice, the wise and steady mentor for the overly passionate Edmund, identifies the source of political corruption as a personal and a moral one: the cultivation of "individual aim[s]" in a society that "discipline[s] the hearts of all men to selfishness" (Lloyd 1: 178). Maurice's answer to social ills is not the further advancement of self-determination, nor is it to involve oneself with "political bodies"; it is to return to the primary site of moral instruction—the family—and there reinforce "an unassuming steadiness of virtue" (1: 185). Even the romantically intoxicated Edmund sees, through his delirium, the need for surrendering individual desires. "We are all unhappy; all complaining; all friendless," he laments. If we "would but annihilate selfishness; regard the interests of others as our own wants, . . . and feel a common identity with mankind at large," we might be content and feel exalted (1: 103–4).

The families of both Gertrude and Edmund fail to teach their wayward children to control their unwieldy passions and involve themselves in a common identity as opposed to an individual one. Gertrude is raised by an unforgiving, tempestuous father who was "gloomily proud and superstitious." He expected absolute obedience from his wife, whose "character was lost in his" (Lloyd 1: 24–25) when it should have been devoted to the family and the community. Edmund's father suffers from a suspicious nature and lets his imagination destroy his marriage and his family. Unable to discern truth from lies, he allows two crafty cousins to question the loyalty and legitimacy of his family. They acquire Mr. Oliver's trust and eventually his estate when they forge his will. Inattentive to familial duty, Mr. Oliver loses his family's property to those not capable of handling financial responsibility or the power that accompanies it.

The ideally supportive family is that of Charles Maurice. Like the Evans family in West's novel, they live in a pastoral haven that is nurturing, safe, and benevolent—far from the corruptions of London and the murky scenes of political discord. Truth, in Lloyd's text, is found only in solitude, not in a dialectical exchange of ideologies or the intellectual dialogues that might take place in a London coffeehouse. It is Charles's intent to bring Edmund into the fold of his idyllic community, draw him away from his self-indulgent love for Gertrude, and allow nature to provide its solace and enlightenment. Gertrude and the principles she espouses strike Charles as dangerously deceptive and out of touch with the needs and wants of the people she purports to illuminate. In an exchange with Edward D'Oyley, Charles levels an accusation that is a common one in Anti-Jacobinism. He claims that Edward's democratic principles are of "wide application" and therefore "superficial, and "negligently imbibed" (Lloyd 1: 85).

The generalizing tendencies of new philosophy are frequently attacked because their universality implies an extension of influence beyond the borders of immediate localities, such as singular families or English villages. Universal principles enable the unmonitored export of ideologies beyond local borders and the infiltration of foreign principles within those borders. If boundaries are allowed to be permeable, Gertrude Sinclair will be only one of the many who will be destroyed by false hopes of personal expansion that only result in self-destruction. Reform, Charles argues, should be a contained event, not an expansive political policy. "Equality of rights," he contends, is a disembedded notion, associated only with legal institutions; it is a distant vision premised on a first principle that has little to do with human happiness (Lloyd 1: 181–84). Ironically, it is Charles who entertains the notion of equalizing property and Edward who questions its usefulness. His "redistribution" would be accomplished, however, not through legislative reform. It would be considered a Christian duty to recognize ownership as stewardship, provide for one's neighbor, and act charitably with money over and above what one needs to support one's own family. In his advocacy of the institution of the family, Charles is aware of the sociopolitical dangers connected to wayward individuals and weak familial structures. Yet he ultimately denies the role of equal rights in gendered domestic relations and the economics of the family; he refuses to acknowledge the impact of law on the individual; and he fails to consider the vulnerability of those who cannot claim the protection property affords.

Charles's concern with personal development is to contain desire and turn thoughts away from the self and toward an immediate, rather than a distant (that is, political), other. His instruction to Edmund centers itself around the following treatise on love that illustrates the danger Anti-Jacobin novelists saw in the powerful and deceptive quality of ardent adoration. To Edmund he asserts that "the intoxication of this passion can never *last.*" If it should, he warns,

> we sink in the dainty slothfulness of personal indulgence—we are attracted as by magic to the silken couch of pleasure, and in the end lose the nerve of manhood—our souls become emasculated; the arm, which

might wield the elements, is palsied with impotence; and if this enchantment cease, shall we look with complacency on an object in the light of a mere human being, whom we have adored as an angel—to whom we have ascribed the mysterious sanctity of divinity, the unceasing power of inebriating the soul! Surely no! Her whom we have worshipped we can never rationally love. (Lloyd 1: 89–90)

It is rational love that Charles successfully arranges for Edmund, his sister Ellen, their cousin Edith, and friend Mr. Alleyne. The alternatives, excessive sexual desire (as described above) and illicit sexual behavior (as exemplified by the affair between Gertrude and Edmund), are both debilitating and disempowering. The seduction of women by French *philosophes* has obvious sociopolitical and economic ramifications in its disruption of inheritance; however, the passion that threatens to blind and then emasculate Edmund Oliver is comparable to the uncontrolled desire that threatens to weaken the entire nation. Moreover, a nation unaware of encroaching dangers and its own vulnerability is indeed susceptible to reform.

Henry James Pye calls on the entire nation in his novel of French infiltration, *The Democrat* (1795), to represent the chaotic quality of political dialogue, the pervasiveness of complaint, and the ultimate refusal of Britain to succumb to the influences of French principles. The contemptible Jean Le Noir, whose self-proclaimed mission it is to bring to Britain the principles of "the Metropolitan See of Sedition and Murder at Paris" (Pye v), is intent on redistributing wealth. His notion of equality, however, is equal portions for all and a slightly larger one for himself. Born in the province of Champaigne, Le Noir fights for the French against the British in America. He eventually deserts the army and only returns to France to join the Jacobin Club and associate with the extraordinary (and violent) Marat and Robespierre. In the midst of the revolution, Le Noir decides he should introduce a "system of equalization and fraternity" to Britain and initiate a campaign to unite France and Britain so that they might bring democracy to the world.

Although Pye's novel unabashedly points to France as the source of political trouble in Britain, the design of his narrative betrays a myriad of internal conflict that has very little to do with France or the so-called French principles. Le Noir travels through England and talks with inhabitants along the way, in hopes of finding sympathetic comrades who will join French forces when they come to "visit" Great Britain. What he finds is an immense array of complaints about social ills, inequalities, and the need for reform. But nowhere does he find a group of Englishmen ready to engage in designing a system to redistribute wealth, except a group of pickpockets who are quite delighted to continue their efforts in "the levelling of rank and equalization of property" (Pye 2: 139). Each of Le Noir's encounters on his trip from the coast to London reveals a specific conflict plaguing the British populace; however, each issue is usually diffused by ironic or silly statements made by the complainer, an intervention by the narrator, or a counterargument by a learned respondent. One of the first Englishmen Le Noir meets is Mr. Edistone, a republican who speaks of the tyranny of the Test and Corporation Acts. Referring to Anglicanism, he argues that religion need not be protected by law. Yet his own desire to see the repeal of the Test and Corporation Acts is a request that the law protect *his* religion. In case the reader does not glean this contradiction, the narrator steps in to amuse us with a report that the republican must end his tirade against the British government run only by "the great" because his daughter calls him to tea with a lord. Although Le Noir is puzzled by the republican's behavior, he continues on his travels, optimistic that he will meet the sort of English people he read about in Voltaire—those who pay little regard to nobility. But all he finds, before ending his travels with his introduction to the company of pickpockets, is "a thousand discordant systems of reform" (2: 106).

The tale of Le Noir's travels—that is, his introduction to British politics—is framed by a story that follows Le Noir from France and testifies to the very real treachery this rather humorous figure is capable of executing. On one of his stops, Le Noir dines with a Dr. Portwell and his friend Mr. Newcomb. Dr. Portwell is also hosting a French nobleman, the Count de Tournelle, and his daughter Adelaide who have both fled France and taken refuge in England. When the count hears mention of Le Noir's name, he relays the tragic account of their flight from France precipitated by Le Noir's deceptive and criminal behavior. In the midst of the revolution, the count and his daughter are driven from their château. Le Noir promises to help them flee but, after securing their trust, steals both the count's property and his daughter. Adelaide is soon freed by a band of Royalists, and they eventually find a safe haven in England; but never have they forgotten the man who betrayed them. Le Noir's philosophical penchant for equalizing wealth is revealed to be no more than common thievery and his grandiose notions of universal, international reform no more than an excuse to flee France when he might be pursued for a crime. Although he is not taken seriously by the English citizens he encounters, his villainous behavior toward the count and his daughter is a reminder that he and other *philosophes* could be inclined to seize property under the guise of economic reform in Britain, as readily as they did in France.

The duplicitous Frenchman in Isaac Disraeli's *Vaurien; or Sketches of the Times* (1797), is a much more insidious and therefore dangerous character than Pye's Le Noir. Described as an "eloquent" and "fascinating" gentleman, both temperate and voluptuous, humble and glorious, submissive and passionate, Vaurien is constituted of a Janus-like character. The effect of Le Noir's infiltration is dangerous, but not excessively so, because he does not disguise his intent, nor does he manage to insinuate himself into a British family. But Vaurien works slowly and steadily to befriend Charles Hamilton, an earnest young man raised in a country vicarage, only to strategize against Charles when they become rivals for the affection (and sexuality) of Emily Balfour. Vaurien fabricates a compromising story about Charles and a former prostitute, sees him discharged from his patron's care, and renders Charles financially dependent. His ultimate plan is to have Charles imprisoned for debt so that Charles will not interfere with his attempt to seduce Emily. Vaurien does not succeed in his plan to seduce Emily, but he does manage to tarnish the concept of "first principles." They are meant to be an immovable basis of a system of ethics in the new philosophy; but Vaurien shows them to be as changeable as his own character and as susceptible to contrivances and deception as the person who espouses them.

The seeds of suspicion that Vaurien imports from France prove to be far more destructive than the rather hollow French principles he purports. Though he speaks as a *philosophe*, his intent is not to institute reform but to introduce fear of betrayal—sexual, emotional, and political betrayal. His ability to tempt corruption on every level makes Vaurien as a sexual seducer a prime suspect for a political spy. Indeed, he does seem to be more proficient at political treason than domestic seduction when at the end of the novel he has failed to seduce Emily but moves on to the recently invaded Holland to begin to ruminate on a new government. In the meantime, Vaurien's manipulations ripple through the lives of all the characters in Disraeli's novel, dividing family members and stifling Christian virtues. Yet as in other Anti-Jacobin novels, the infiltration of foreign evils is only made possible through the deficiencies of the family. In the case of the Belfields, it is Lord Belfield's republicanism that has corrupted his wife and left her not only vulnerable to the wiles of Vaurien but also willing to aid Vaurien in his attempted seduction of Emily. Lord Belfield shirks his responsibilities as a noble lord of royal blood from France and England in numerous ways. He does not command the respect of a patriarch, as he should for social stability, and he leads young Charles down a thorny path by introducing him to his fellow philosophers: Mr. Subtile, Mr. Reverberator, Dr. Bounce, Mr. Rant, Mr. Libel, Mr. Dragon, and Mr. Sympathy, all figures based on prominent English reformers.

Yet Charles learns more about nature, instinct, and humanity from his childhood in the country and his recent experiences in London than he does from philosophy, which is unequivocally equated, in this text, with contrivance and duplicity. Charles is more aware than his philosophical acquaintances, for example, that in spite of Vaurien's admission to being a failure at domestic treason, acts of sexual transgression, such as adultery, have sociopolitical ramifications. When Vaurien praises the freedom of sexual libertinism, Charles observes that "the cruelty of adultery is propagated through a generation" (Disraeli 1: 290); he is cognizant of the problems encountered by a family who must deal with the social and financial consequences of an illegitimate birth. He reminds us that clarity of paternity is essential to the process of inheritance and the determination of rightful claims of ownership. Charles's observation is a particularly pertinent one in this text because Disraeli makes a point of drawing direct correspondences between revolutionary events in France and reform movements in Britain. Vaurien's threat as a seducer is all the more urgent for the English conservative, when he or she considers the dangerous precedent set by the convention of revolutionary France when it passed legislation in November 1793 that guaranteed illegitimate children equal rights of inheritance (Hunt 66). The legislation seemed to condone unrestricted personal behavior and made it more difficult to control and concentrate wealth. Other correspondences between Britain and France, in Disraeli's novel, seem to be urgent warnings of possible violence. Vaurien and the team of philosophers plot a massacre and an assassination of the king. Yet, in Disraeli's novel, as in other Anti-Jacobin texts, it is still the impact of French principles, new philosophy, or English Jacobinism on personal behavior and familial bonds that poses the greatest threat to British society.

A pervasive complaint in Anti-Jacobin discourse is that philosophy abstracts and generalizes whereas moral responsibility is a private and personal matter. The distance of abstraction allows for the corruption and deception exhibited by Fitzosborne, Vallaton, Vaurien, and other seductive *philosophes;* but it also ignores the intimate needs of families. Since status is conceptually no longer a reliable indicator of moral fortitude, by the end of the eighteenth century, fulfillment of one's familial role, gendered responsibilities, and social duties are the criteria by which virtue is measured in the Anti-Jacobin novel (Armstrong 3–4). The menace of sexual behavior that threatens familial bonds was the danger of the emerging individual, claiming self determination and demanding a reconstitution of the body politic. Enclosure of the family becomes necessary when threatened by attempts to set the boundaries of the self that distinguish the individual from the "other" and enable agency. Although the actual extension of franchisement that was envisioned by reformers was quite limited (it did not include women and other financial dependents), responses to the empowered individual were reactions to the inevitable evolution of contract theory as the paradigm for political authority that was to replace the model of inheritance. The "French threat," in the Anti-Jacobin novel, was not so much a fear of French influence or revolution, as it was an uneasiness with reforms within Britain and the reconceptualization of property and ownership in contract theory.

NOTES

1. Although Sir Henry Maine wrote in 1859 that the progress of law has been a "movement *from Status to Contract*," numerous studies have shown that contract theory has not fulfilled its initial promise of subordinating status. Gender, class, and economic forces continue to affect access to political agency. See Maine, 100. See, also, work by Habermas, Pateman, and Unger.

2. For an introduction to the Anti-Jacobin novel and a discussion of its conservative ideology (especially as a precursor to Jane Austen's conservatism), see Butler, 88–123.

3. Price's sermon was delivered on November 4, 1789, to the Society for Commemorating the Revolution in Great Britain at the Meeting-House in the Old Jewry.

4. In her introduction to Wollstonecraft's *A Vindication of the Rights of Men*, Eleanor Louise Nicholes points to the dispute over the repeal of the Test and Corporation Acts as a primary catalyst for Burke's fevered response to Price in *Reflections*. See, also, Deane 13–14 and Cone 300–313.

5. The Corporation Act (13 Charles II, Stat. 2, c.1) was passed in 1661 and the Test Act (25 Charles II, c.2) was passed in 1673. Both required sacramental tests to prove affiliation with the Church of England before one could be elected to a corporation office or any civil or military office. See Davis.

6. On the importance of universal benevolence versus charity, see Radcliffe.

7. See Jordan, Ferguson, and Kelso.

8. The protagonist of this novel, "Edmund Oliver," is thought to be based, in part, on Samuel Coleridge. "Charles Maurice," it has been suggested, is Robert Southey, and "Roger Oliver," William Blake.

The Anti-Jacobin; or Weekly Examiner. 5th ed. London: J. Hatchard, 1803.

Armstrong, Nancy. *Desire and Domestic Fiction: A Political History of the Novel.* New York: Oxford UP, 1987.

Baker, Keith Michael. "Ideological Origins of the French Revolution." *Modern European Intellectual History.* Ed. Dominick LaCapra and Steven L. Kaplan. Ithaca: Cornell UP, 1982.

Boswell, James. *The Journal of a Tour to the Hebrides. The Life of Samuel Johnson, LL.D. together with a Journal of a Tour to the Hebrides.* Ed. Percy Fitzgerald. 3 vols. London: Bickers and Son, 1874.

Burke, Edmund. *Reflections on the Revolution in France.* New York: Penguin, 1969.

Butler, Marilyn. *Jane Austen and the War of Ideas.* Oxford: Clarendon, 1975.

Cone, Carl B. *Burke and the Nature of Politics: The Age of the French Revolution.* Louisville: U of Kentucky P, 1964.

Davis, Thomas, ed. *Committees for the Repeal of the Test and Corporation Acts: Minutes 1786–90 and 1827–8.* London: London Record Society, 1978.

Deane, Seamus. *The French Revolution and Enlightenment in England, 1789–1832.* Cambridge: Harvard UP, 1988.

Disraeli, Isaac. *Vaurien; or Sketches of the Times.* London, 1797.

Ferguson, Margaret W., Maureen Quilligan, and Nancy J. Vickers, eds. *Rewriting the Renaissance.* Chicago: U of Chicago P, 1986.

Filmer, Sir Robert. *Patriarcha and Other Political Works.* Ed. P. Laslett. Oxford: Basil Blackwell, 1949.

Godwin, William. *Enquiry Concerning Political Justice.* 3d ed. Harmondsworth: Penguin, 1985.

Habermas, Jürgen. *Structural Transformation of the Public Sphere.* Trans. Thomas Burger and Frederick Lawrence. Cambridge: MIT P, 1989.

Hamilton, Elizabeth. *Memoirs of Modern Philosophers.* 3d ed. London: G. G. and J. Robinson, 1801.

Hufton, Olwyn H. *Women and the Limits of Citizenship in the French Revolution.* Toronto: U of Toronto P, 1992.

Hunt, Lynn. *The Family Romance of the French Revolution.* Berkeley and Los Angeles: U of California P, 1992.

Jordan, Constance. *Renaissance Feminism.* Ithaca: Cornell UP, 1990.

Kelly, Gary. *The English Jacobin Novel, 1780–1805.* Oxford: Clarendon, 1976.

Kelso, Ruth. *Doctrine for the Lady of the Renaissance.* Urbana: U of Illinois P, 1956.

Lloyd, Charles. *Edmund Oliver.* London, 1798. Oxford: Woodstock, 1990.

Mackintosh, Sir James. *Vindiciae Gallicae.* London: G. G. and J. Robinson, 1791.

Maine, Sir Henry *Ancient Law.* London: J. M. Dent and Sons, 1917.

Paine, Thomas. *Rights of Man.* London: J. S. Jordan, 1791.

Pateman, Carole. *The Sexual Contract.* Stanford: Stanford UP, 1988.

Pocock, J. G. A. "Burke and the Ancient Constitution: A Problem in the History of Ideas." *Politics, Language, and Time: Essays on Political Thought and History.* New York: Atheneum, 1971.

Price, Richard. "A Discourse on the Love of Our Country." Oxford: Woodstock, 1992.

Pye, Henry James. *The Democrat*. New York: James Rivington, 1795.

Radcliffe, Evan. "Revolutionary Writing, Moral Philosophy, and Universal Benevolence in the Eighteenth Century." *Journal of the History of Ideas* 54 (April 1993): 221–40.

Schochet, Gordon J. *Patriarchalism in Political Thought*. London: Basil Blackwell, 1975.

Unger, Roberto Mangabeira. *The Critical Legal Studies Movement*. Cambridge: Harvard UP, 1983.

West, Jane. *A Tale of the Times*. London, 1799.

Wollstonecraft, Mary. *A Vindication of the Rights of Men*. Ed. Eleanor Louise Nicholes. London: J. Johnson, 1790. Gainesville: Scholars' Facsimiles and Reprints, 1960.

Desiring the Foreign Self
Identity (Com)modification
and the Early Grand Tour

David R. Evans

In the context of the intense political and sociocultural conflicts that lasted throughout the seventeenth century in England, numerous books of travel theory formulating the "Grand Tour" served certain segments of the aristocracy and gentry as an exclusive and exclusionary discourse, building a wall between them and those groups encroaching on their dominance. Such works as James Howell's 1642 *Instructions for Forreine Travell,* Thomas Neale's 1643 *A Treatise of Direction How to travell safely and profitably into Forraigne Countries,* and Jean Gailhard's 1678 *The Compleat Gentleman: Or Directions For the Education of Youth As to their Breeding at Home and Travelling Abroad* advanced the material, sociocultural, and political interests of the traditional ruling classes in the face of intensifying criticism and outright rejection of the tropes that had hitherto underwritten their power.

Travel literature as a whole attempted to restructure two inevitably linked types of authority. Delineating the doubly beneficial nature of foreign travel, John Evelyn remarks in his 1652 *The State of France* that "the vertues which our Traveller is to bring home when he doth *Repatriare* . . . are either publick, such as namely concern the service of his Country; or Private, and altogether personall, in order to his particular advantage and satisfaction" (sig. B2r). Institutional, overtly political authority often came to be located in firsthand experience, what Howell calls "one's own *Ocular* view" (5), rather than inborn "superiority." This trend obviously benefited the popularity of European travel, exemplified by Restoration panegyrics, which regularly praise Charles II for the practical wisdom he gained during his European exile rather than his mystified innate superiority to his subjects.[1] As Evelyn suggests, the Grand Tour and its attendant discourses also helped to construct and assert a more personal authority, which was attributed to distinctive modes of behavior and stylistic consciousness obtainable from experience abroad, such as dancing, fencing, musical competence, and fluency in foreign languages.

In underscoring *both* the public, politically oriented *and* the private, socially centered enhancements that experiences abroad could provide, travel writers obviously conceived of traveling, and justified its practices, fundamentally as a mode of education. Such education was limited to a select few, however. For travel writers, an individual qualified to undertake the Grand Tour inevitably was a member of the aristocracy or upper gentry, a "gentleman" in the narrow, familial, and class-based sense. In 1671, Edward Leigh, citing Francis Bacon, states that, while determining "whether Travel be necessary to an ingenious man," it is crucial to understand that "those who would travel must be young and strong, rich and well borne to get any good by their Travells" (13–14). The distinction travel writers make between the "rich and well borne" and those not so blessed is crucial to the general educational purpose of experience abroad. For travel writers, polishing a "gentleman" was the stated purpose of the Grand Tour in the latter part of the seventeenth century.

The economic mobility that threatened this traditional definition of the gentleman, and its consequent social effects, were in the broadest sense the reasons why it was necessary to promulgate this mode of distinction. However, the travel writers' project was fatally flawed from its inception, for in formulating and publicizing the criteria for successful travel, travel writers converted its benefits into commodities, packaged for ready cultural consumption by a much wider group than their (apparently) intended audience. The vision of foreign travel articulated in Grand Tour literature ironically created the desire to travel among literate classes beyond the traditional aristocracy and gentry, because travel writers are quite explicit and convincing in enumerating the considerable benefits that could accrue to the successful traveler. Therefore, placing the benefits of foreign travel into the symbolic economy of late-seventeenth-century society rendered them susceptible to appropriation by anyone with sufficient wealth and desire to undertake a journey, without regard to the source of the wealth or the desire. The Grand Tour is thus implicated in crucial issues of class and personal identity that stand out as defining characteristics of a period when tradition and privilege were sites of deep, bitter, and occasionally violent cultural conflict.

The social skills and knowledge that were in theory exclusively available to those who had traveled in Europe were granted a peculiar privilege during the 1630s and beyond, as the interests of the court party enhanced the value attached to foreign acquirements. This cultural privilege became especially powerful during the Restoration, when the prestige accruing to European travel received a significant impetus from the interests of the returned Royalist exiles. They clearly sought to validate their traumatic experiences by rewriting them as a positive form of education, generally divorced from their context in the tumultuous divisions of the civil wars and interregnum.[2] However, even as it was constructed before the Restoration, the whole practice of the Grand Tour can be read as a ploy, first to retain and then to reoccupy the cultural as well as the political center of English life. The assumptions that travel writers made about their audience, the things they valued, and the goals they propounded for foreign travel all served directly to (attempt to) augment the cultural ascendancy of the traditionally minded segments of the aristocracy and upper gentry.

Writers on the Grand Tour, and everything attendant upon it as a practice and a concept, used educational travel as a significant strategy of containment perpetuated by hitherto dominant classes in the face of a new social order. This new order acknowledged—in fact in many ways was a result of—the emergent power of the "Puritan bourgeoisie" during the course of the seventeenth century. Travel writers promulgated foreign travel as a practice that could provide partakers with social distinction, hence "superiority," relative to nontravelers: as Baptist Goodall notes in his poem *The Tryall of Travell*, "Civility breeds by experience made" (sig. E2r). More coherently, James Howell asserts that "courtesie is the chiefest cognisance of a Gentleman, which joyned with discretion, can only Travaile all the World over without a Passeport" (60). Like Howell, many other writers constantly show how foreign travel was the source of such worldly "courtesy" and hence granted the gentility that could open the doors to public and private authority.

This vision of foreign travel as an important educational experience for the gentry and aristocracy, one that assured their performative gentility and hence their social superiority, contained a critical contradiction upon which the Grand Tour, as it was originally conceived, soon came to founder. As Susan Staves has remarked in an interesting analysis of *The Man of Mode*, this contradiction appears in the fact that "much contemporary courtesy literature paradoxically idealized gentility as a natural phenomenon that could not be achieved by effort, yet at the same time that courtesy literature appeared to present universally accessible step-by-step directions as to how to construct a genteel identity" (123). In his analysis of Elizabethan courtesy literature, Frank Whigham addresses this paradox by suggesting that social mobility evoked from the upper classes "the presentation of difference in degree as difference in kind, of contingent difference as absolute" (67). Things that could be *learned*, in other words, came to be represented as things that were "natural" and therefore assumed to be eternal and unchangeable. I would add that, at least in travel literature, the transforming effects of education are presented explicitly as only available to classes whose social position is already assured, the "young and strong, rich and well borne." Supporting Whigham's contention, in *The Compleat Gentleman*, published in 1622, Henry Peacham remarks that, "Nobilitie being inherent and Naturall, can have (as the Diamond) the lustre but onely from it selfe: Honors and Titles externally conferred, are but attendant upon desert, and are but as apparell, and the Drapery to a beautifull body" (3). Insistence on the essential nature of nobility by conservative writers such as Peacham diffused the idea that social hierarchy was a God-given fact of existence, not a social construction. However, the paradox posed by the educational aims of courtesy and travel literature remains, and ultimately, the educational aspect of the Grand Tour came to dominate over any insistence on inherent nobility.

In his *Outline of a Theory of Practice*, Pierre Bourdieu provides a theoretical explanation for both why and how such mystifications of the social order function to construct the cultures in which they appear. Bourdieu argues that "Every established order tends to produce (to very different degrees and with very different means) the naturalization of its own arbitrariness. . . . The instruments of knowledge of the social world," for example conduct and travel books, "are in this case (objectively) political instruments which contribute to the reproduction of the social world by producing immediate adherence to the world, seen as self evident and undisputed, of which they are the product and of which they reproduce the structures in a transformed form" (Bourdieu, *Outline* 164). Widely articulated affirmations of the existence of inherent nobility and its social primacy, thus, would have served to evoke assent from people who were not even aware that they were submitting to a contingent institution. If we accept Bourdieu's model of social reproduction, repetition of certain "facts" as facts would cause them to be accepted as commonsense truths. Bourdieu's term for the worldview that creates and is in turn created by this experience is *doxa*, where the configuration of "the world of tradition [is] experienced as a 'natural world' and taken for granted" (164). Most broadly, the *doxa* is the entire epistemological condition of a society that has not yet been exposed to a revealing critique of its current ruling assumptions.

One of the signal characteristics of the seventeenth century, however, was that England's ruling assumptions came increasingly under an attack that revealed their nature as social constructions rather than natural givens. New class definitions emerged—or at least were made imaginable—as a consequence of critiques by groups like the Diggers and the Levellers.[3] This social reordering was also particularly evident in the rise of a significant, wealthy middle class, centered in the City of London, whose leanings were distinctly puritan and whose ties were not to the traditional source of power and influence, the land. Moreover, the English people's experiences of the 1640s and 1650s, when they were ruled not by a king but by a parliament, and then by a military man, had clearly demonstrated the fragility of a wide variety of assumptions that had hitherto governed social and political relations.[4] By the late 1670s, in a book that tellingly repeats the conservative Peacham's title *The Compleat Gentleman,* Jean Gailhard recognizes that though class definitions *might* inhere in the order of nature, other factors not necessarily directly connected to family were much more important in defining a "Gentleman." His discussion is basically premised on the idea that distinguishing behavior—and hence distinction—is substantially the result of "Breeding." This is a marvelously ambiguous term, with its connotations of genetic inheritance, but Gailhard clearly includes within his definition what we might call "upbringing," or education, as well as mere birth (in the sense of "born *and* bred"):

the chief thing I propound herein to myself, is to shew the necessity, benefit, and excellency of a good Breeding, becoming none so much as a Gentleman, who, *by his Vertue and Merit, more than by his Extraction, should be raised above the Commonalty;* for Vertue first of all made a difference between man and man, there being an equality between all the Children of *Adam,* as to Birth and Nature; and certainly when the Nobility and Gentry wants merits to Command, and Abilities to Govern, they must change place with the lower sort of People, whom

Parts and Virtue, (though not without favour) will raise to the greatest Charges and Dignities in the Land. (Gailhard sigs. I.A8r–A8v, emphasis added)

As Gailhard's statement makes clear, the emergence of groups ready to contest, or even deny, the legitimacy of inherent class distinctions and other forms of social hierarchy made it necessary for the upper classes to demonstrate, not merely assert, their "merits to Command and Abilities to Govern."[5] The various challenges to their power evoked a variety of responses from the traditional aristocracy and gentry, who naturally sought to "defend[ ]the integrity of the doxa," as they were, of course, the groups most profiting from the status quo. "[S]hort of this," Bourdieu continues, the "dominant classes" will try to "establish[ ] in [the *doxa's*] place the necessarily imperfect substitute, *orthodoxy*," the more or less openly theorized and justified set of ideas on which a particular culture grounds its social arrangements (Bourdieu, *Outline* 169; see also 94 and passim). In the 1640s and 1650s, the "lower sort of people" had ruled, or at least entered into the ruling structure, and the traditional ruling classes needed a response adequate to the task of preventing such a thing from happening again.

Given these changes, and the fact that foreign travel was widely and openly promulgated as a mode of education for the upper classes, it is useful to apply Bourdieu's theoretical metaphor of "symbolic capital," from the *Outline of a Theory of Practice*, to an analysis of the sociocultural and political aims of the Grand Tour. Bourdieu opposes "symbolic capital," signified by modes of behavior, "honour," and so on, to "economic capital," which consists of the possession of monetary wealth (e.g., 48; 171–83). He suggests that symbolic capital functions in much the same ways as, and often more effectively than, economic capital, providing the possessor with the ability to obtain prestige, advancement, and even material goods unavailable to those who lack it. In fact, Bourdieu argues, "Wealth, the ultimate basis of power, can exert power, and exert it durably, *only* in the form of symbolic capital" (195), thus according symbolic capital a vast power in the day-to-day negotiations undertaken in any society. The influence of symbolic capital is particularly significant in a stratified, still semifeudal society such as early seventeenth-century England. In such a society, the symbolic economy trading in modes of behavior, stylistic consciousness, aesthetic taste, and so on would, perforce, deny cash even the value placed on it in more overtly capitalist societies of the type arguably emerging in England later in the century.

Symbolic economies logically enough provide the greatest advancement to those who most effectively accumulate and exploit their stock of symbolic capital by competently deploying it in the sociocultural arena. In its role as a form of education for the upper classes, foreign travel served, first, as an opportunity to accumulate such a stock, and then as an ongoing storehouse of the wisdom and skills necessary to ensure that stock's maximally effective exploitation at home. Moreover, as Bourdieu points out, institutionalized education tends to affirm, rather than subvert, the dominant order of the society those institutions inhabit by "reproducing the hierarchies of the social world in a transformed form."[6] Though Bourdieu's analysis particularly considers schools and other contemporary institutions, a metaphorical reading of the Grand Tour as a cultural practice shows that it was indeed institutionalized in a fairly literal way—in fact, like a school, it had a specific "curriculum," which is outlined by Howell, Neale, Gailhard, and many other writers.

Successful exploitation of the symbolic capital he accrued by following this curriculum would help to advance the young man just returned from his travels into a more advantageous position in the elite to which he already belonged and to augment the political and social authority he already possessed. As Howell remarks in *Instructions for Forreine Travell*, proper social refinement could enable the young traveler to ascend politically and socially upon his return to England, since, along with his "Noble extraction," such refinement would ensure he would be "like to be a Star of the greatest Magnitude in the sphere of his owne Countrey" (22–23). Conceptually echoing Howell, Richard Lassels states in *The Voyage of Italy* that "the nobleman by long traveling, having enlightened his understanding, comes home like a glorious *Sunn*, and doth not onely shine bright in the firmament of his country, the *Parliament house*; but also blesseth his inferiours with the powerfull influences of his knowing spirit" (sig. A VI v). Expanding this argument to the structure of the culture at large, it is clear that such political and social positions could be maintained by an entire class if Edward Leigh's "young and strong, rich and well borne" men could all "profit" enough from their educational travels to "shine bright" in the Parliament house.

Many of the particular practices travel writers advocate in delineating this pursuit of refinement and authority fit neatly into Bourdieu's theory of symbolic capital and its functions (particularly) in a precapitalist society. Travel writers' class assumptions overwhelmingly valorize the symbolic as opposed to the pragmatic benefits to be gained abroad, often explicitly juxtaposing them in ways that favor symbolic acquisitions.

During this period, books on the Grand Tour practically *never* mention foreign travel as a possible source of material wealth, a glaring and significant omission.[7] Rather, these writers concentrate on aspects of behavior and acquired wisdom and experience, which in themselves are much more satisfactorily theorized as symbolic rather than material, regardless of their ultimate (though often hidden) material benefits. In his *Treatise,* Thomas Neale insists that the traveler should eschew what we now think of as the "Protestant work ethic" in language that rejects the kind of pragmatic aims associated with the pursuit of "economic capital." As he concludes his book, Neale directs, "Avoid also the distraction of businesse, which often hindreth the intents of a travellour": "For a judicious man undertaketh not his peregrination, to be pragmaticall after the manner of lawyers, but when his leasure serveth him, that he may observe by action; because he often, which is so busy in the practique part, can hardly learne anything, whilst he doth spend his time in superficial follies, or needlesse businesse, and so loseth both science and experience" (163).

Neale's emphasis on the leisurely nature of proper foreign travel fits nicely into Bourdieu's model describing the accumulation of symbolic capital. "As well as material wealth," writes Bourdieu, "*time* must be invested, for the value of symbolic labour cannot be defined without reference to the time devoted to it, *giving* or *squandering time* being one of the most precious of gifts. It is clear that in such conditions symbolic capital can only be accumulated at the expense of the accumulation of economic capital" (*Outline* 180; footnote omitted). Though Neale's book is pervaded by metaphors of consumption and profit (e.g., 27, 39, 50, 62, 66, and 161), it is clear from his disavowal of lawyerly pragmatism that the kind of profit he has in mind is symbolic rather than literal, a conclusion reinforced by his dismissal of "needlesse businesse."

Bourdieu notes that "all societies" rely extensively on "the seemingly most insignificant details of *dress, bearing,* physical and verbal *manners*" to embody the "arbitrary content of the culture" (*Outline* 94). The more specific goals travel writers outline for the young traveler further emphasize that the Grand Tour was an important nexus of a symbolic acquisitiveness that directly assisted in this process of embodying the arbitrary by teaching the ruling classes to perform socially in ways unavailable to other groups. Gailhard's dedicatory epistle "To the Honorable Sir Thomas Grosvenor Baronet," whom he accompanied on the Grand Tour, reveals his pleasure in Grosvenor's particular endeavors: "And with your close following Riding the great horse, Fencing, Dancing, Drawing Landskips, and Designing; Learning upon the Gitar, the French and Italian Tongues, and following other Exercises, to acquire those Accomplishments, which do so much become a Gentleman of your Age, Estate and Quality: It is very hard to find one as you; who would take so much pains, and be so exact in making Observations about Persons, Places and Things" (sig. II.A3r).

Gailhard later notes that, "As the world goes, *Dancing* is an Exercise becoming a Gentleman, it being one of the essential parts of an Outlandish, French breeding: so that as a Gentleman who there goeth into company, hath daily occasions of practising it, it would be a shame for a young Gentleman not to have some skill in't" (2:48). Neale's generalized distaste for lawyerly pragmatism expresses itself more concretely in lists of pursuits for the foreign traveler such as Gailhard's, pursuits that are clearly intended to polish one for "go[ing] into company," not to provide one a vocation. Again, in 1701, Ellis Veryard describes the curriculum of the Grand Tour in almost identical language, while also moving toward advocating artistic connoisseurship of the type considered by Bourdieu: "In *France*, young Gentlemen usually learn Dancing, Fencing, Riding, and Mathematicks, where they find expert Masters at easy Rates. In *Italy*, their Musick, Architecture, Sculpture, and Painting, are in great esteem; and, indeed, it has always produc'd Men of more than ordinary Skill, whose Names and Works will be transmitted to Posterity as durable monuments of their noble Performances" (Veryard sig. B2v).

The courtly pursuits and the polishing of taste valorized by writers on the Grand Tour clearly aim at creating gentlemen whose activities and comportment symbolize and embody the values of aristocratic society. Gailhard's and Veryard's emphasis on the "gracefull" and "ornamentall" nature of these occupations agrees with their fundamentally leisure-class nature; uselessness is a key aspect of many forms of symbolic capital.[8] Like "the collection of luxury goods attesting the taste and distinction of their owner" (Bourdieu, *Outline* 197), luxury behaviors, "the ease which is the touchstone of excellence" (Bourdieu, *Distinction* 66), add to the stock of symbolic capital available to the possessor to abet his pursuit of sociocultural advancement or domination. Thus, certain groups came to be tied to practices such as fencing, dancing, manners, and good command of languages, which, as it were, "naturalized" their superiority—and many of these practices could be learned primarily through foreign travel.

This notion of naturalizing one's superiority through the Grand Tour appears even in travel writing's broadest articulations of the goals to be pursued abroad. Toward the end of *Instructions for Forreine Travell*, Howell provides a sweeping summary of the curriculum the young traveler should pursue in his travels: "From the *Italian* he will borrow his *reservedness*, not his *jealousie* and *humor of revenge*; From the French his *Horsemanship* and gallantnesse that way, with his *Confidence*, and nothing else: From the *Spaniard* his *Sobriety*, not his *lust:* From the *German* (cleane contrary) his *Continency*, not his *Excesse*, the other way: from the *Netherland* his *Industry*, and that's all" (190).

Howell's list of the stereotypical virtues to be pursued in the various nations of western Europe is very similar to those other writers provide as they urge the young traveler to "Cull out the Choice of flowers in the fields / So decke thy witts with that each climate yields" (Goodall sig. D2r). Thomas Fuller's Restoration poem, *A Panegyric to His Majesty, on His Happy Return* (London, 1660), praises that ultimate gentleman traveler Charles II in very similar terms:

> Garbling mens manners You did well divide,
> To take the *Spaniard's wisdom*, not their *pride*.
> With *French activity* You stor'd Your Mind,
> Leaving to them their *Ficklenesse* behind;
> And soon did learn, Your *Temperance* was such,
> A sober *Industry* even from the Dutch.
> (2)

Gailhard formulates goals similar to those propounded by Howell and Fuller in more general terms. At the same time, he warns the reader against falling into the trap of becoming denaturalized, which again demonstrates his entanglement in questions of essential and constructed identity:

> when a man is abroad, he studies the tempers of men, and learns their several fashions; . . . not forgetting himself to be an Englishman, nor with becoming a Frenchman, an Italian, or a German, but building upon the true foundation of an Englishman, and making use of the different ways of those several Nations, as Ornaments only, and not as a bottom; for why should he transform himself into, and, as it were, become a Foreigner, who is to live in *England* all the rest of his days: it is enough for him as it were to squeeze the quintessence of what ways, manners, and other good things those Countries do afford. (Gailhard 2:4)

Travel writing thus constantly figures Continental Europe as a sort of supermarket of desirable and undesirable behavioral characteristics, from which the young, upper-class English traveler should select the "best things," "squeeze the quintessence," to assist him in his search for social refinement and the power that comes with it. Packaged and validated by the process of being canonized in travel books, these best things were made available for consumption by those who read them.

Unfortunately for the traditionally minded aristocracy and upper gentry, however, their project for cementing political and sociocultural authority through foreign travel was built on a fragile foundation. One of the Grand Tour's major weaknesses as an exclusive and exclusionary method of sociocultural domination is ironically embedded in the very strategy that made that function possible in the first place. If we view the specific and general behaviors travel writers discuss as symbolic commodities — which, like literal commodities, are subject to exchange and consumption in the cultural economy — this shortcoming immediately becomes clear. As Martyn J. Lee points out, "in the modern consumer marketplace the social meanings that attach themselves to commodities are, in the first instance, supplied by such institutions as advertising, marketing, and similar promotional organisations" (16–17). Though the middle of the seventeenth century was certainly not the modern consumer marketplace, Lee's observation provides a compelling rationale for reading books such as Howell's *Instructions* and Neale's *Treatise* as a form of advertising that imparts "social meaning" to the behaviors they advocate. Because it delineates the advantages a young man could obtain by going abroad and advocates foreign travel on the basis of its ability to provide those advantages, travel writing, like any other type of "advertising," can be read as an attempt to create the desire among its readers to consume the commodity it represents. Moreover, travel writing is overt in its process of imparting social meanings to its commodities, giving significance that "could only be read by those who possessed a knowledge of the object-code" (McCracken 20) it imparted. In a society partly constructed by the vision advanced by travel writing, then, the impression made by a young man displaying a good command of foreign languages, graceful dancing, a sense of stylish dress, and similar qualities was likely to be inflected by the interpretations inscribed by travel writers. Of course this process of imposing social meaning on such behaviors was necessary in order for the Grand Tour to function in the first place. If the returned tourist entered a culture that was unaware that his markers of "superiority" in fact *did* signify his superiority, they would not work as intended: symbolic capital simply cannot be recognized without some form of publicity.

Travel literature's commodifying and advertising function in seventeenth-century society explains the reasons for the Grand Tour's limited utility as a mode of sociocultural domination. As I suggested above, in the seventeenth century one version of England's *doxa* was in the process of being replaced by orthodoxy, the more self-conscious construction of a social order whose ostensible transcendence had been permanently revoked. This change was a process in which travel writing and the Grand Tour were deeply implicated. In response to threats to their dominance, members of the traditional aristocracy and gentry accumulated a new kind of symbolic capital, through travel and other practices, which served to distinguish them from their "inferiors." For the ruling classes, the difficulty arose from the fact that, as Bourdieu points out, economic and symbolic capital have a hidden convertibility (e.g., *Outline* 179). To these classes' benefit, the symbolic capital provided by the Grand Tour was convertible fairly readily into hard money via the continued domination of the social and political landscape it could enable. To their detriment, Bourdieu's analysis also suggests that economic capital is convertible into symbolic capital, because symbolic capital, in a roundabout way, can be purchased. By turning the benefits available from the Grand Tour into explicitly commodified cultural objects, travel writers simply made them subject to purchase.

Generally speaking, it is in the dominant classes' interests to obscure this interconvertibility, because their position depends upon maintaining a symbolic advantage. Seventeenth-century travel writing nevertheless occasionally lays bare the mechanism through which symbolic and economic capital are exchanged. A particularly explicit example of this revelation occurs when Howell discusses the financial needs of a young traveler: "And for his owne expences, he cannot allow himselfe lesse than 300 l.," in addition to "fifty pounds a piece *per annum*" (49) for each servant who attends him—"a Cook, a Laquay, and some young youth for his Page, to parley and chide withall" (48). This passage reveals both that Howell's plan involves an obvious though fairly complex exchange of money for symbolic capital and his assumption that only the very well-to-do could undertake the Tour in the first place. Similarly, William Mountague's self-characterization as a liberal spender in the Low Countries in his *The Delights of Holland* (sigs. A2v–A3r) shows his crucial awareness of how *expense* is an inverted form of symbolic acquisition. More importantly, the fact that many writers advocate taking lessons, which explicitly involve an exchange of money for cultural competence (as shown by Veryard's phrase, "expert Masters at easy rates") also shows the process through which cash can be converted into symbolic capital through an elaborate series of transactions.

From the point of view of classes benefiting from the social status quo, this symbolic economy can appear to be a closed system, characterized by the constant interchange of literal and symbolic capital in an infinite regress all the way back to the original "ennobling" or "enriching" event. However, the existence of this originary event exposes the permeability of the social barriers that at first appear impassable. In fact, aristocrats had been buying symbolic capital with money all along. The interconvertibility of economic and symbolic capital in the final analysis enables broadening participation in practices, such as the Grand Tour, that are instrumental in accumulating symbolic capital. Commodities, even symbolic ones, can be bought for money once it becomes apparent that they *are* commodities and not some mysterious other thing that is not subject to economic power. Ultimately, therefore, any social practice that serves to distinguish one class from another is subject to being undermined as soon as the excluded group discovers that this practice is desirable and then attains the financial means to imitate it and sufficient time to make that imitation convincing. The widening publicity surrounding the Grand Tour led to obvious commodification of the exclusionary, mystifying practices of the upper classes. Increasing economic power among the middle classes consequently allowed them to imitate the aristocracy by undertaking distinctive practices such as the Grand Tour, which had been made desirable to them by the same texts initially written to show how these groups could be shut out. The practice of the Grand Tour thus became an ironic participant in the class mobility it appears to have been designed to repress, as the patina of longstanding nobility gave way to the fashionability of a foreign education that enhanced social performance.[9]

Thus, though the strategy of publishing books of travel theory and accounts of foreign journeys became vital to figuring travel in terms of symbolic capital, the same strategy ultimately contained the seeds of its own destruction. Frank Whigham also notices this phenomenon in his discussion of the narrower and less overtly economic world of Elizabethan courtesy literature; by making available the instructions necessary to accumulate symbolic capital, both courtesy and travel literature enabled those they were trying to shut "out" to come "in" to the circle such works defined. Books such as Howell's *Instructions* obviously if not openly valorized foreign travel as a mode of accumulating sociocultural prestige. As Whigham points out, such valorization implies that "[t]he circulation of the texts would have to have been restricted for the recuperation [of the courtier] to be effective. For all too many of the assheads [Castiglione derides in *The Courtier*] could read, and in fact they soon learned to use elitist texts for their own purposes" (19). Since the circulation of travel literature was not restricted, the natural consequence of its exclusionary project was that the desire to go on the Grand Tour disseminated more and more widely throughout English culture. Such spreading desire, coupled with an increasing number of people economically able to undertake foreign travel, therefore rendered the Grand Tour progressively less useful as a mode of domination. This process was abetted by the steadily increasing number of travel books published as the seventeenth century wore on,[10] which in turn (circularly) testify to the eroding exclusivity of the Grand Tour. The socioeconomic transformations that rendered the Grand Tour project necessary in the first place ultimately led to its destruction as a particularly exclusionary activity, since the desirability of foreign travel spurred competitive desires among various classes. Like Whigham's Castiglionesque "malapert assheads," well-to-do merchants from London could read, and putting works that showed the value of foreign travel into their hands inevitably led them to go abroad themselves. Such self-destruction is the consequence of the passage from *doxa* to orthodoxy, from the taken-for-granted to the openly theorized. Creating the desire to go abroad, travel writers undermined their own hegemonic act, as desire is not limited to the aristocracy. When the traditional gentry and aristocracy commodified the Grand Tour and its behaviors, they played right into the hands of the middle classes—whose business, after all, was commodities.

NOTES

1. See David R. Evans for a full version of this argument. Also, the slightly later formation of the Royal Society both indicated and abetted the increasing value and legitimacy accorded to firsthand experience over reading and "innate superiority" of the type that had hitherto underwritten upper-class epistemological domination. I am grateful to Douglas Hollinger's dissertation-in-progress at Texas Christian University for helping to clarify the Royal Society's appropriation of "gentlemanly" travel for empiricist, scientific ends. See also Michael McKeon, 101 and passim.

2. See Evans (60) for how this process worked in poetic representations of Charles II.

3. Such changing definitions also owed a great deal to the more historically remote activities of nonaristocratic status seekers attempting to gain a seat "at the table of the great," such as those Stephen Greenblatt considers; in particular, Thomas More (11–73).

4. On the collapse of these ruling assumptions see, for example, Christopher Hill's analysis, which provides a good summary of much of his thinking on the Restoration. The exact nature of the events of the midcentury is, of course, intensely contested ground, as witnessed by J. C. D. Clark's arguments with Hill and others. However, regardless of the *structural* implications of the civil wars and Charles I's execution, it

seems abundantly clear that they had considerable, and long-lasting, psychological and epistemological consequences for the way different social classes interacted after the Restoration.

5. Whigham makes a similar point about performative superiority within the smaller context of the Elizabethan court (5, and 32: "Elite status no longer rested upon the absolute, given base of birth, the received ontology of social being; instead it had become a matter of doing, and so of *showing*").

6. This theory of education is the broadest underlying theme of Bourdieu's *Distinction*, and it is specifically articulated, among other places, at 387. Jon Guillory extensively discusses Bourdieu's analysis of educational inculturation into dominant social structures and its consequences in the realm of sociocultural domination (56–59 and passim).

7. An exception to this generalization is Goodall, who addresses not only aristocratic young travelers but also merchants and others who traveled in pursuit of much more literal profits.

8. The continuing validity of this point is demonstrated, I believe, by the often vastly different amount and kind of prestige that accrues to an education at an eminent liberal arts college, as compared to the (likely equally good) education available in a more technical field at a land grant university.

9. Grant McCracken discusses this shift as more literally embodied in the prestige accruing to consumer goods, particularly 31–43.

10. This increase can be traced easily in Edward Godfrey Cox, and R. S. Pine-Coffin, as in critical works such as that of Charles Batten.

WORKS CITED

Batten, Charles. *Pleasurable Instruction: Form and Convention in 18th-Century Travel Literature.* Berkeley and Los Angeles: U of California P, 1978.
Bourdieu, Pierre. *Distinction: A Social Critique of the Judgment of Taste.* Trans. Richard Nice. Cambridge: Cambridge UP, 1984.
———. *Outline of a Theory of Practice.* Trans. Richard Nice. Cambridge Studies in Social Anthropology 16. Cambridge: Cambridge UP, 1977.
Clark, J. C. D. *Revolution and Rebellion: State and Society in England in the Seventeenth and Eighteenth Centuries.* Cambridge: Cambridge UP, 1986.
Cox, Edward Godfrey. *A Reference Guide to the Literature of Travel. Volume 1, the Old World.* University of Washington Publications in Language and Literature, Volume 9. Seattle: U of Washington, 1935.
Evans, David R. "Charles II's 'Grand Tour': Restoration Panegyric and the Rhetoric of Travel Literature." *Philological Quarterly* 72.1 (winter 1993): 53–71.
E[velyn], J[ohn]. *The State of France, As It Stood in the IXth Yeer of this Present Monarch, Lewis XIIII.* London, 1652.
Fuller, Thomas. *A Panegyric to His Majesty, on His Happy Return.* London, 1660.
Gailhard, Jean. *The Compleat Gentleman: Or Directions For the Education of Youth As to their Breeding at Home and Travelling Abroad. In Two Treatises.* London, 1678.
Goodall, Baptist. *The Tryall of Travell or, 1. The Wonders in Trauell, 2. The Worthes of Trauell, 3. The Way to Trauell. In three bookes Epitomiz'd.* London, 1630.

Greenblatt, Stephen. *Renaissance Self-Fashioning.* Chicago: U of Chicago P, 1980.

Guillory, Jon. *Cultural Capital: The Problem of Literary Canon Formation.* Chicago: U of Chicago P, 1993.

Hill, Christopher. *Some Intellectual Consequences of the English Revolution.* Madison: U of Wisconsin P, 1980.

Howell, James. *Instructions for Forreine Travell. Shewing by what cours, and in what compass of time, one may take an exact Survey of the Kingdomes and States of Christendome, and arrive to the practicall knowledge of the Languages, to good purpose.* London, 1642.

Lassels, Richard. *The Voyage of Italy, or A Compleat Journey through Italy. In Two Parts. With the Characters of the People, and the Description of the Chief Towns, Churches, Monasteries, Tombs, Libraries, Pallaces, Villas, Gardens, Pictures, Statues, and Antiquites. As Also of the Interest, Government, Riches, Force, &c. of all the Princes. With Instructions concerning Travel.* Paris, 1670.

Lee, Martyn J. *Consumer Culture Reborn: The Cultural Politics of Consumption.* London: Routledge, 1993.

Leigh, Edward, Esq. *Three Diatribes or Discourses. First of Travel, Or a Guide for Travellers into Forein Parts.* London, 1671.

McCracken, Grant. *Culture and Consumption: New Approaches to the Symbolic Character of Consumer Goods and Activities.* Bloomington: Indiana UP, 1990.

McKeon, Michael. *The Origins of the English Novel 1600–1740.* Baltimore: Johns Hopkins UP, 1987.

Mountague [or Montague], William. *The Delights of Holland: Or, Three Months Travel about that and the other Provinces, With Observations and Reflections on their Trade, Wealth, Strength, Beauty, Policy, &c. Together with A Catalogue of the Rarities in the Anatomical School at Leyden.* London, 1696.

Neale, Thomas, of Warneford. *A Treatise of Direction How to travell safely and profitably into Forraigne Countries.* London, 1643.

Peacham, Henry. *The Compleat Gentleman Fashioning him absolute in the most necessary & commendable Qualities concerning Minde or Bodie that may be required in a Noble Gentleman.* London, 1622.

Pine-Coffin, R. S. *Bibliography of British and American Travel in Italy to 1860.* Biblioteca di bibliographica italiana 76. Florence: L. S. Olschki, 1974.

Staves, Susan. "The Secrets of Genteel Identity in *The Man of Mode:* Comedy of Manners vs. the Courtesy Book." *Studies in Eighteenth-Century Culture* 19 (1989): 117–28.

Veryard, E[llis], M.D. *An Account of Divers Choice Remarks, As Well Geographical, as Historical, Political, Mathematical, Physical, and Moral; Taken in a Journey Through the Low Countries, France, Italy, and Part of Spain, With the Isles of Sicily and Malta, As Also, A Voyage to the Levant.* Exon, 1701.

Whigham, Frank. *Ambition and Privilege: The Social Tropes of Elizabethan Courtesy Literature.* Berkeley and Los Angeles: U of California P, 1984.

4

Re-viewing the Subject

Blaming the Audience, Blaming the Gods

Unwitting Incest in Three Eighteenth-Century English Novels

Jones DeRitter

Depictions of incest in English narrative forms moved in and out of fashion several times between the sixteenth and the nineteenth centuries. The dramatic literature of the English Renaissance explored nearly every conceivable variation of this theme, and many Gothic novels and Romantic narrative poems exhibited similar (if somewhat more narrowly focused) interests. In recent years, some critics have argued or simply asserted that the early English novel is also preoccupied with incest, but very few of those critics have attempted either to explain the significance of this widespread preoccupation or even to provide a convincing demonstration of its existence.[1] This essay began as an attempt to address these two questions, but my investigation has led me to conclude that the early English novel is not in fact extraordinarily concerned with this topic. And since the first question could not be pursued without a positive response to the second, this conclusion meant that I needed to take a closer look at the original premise of the discussion.

If we wished to defend the notion that the early English novel was extraordinarily interested in the topic of incest, we would need to be able to demonstrate that there is a large number of novels from this period in which some version of incest is used to complicate the writer's plot. In the case of the seventeenth- and eighteenth-century English novel, there is no such evidence.[2] The use of incest as a plot device occurs much less frequently in English fiction written between 1685 and 1789[3] than it does in English stage plays of either the sixteenth or the seventeenth century,[4] and nowhere within this longer period is there a cluster of early English novels-with-incest that would justify a comparison to the simultaneous explorations of this topic by Romantic and Gothic writers between 1790 and 1825.[5]

Although the early English novel is not in fact preoccupied with incest, it is relatively easy to understand why that impression has taken hold. When the topic is raised, almost any student of the genre can cite Daniel Defoe's *Moll Flanders* (1722), Henry Fielding's *Joseph Andrews* (1742) and *Tom Jones* (1749), and perhaps even Fanny Burney's *Evelina* (1778) as early novels that present their readers with real or imagined incestuous relationships. There may not be many such examples from this genre,[6] but they are disproportionately represented on the list of required texts for the period. And since that is the case, we may be able to make a relatively minor semantic adjustment to the original question and proceed according to the original plan—in other words, instead of asking why the early English novel as a whole was preoccupied with the subject of incest, we might simply ask why Defoe, Fielding, and Burney were each interested enough in this topic to use it as a plot complication.

Not only does this reformulation avoid the inaccuracy that plagued some earlier discussions of this issue; it also quite fortuitously eliminates much of the potential for confusion that is created by larger groups of less homogeneous examples. Although the vast majority of actual incestuous relationships in the modern world follow a single pattern—one in which female children and adolescents are sexually abused by older male relatives—early modern literary treatments of this topic present us with a bewildering variety of situations. Some Jacobean plays present two hapless paragons struggling with sexual desires that preceded their awareness of family ties, while others present virtuous heroines threatened by villains whose sacrilegious lusts help to define their monstrosity. Many Gothic novels and a few Romantic closet dramas (Percy Shelley's *The Cenci*, for example) employed a version of this second plot to heighten the sense of villainy associated with certain fathers or father figures, while in Percy Shelley's *Laon and Cythna* (1817) and Byron's *Manfred* (1817), consensual sibling incest is treated as a higher form of love than more traditional exogamous relationships. The incestuous elements in these encounters can be real or imaginary, depending upon whether the connection between the characters was genuine or merely supposed, and the connection itself can be defined either in terms of consanguinity or in terms of pseudofamilial ties based on contractual obligations associated with marriage or guardianship. On a more immediate level, incestuous unions can be witting or unwitting, depending upon whether the participants knew of their familial or allegedly familial connections beforehand, and such unions can be consummated or only intended, depending upon whether the writer wishes merely to take his or her characters to the brink of disaster or, alternately, to throw them off the cliff.

As this range of possibilities might suggest, generalizing about literary treatments of incest is a risky business, and one that calls for the drawing of careful distinctions, not only between the kinds of events depicted but also between the effects created and the purposes served by different episodes. This essay focuses on three treatments of unwitting incest by canonical eighteenth-century English realists. In *Moll Flanders*, Defoe's eponymous heroine inadvertently marries her half-brother and has three children with him; in *Tom Jones*, Henry Fielding's title character enjoys a brief tryst with a woman who is thought to be his mother; and in *Evelina*, an indigent Scottish poet named Macartney tells Fanny Burney's heroine how his courtship of a young Frenchwoman ended in disaster when he wounded her father and then discovered that her father is also his father. In the terms established above, only *Moll Flanders* presents us with real incest, but all three cases are defined as incestuous by an actual or supposed blood relationship. Similarly, in *Moll Flanders* and *Tom Jones*, the incestuous or supposedly incestuous relationship is consummated, while in *Evelina* it is only intended; in all three cases, however, the desire precedes any knowledge of a real or supposed connection. In other words, what these three episodes have in common is a situation in which a real or intended sexual relationship between two consenting adults is suddenly redefined by the discovery of a real or alleged consanguinity.

In the Western literary tradition, the best known instance of unwitting incest occurs in *Oedipus the King;* for reasons that have less to do with Sophocles than with twentieth-century American and European intellectual history, there is no need to summarize the plot of the tragedy. The model for interpreting this fictional paradigm was established by Sigmund Freud, whose *Introductory Lectures on Psychoanalysis* includes an account of an imaginary (male) spectator's response to the suffering of Sophocles' hero:

He reacts as though by self-analysis he had recognized the Oedipus complex in himself and had unveiled the will of the gods and the oracle as exalted disguises of his own unconscious. It is as though he was obliged to remember the two wishes—to do away with his father and in place of him to take his mother to wife—and to be horrified at them. And he understands the dramatist's voice as though it were saying to him: "You are struggling in vain against your responsibility and are protesting in vain of what you have done in opposition to these criminal intentions. You are guilty, for you have not been able to destroy them; they still persist in you unconsciously." And there is psychological truth contained in this. Even if a man has repressed his evil impulses into the unconscious and would like to tell himself afterwards that he is not responsible for them, he is nevertheless bound to be aware of this responsibility as a sense of guilt whose basis is unknown to him. (331)

I quote this passage at length because I believe that we need to distinguish between what the passage says and what I take to be a common misapprehension of Freud's reading. Because Sophocles' plot has become fused in the popular imagination with the master narrative of classical psychoanalysis, most readers have tended to attribute to Oedipus himself the transgressive desires that Freud attributes only to the spectator watching the play. In the wake of this persistent misunderstanding, we may need to be reminded that Oedipus did not deliberately kill his father; rather, he killed an armed and angry man who challenged him to fight. By the same token, if he did not know that Jocasta was his mother when he married her, on what basis do we label his desire for her—as opposed to the sex act itself—incestuous?

To a Freudian critic who was not Freud himself, both Oedipus's subsequent violence against himself and his ultimate acceptance of his fate might suggest that the character was aware of his own transgressive desires, and that he accepted his fate as an appropriate punishment for both his crimes and the impulses that prompted them. However, Freud himself seems unwilling to take this step:

[F]undamentally [*Oedipus the King*] is an amoral work: it absolves men from moral responsibility, exhibits the gods as promoters of crime and shows the impotence of the moral impulses of men which struggle against crime. It might easily be supposed that the material of the legend had in view an indictment of the gods and of fate; and in the hands of Euripides, the critic and enemy of the gods, it would probably have become such an indictment. But with the devout Sophocles . . . [t]he difficulty is overcome by the pious sophistry that to bow to the will of the gods is the highest morality even when it promotes crime. (331)

In the pages that follow, I argue that Freud's two responses to Oedipus—that is, both his hypothesis that the play inspires a kind of guilty empathy in the generic spectator and his sardonic indictment of the gods who ordained this appalling sequence of events—are anticipated by the ways that these three eighteenth-century English novelists deploy the paradigm of unwitting incest in their own plots.

Many of the critics who have written about early modern literary treatments of incest have neglected or resisted what they perceive as the Freudian perspective on this topic, preferring anthropological or historical perspectives instead. The best defense of this position is provided by Richard McCabe, who argues that the universalizing tendencies of both the psychoanalytical and the anthropological perspectives inevitably work against the effort to understand the relationship between these literary works and their respective sociohistorical contexts (4–9). As I suggest above, I believe that we should distinguish between Freud's reading of unwitting incest and a more recognizably Freudian interpretive strategy that would focus on the personality of either a character or an author;[7] in this section of my discussion, I argue that one benefit of this distinction is that the model defined by Freud's response to *Oedipus the King* allows us to shift our attention away from the characters and toward the audience and thus toward the historical moment that provided the context for the initial success of the text in question.

At least since 1975, social historians have explored the demographic changes that took place in early modern England and concluded that the institution of the patriarchal family—which in a postfeudal society had served as the single most important determinant of the individual's social and economic destiny—had lost some of its influence (Laslett 19). For Defoe, Fielding, and Burney, and for the eighteenth-century English reading public as well, we can hypothesize that the paradigm of unwitting incest could have served as an economical way of placing new means of constructing and validating individual identities in competition with the more conventional processes determined by the political structure of the traditional family.

In each of the three episodes considered here, the incestuous encounter grows out of an unsettled situation in which an unattached and impoverished protagonist attempts unsuccessfully to claim a degree of legitimacy for herself or himself. In the particular case of *Moll Flanders*, the chain of circumstances leading to the marriage between Moll and her half brother begins at a moment when her public identity is especially tenuous. Shortly before she meets her third husband, her second husband flees to France to escape his creditors, and Moll finds herself rapidly running out of money. Although she hopes to find a new husband, her second marriage is still nominally in force, and that would of course make any subsequent marriage illegal. Partly for this reason, and partly because she dislikes the company in which she finds herself, she tells her readers that she has resolved "to make a new Appearance in some other Place where I was not known, and even to pass by another Name if I found Occasion" (Defoe 122). The marriage that follows from this turns out to be the final act of a desperate con game played by not one, but rather two only apparently respectable individuals.

The eventual discovery that Moll's third marriage is incestuous coincides with and follows from the discovery of Moll's long-lost mother, and the debate over what Moll should do with her new knowledge is initially presented as a disagreement between the mother and daughter. The series of conversations that leads to the discovery introduces Moll's mother as having redeemed herself from her past errors; after telling Moll that many of the most eminent persons in Virginia were transported felons, she reveals that she herself had been imprisoned in Newgate, but that once she was released, "she very luckily fell into a good Family, where, behaving herself well, and her Mistress dying, her Master married her, by whom she had my Husband and his Sister, and that by her Diligence and good Management after her Husband's Death, she had improved the Plantations to such a degree as they then were, so that most of the Estate was of her getting, not her Husband's" (136). In certain respects, the details of this story echo several of the circumstances in Moll's early adulthood. Falling into a good family and marrying her master recall certain aspects of Moll's first marriage, and her mother's diligence and good management in widowhood recall her own relative prosperity immediately after the death of her first husband. On the other hand, repentance and the desire to behave well are somewhat alien to Moll at this point; as numerous critics have pointed out, it is her immediate material interests, not her feelings, that prompt her to each of her first three marriages. Thus it is somewhat ironic that the good behavior of Moll's mother conspires with the more worldly ambitions of her daughter to produce the incest crisis in the novel, and that the mother's story of her reformation becomes the means by which the daughter's latest settlement with the world is permanently disrupted.

For three years after her initial discovery, Moll keeps her knowledge to herself, and although she is faced "with the greatest Pressure imaginable" throughout this period, she nonetheless takes the time to satisfy her curiosity about her mother's life: "During this time my Mother used to be frequently telling me old Stories of her former Adventures, which, however, were no ways pleasant to me; for by it, tho' she did not tell it me in plain terms, yet I could easily understand, joyn'd with what I had heard myself, of my first Tutors, that in her younger Days she had been both WHORE and THIEF; but I verily believe she had lived to repent sincerely of both, and that she was then a very Pious sober and religious Woman" (Defoe 137). By balancing Moll's childhood impressions of her lost mother with her adult judgments of the woman before her, this passage both indicts and excuses the older woman. Furthermore, since Moll herself dates from the period when her mother was whoring and thieving, the equivocal nature of Moll's own social status is reflected in her ambivalence about her mother; she refers directly to "liv[ing] . . . in open avowed Incest and Whoredom, and all under the appearance of an honest Wife" (137), but submerged in this comparison is another, equally troubling question of whether she is the dutiful daughter-in-law of a pious, sober, and religious woman or the irredeemable bastard child of a convicted felon. Of course, this all begins with the incest itself; set against the sudden transformation of husband and wife into brother and sister, the shift that requires both Moll's mother and Moll herself to confront the image of themselves as whore and bastard seems almost beside the point. Still, as the episode develops, the reader may be apt to conclude that it is the husband's reaction, not that of Moll and her mother, that ultimately drifts off into irrelevance.

What can be made of all this? In an essay published in 1989, Ellen Pollak argues that Defoe uses the paradigm of unwitting incest to keep Moll from succeeding in her attempt "to undo the categories of gender [and] to control her own [economic] circulation" (18). Starting from the anthropological perspective defined by the works of Claude Levi-Strauss and Gayle Rubin, Pollak asserts that the incest taboo is primarily a means by which society ordains the control and distribution of female children by patriarchal authorities (7). In her view, Moll's efforts to escape or resist the strictures of a society that condemns unattached women to poverty and powerlessness is circumscribed by the disastrous end of the third marriage, so that "however anti-institutional [her] subsequent violations of social law may seem to be, they are already inscribed within the limiting conditions of patriarchal heterosexual exchange" (17). Pollak's notion that the incest episode defines an outer limit for Moll's transgressive behavior has been seconded by Nelson; however, where Pollak sees Moll's third marriage as a "refusal of cultural obligation" (Pollak 16), Nelson points out that this refusal is more accidental than deliberate and suggests instead that the incestuous marriage is Defoe's idea of an appropriate punishment for "Moll's willingness to commit other kinds of 'cheat' on procreation and marriage" (Nelson 146).

It seems to me, however, that neither of these claims can adequately account for the roles played by Humphrey and Moll's mother in this episode. Humphrey is no less willing than Moll to bend the rules of courtship to suit his own purposes, and Moll's mother is arguably more blameworthy than either of her children, since it is her checkered marital history that created the possibility that the two half-siblings later turn into a disastrous reality. Nelson suggests that the novelist wishes to condemn Moll's sexual or social transgressions here, but even if that is the case, the sins of the daughter alone would not be enough to create the conditions for this encounter; and since the mother has already repented of her past errors, such a punishment sends a curiously mixed message, one that lends itself more easily to Freud's indictment of the gods than it does to the more localized system of rewards and punishments described by Nelson. In the long run, I believe that sorting through these shades of culpability will be less valuable than returning to Freud's two responses to Sophocles.

If we approach the incest episode in *Moll Flanders* with these ideas in mind, we might begin by asking whether Defoe's readers, like Freud's imaginary playgoer, will understand both the appeal and the risks of Moll's courtship gambit in terms other than those she applies to it. The similarities between Moll's career and her mother's have already been noted, but there are indications that Humphrey also resembles his wife and half sister in certain important respects. Although Moll herself suggests repeatedly that she is in control of her courtship, neither she nor Humphrey ends up receiving as much from the marriage as she or he expected;[8] as Moll puts it, "his Circumstances were not so good as I imagined, as on the other hand he had not bettered himself by marrying so much as he expected" (Defoe 129). The parallelism here signals a rough equivalence that is reflected in various stylistic devices employed throughout the account of their courtship, beginning with Moll's preliminary announcement that she intends to "Deceive the Deceiver" (123), continuing with her repeated references to "jesting" on her part and "good Humor" on his, and culminating in the poetic interchange where Moll first reveals that she is indeed poor. In this last instance, their ability to rhyme to-gether helps to suggest a level of sympathy between these two individuals that has been notably absent in her previous relationships.

Although this sympathy seems to anticipate certain relatively recent in-sights into the origins and persistence of the incest taboo,[9] it seems un-likely that we are supposed to regard Moll's regard for Humphrey as a species of endogamous desire. Ultimately, Moll runs into trouble not be-cause she wants to marry someone like herself, but rather because she be-lieves that she can manipulate certain social conventions to suit her own purposes, and because she accomplishes that goal by offering the world a fictional identity. The consequences of her success suggest that the creation of any new identity is a betrayal of the past in general and one's parents in particular; this is presumably why Defoe arranges to have the incest crisis precipitated by the personal testimony of Moll's mother. Essentially, the transgressive impulse here is social, not sexual; it is not the desire to marry the wrong individual, but the child's desire to reinvent herself, without interference from her parents, that in Defoe's fictional world leads to disaster.

Of the three instances considered in this essay, Defoe's use of the para-digm of unwitting incest is the most conservative. *Moll Flanders* treats the patriarchal structures of the early eighteenth century with the same sort of deference that Freud attributes to Sophocles. Although the episode is structured so that neither Moll's mother nor her children can be held en-tirely responsible for what happens, both the utter lack of information about Moll's father and the convenient incoherence of Humphrey once the mistake is discovered suggest an unarticulated link between the possi-bility of making such errors and the social strategies of women who are left to (or forced to fall back upon) their own devices. In Fanny Burney's *Evelina*, the incestuous encounter is arranged so that it presents masculine misconduct, not feminine resiliency, as the more serious threat to the so-cial fabric. By so doing, the novelist recasts the moral valence attached to the episode, so that the blame attached to the audience in the earlier novel is shifted in this case to the eighteenth-century secular equivalent of a ca-pricious god—that is, to the arrogant and irresponsible Sir John Belmont.

As both Mary Poovey and Irene Fizer have shown, both Evelina's struggle to obtain her father's acknowledgment and her father's deep ambivalence toward his newly legitimated daughter have distinctly in-cestuous overtones; given this deep structure, it is perhaps remarkable that Burney chose to include a subplot in which the possibility of a more literally incestuous connection is used to further complicate her plot. Like Moll Flanders and Tom Jones, Burney's illegitimate Mr. Macartney is trying to make do with too little money in a strange place when he blunders into apparent incest and (in his case) what looks like attempted parricide. The situation is later resolved by the discovery that his beloved Polly Green is not his sister and not Sir John's daughter, but rather an unwitting imposter who through no fault of her own has usurped Evelina's rightful place as the legal heir to the Belmont fortune. At first glance, this wholesale rearrangement of the blood and social ties between these characters at the end of the novel seems calculated to establish a situation in which none of them can be blamed for the difficulties they have created for each other. In fact, however, it is Sir John who ultimately foots the bill for all of this confusion, and the text suggests that this is no more than he deserves.

As Margaret Doody has suggested, Macartney's chief value to Burney's plot is that he provides occasions for Evelina to discover her personal sense of honor and to test it against her wish to be accepted into polite society (62). This personal commitment is important not only for its own sake, but also because it leads eventually to the social acceptance not of Evelina, but rather of Macartney and his new bride. When Polly Green's low birth is finally revealed, Sir John arranges to have Macartney marry her at the same time that Lord Orville marries Evelina. As Mrs. Selwyn explains, the simultaneous weddings will prevent or at least postpone any public exposure of Miss Green's background or Sir John's past behavior, because "at first, it will only be generally known that *a daughter of Sir John Belmont* is married" (Burney 360).

Fizer notes that the necessity of paying for the second wedding (and of providing the second couple with a place to live and a degree of legitimacy) constitutes an appropriate punishment for Sir John's rakish past (88), but the personal relationship between Evelina and Macartney takes this process even further by confirming that Macartney and Polly Green will be full-fledged and visible members of Evelina's social circle. Shortly after the plans for the marriages are announced, Orville tells Macartney of his wish that "the first guests we will have the happiness of receiving may be Mr. and Mrs. Macartney" (Burney 364–65); since this invitation occurs immediately before Evelina's first and least satisfactory interview with the repentant Sir John, the contrast between the sociability of the younger generation and the inability of Sir John to deal with the same set of changes could not be stronger.

The paradigm of sibling incest continues into the new arrangements, because the woman who is publicly regarded as "a daughter of Sir John Belmont" has been married to a man whom the other daughter of Sir John Belmont acknowledges as her brother. Moreover, since (as Doody points out) Macartney seems at times to be nursing some sort of erotic attachment to Evelina (62), and since (as Fizer points out) Orville claims for himself the role of Evelina's brother shortly before he proposes to her (97–98), the incestuous connections here run in nearly every conceivable direction.[10] The lines of authority in the traditional family structure are supposed not only to control the sexual activity of daughters but also to control or at least to direct the sexual activity of sons. The vision of all these married brothers and sisters socializing happily at Evelina's childhood home while the patriarch contemplates *his* guilt elsewhere seems to parody the internecine disaster that drove Moll Flanders back to the sexual marketplace and her brother-husband to invalidism.

To put the finishing touches on this picture, we need only recall that Macartney—who is, as far as we know, the only son of the patriarch—has been treated all along as a problem rather than a solution. If he is not quite as bad as the "little bourgeois imitation Hamlet" that Doody sees (62), he is certainly something other than the hero or highwayman he sees in his own mirror, and Mrs. Selwyn's epithet of "all-dismal" (Burney 360) seems entirely appropriate. His literary efforts are an embarrassment to all concerned, and his Oedipal assault on Sir John does nothing to resolve the conflicts at the heart of the novel. Generally speaking, Burney uses Macartney as the novelistic equivalent of Susannah Centlivre's Marplot: even when his motives are fundamentally good, his unintelligent self-absorption makes him far more exasperating than helpful. Forcing Sir John Belmont to accept this figure as both his son and his son-in-law is an ingenious comic punishment for the transgressive patriarch.

I save my discussion of *Tom Jones* for last because I want to use the examples of *Moll Flanders* and *Evelina* to frame my argument about Fielding's use of unwitting incest in his masterpiece. Essentially, I wish to suggest that although the critical consensus on this issue has been that this episode uses this paradigm in the same conservative, masculinist way that Defoe uses it in *Moll Flanders*, the details of this episode reveal many of the same parodic elements that Burney brings to her treatment of this issue in *Evelina*. Some of Fielding's supporters have described the incest scare in *Tom Jones* as a means of demonstrating his sincerity as a moralist without compromising his comic vision of life; meanwhile, some of the novelist's detractors have attacked him on the grounds that he treats the issue of incest with insufficient seriousness.[11] My own view is that Fielding does *not* ultimately regard this particular version of incest as a serious moral crisis, or even as the proper occasion for serious reflections.

Tom's first response to the erroneous discovery that he has committed incest is a self-lacerating soliloquy—"why do I blame Fortune? I myself am the cause of all my Misery" (Fielding 916)—which has been generally construed as an indication that he has at last achieved some degree of self-knowledge. It is certainly true that, like most fictional characters (and, for that matter, like most human beings), Tom needs to reflect on his behavior a bit more than he does. However, the more relevant issue here is whether Tom needs to obtain the particular sort of self-awareness that might be generated by the fear that he has accidentally slept with his mother. In my discussion of Defoe and Burney, I describe two different ways of assigning moral responsibility for such encounters: that of blaming the audience (the readers who approve of Moll's independence and resourcefulness in maneuvering Humphrey into marriage), and that of blaming the secular gods (in this case, Sir John Belmont, the parent whose promiscuous behavior deprives his children of a stable and clearly delimited sense of their family relationships). Over the next few pages, I examine the incest scare in *Tom Jones* with these two possibilities in mind.

Because Tom's brief tryst with Jenny Waters follows the Oedipal plot rather closely, it seems safe to assume that many Freudian critics (though again, not Freud himself) would see in this episode an expression of every man's childhood desire to replace his father in his mother's bed. Following the example of Pollak and Nelson, we might complicate this slightly by suggesting that the reader's emotional investment in Tom's happy-go-lucky hedonism carries with it a wish to be freed of his or her attachment to conventional morality and conventional family structures. Of course, other critics might see this episode as an indictment of Jenny Waters, the supposed parent of Fielding's protagonist whose apparent carelessness echoes that of Moll's mother and Sir John Belmont.[12]

If we look at this episode closely, however, we encounter a number of details that seem calculated to subvert both of these ways of apportioning blame for the doings at Upton. In the first place, the "discovery" that Tom has supposedly committed incest is made and announced by Partridge, the superstitious and frequently mistaken Jacobite who was himself falsely accused and convicted of being Tom's father. When the narrator indicates that Partridge first arrives at Newgate to give Tom this news "look[ing] as he would have done had he seen a Spectre" (Fielding 915), he reminds us of the little barber's absurd credulity and thereby warns us to consider the source of what we are about to hear. And where Partridge has consistently displayed a tendency to garble and misinterpret the little information he has at his disposal, Tom's supposed mother often seems to be wiser than he knows. When she writes to inform Tom that he is not a murderer, Jenny assures him in her postscript that "whatever other grievous Crimes you may have to repent of, the Guilt of Blood is not among the Number" (917). Her wording alludes to the alternate meaning of *blood* as kin, thereby inadvertently strengthening the suggestion that Partridge is once again mistaken.

Since any incestuous act constitutes a challenge to conventional morality and therefore to the patriarchal authorities charged with enforcing that morality, no reader should be surprised to discover Partridge running to Allworthy to tell him about the alleged disaster. Nor should Allworthy's righteous anger, much of it apparently directed at Jenny, seem improper or unexpected. What *is* shocking, however, is Jenny Waters's peremptory dismissal of Allworthy's ill temper. Instead of listening to another of the squire's lectures on sexual continence, she simply asks him "to be pleased to wave all Upbraiding me at present, as I have so important an Affair to communicate to you concerning this young Man" (Fielding 939)—and with that, she clears up the mystery of Tom's parentage and exposes the various plots against him as well.

Thus, although the incest scare in *Tom Jones* seems like a climax when it occurs, it ultimately seems to be little more than a calculated feint in the direction of a rather Draconian morality. When Tom makes love to Jenny Waters at Upton, he has no idea that she had once claimed to be his mother and no reasonable expectation that he will ever be either restored to Allworthy's favor or married to Sophia Western. Under these circumstances, this episode has to be considered perhaps the least blameworthy of Tom's sexual adventures, and it seems safe to suggest that the real thematic issue raised by Tom's behavior at Upton is not that of "Incest— with a Mother!" (Fielding 916), but rather the more general question of "How came this Muff here?" (548)—a question that is raised when Tom and Jenny are interrupted by the unexpected arrival of Sophia and several others at the inn[13] and that resonates in both directions from the center of the novel.

Critics who misread the incest scare in *Tom Jones* tend also to conclude that the hero's illicit sexual activities endanger him because they show him to be incapable of living up to the code of conduct articulated by

Allworthy in the early chapters of the novel. In fact, however, it is quite possible to argue that Tom's involvements with Molly Seagrim, Jenny Waters, and Lady Bellaston are problematic not because they dramatize Tom's supposed refusal to adopt the virtuous patriarch's code as his own, but rather because they illustrate his apparent inability to subordinate his physical desires to his emotional commitments. (If Fielding's readers are supposed to be prompted to guilty reflections by Partridge's discovery, those reflections would presumably proceed along these lines.) This is why the relationship between Tom and Sophia is the last to be resolved in the novel. The threat of incest becomes irrelevant even before Tom is released from prison, not merely because Jenny Waters is not Tom's mother, but because what Sophia thinks of Tom's promiscuity is ultimately more important than what Tom's uncle and adoptive father thinks of it. In the final analysis, the primary purpose of the incest trick in *Tom Jones* is to give Fielding's readers a reason to shift their attention away from the simple regulation of desire by the patriarch to the broader question of whether and how Tom's desire can be made to coincide with his commitment to Sophia.

In the final paragraph of his essay concerning the motif of unwitting sibling incest in English, German, and French eighteenth-century sources, W. Daniel Wilson makes the claim that "despite rationalist demolitions of the incest taboo, eighteenth-century literati remained bound by it" (263). Since neither Defoe, nor Fielding, nor Burney chose to critique the incest prohibition itself, the statement can certainly be applied to the three novels under consideration here. At the same time, however, this statement seems to me to be more than a little misleading. To one degree or another, each of these novels has raised questions about conceptions of filial and social duties, about parental conduct and responsibilities, and about the social regulation of individual desires and the orderly transfer of wealth and power from one generation to another. But even if Defoe, Fielding, and Burney are asking some of the same questions, their responses do not lead to anything like consensus. Where Defoe appears as a cultural conservative who uses the plot device of unwitting incest as a trap to be sprung on his readers, Burney appears as a sly progressive who uses the taboo to force her fictional patriarch to acknowledge more connections and accept more responsibility than he seems inclined to do.

Fielding, of course, goes even further. In *Tom Jones*, the false accusation of incest becomes the means by which his patriarch learns that he has been mistaken and misled. It is also the means by which the reputation of the often-vilified Jenny Waters is finally rehabilitated, and the means by which his hero is prevented from fulfilling the prophecy that he was born to be hanged (118). By resolving all of the difficulties that had estranged Tom and Allworthy, the incest scare also refocuses the reader's attention on the relation between Tom and Sophia. If, as the anthropologists and psychoanalysts like to suggest, the incest taboo is directly related to the patriarch's need to maintain control over his wife and his children, there is more than a little irony in Fielding's willingness to use it here as a means of getting Allworthy out of the way.

What is most striking about the episodes of unwitting incest in *Tom Jones* and *Evelina* is the way that both Fielding and Burney manage the shift from blaming the audience to blaming the resident patriarch. To be sure, in both cases, the blame is rather attenuated. Given the conspiracies working against him, Squire Allworthy's errors are very excusable, and he remains a good and honorable man despite his inability to see through the guises of hypocrites. Similarly, Burney's Sir John Belmont seems thoroughly chastened by the last-minute discoveries that help to close out the novel, and despite his errors, Evelina still yearns for his acknowledgment and approval. It should nonetheless be clear that in each case, the ultimate happiness of the protagonist depends at least to some extent on the patriarch renouncing his authority and his ability to judge his child too harshly, and that the incest scare in each novel helps to induce that necessary renunciation. Burney and Fielding may well be bound by the prohibition against incest, but they each find ways to use that prohibition to produce necessary alterations in the behavior of the very individual that the taboo was originally designed to serve.

NOTES

1. This issue has been addressed directly and defended in some detail by W. Daniel Wilson (249) and T. G. A. Nelson (127); by way of contrast, both Margaret Doody (277) and Alan Richardson (758) present this claim without further elaboration, apparently assuming that the question has already been settled.

2. The essays by Wilson and Nelson are both entertaining and informative, but each critic seems to view the number of examples he has found as being larger and more significant than it actually is. Of the hundreds of prose narratives published between 1680 and 1778, Nelson identifies approximately fifteen that use incest as a plot device; meanwhile, Wilson notes that there are "almost thirty" literary treatments of unwitting sibling incest between 1689 and 1803, but his pool of possible examples includes plays, philosophical treatises, and purportedly factual histories as well as prose fiction, and it encompasses not only English literature but German and

French sources as well. The weakness of these claims can be exposed by comparing them either to Lois E. Bueler's list of forty-two English plays written between 1559 and 1658 that deal with incest (117–18), or even to Anne Dalke's discovery that there are at least seven American novels written between 1795 and 1812 that present versions of unwitting incest (189).

3. The choice of dates is not entirely arbitrary: the relatively swift downfall and expulsion of James II from England coincides with Aphra Behn's loss of access to the London stage and hence her first great success as a novelist, while the events leading up to the storming of the Bastille were accompanied by the literary wars between the Jacobin and anti-Jacobin novelists in England, and on that basis can be used (tentatively, at least) to demarcate the boundary between eighteenth- and nineteenth-century English realisms. In his essay, Nelson defines the "early novel" as being written between 1680 and 1770.

4. In addition to Bueler's list (see n. 2 above), a new book by Richard McCabe extends the study of English incest plots into the Restoration period by connecting plays by Behn (141), Dryden (264–91), Nathaniel Lee (273–77), and others (McCabe 346 n. 2) to the works of their Jacobean and Caroline predecessors. At the end of his discussion of the Restoration plays, McCabe comments in passing that "although incest remains a comic possibility in the novels of Fielding, it was not until the Gothic and Romantic periods that it again emerged as a major focus for the examination of human nature" (291).

5. Alan Richardson's "The Dangers of Sympathy: Sibling Incest in Romantic Poetry" describes the role played by incest in poems by Coleridge, Wordsworth, Southey, Byron, and Percy Shelley. Richardson's focus on sibling incest prevents him from citing Percy Shelley's *The Cenci* (1819) as part of the larger pattern. A brief list of Gothic novels from this period that make use of this theme would include Mary Wollstonecraft's *Mary* (1791), Matthew Lewis's *The Monk* (1796), Mary Shelley's *Frankenstein* (1819) and her suppressed *Mathilda* (written 1819).

6. In addition to these four novels, Nelson cites Aphra Behn's *Love-Letters Between a Nobleman and His Sister* (1684–87), Delariviere Manley's *The New Atlantis* (1709), Eliza Haywood's *The Fortunate Foundling* (1744), Sarah Fielding's *David Simple* (1744), Sarah Scott's *A Description of Millenium Hall* (1762), Frances Sheridan's *Miss Sidney Biddulph* (1767), and the anonymous *Genuine Memoirs of the Celebrated Miss Maria Brown* (1766) as examples of the early novel's fascination with incest.

7. I have in mind here the kind of traditional psychoanalytic criticism best exemplified by Ernest Jones's reading of *Hamlet* or Norman O. Brown's interpretation of the works of Jonathan Swift in *Life Against Death*.

8. Moll's account of these matters (124–32) is not entirely consistent. It is certain that Moll gives her new husband £500 in gold, bank bills, and linen instead of the estate of £1,500 a year that had been reported to him by her friend's husband; what is less certain is whether her new spouse fully believed in her wholly imaginary fortune. Similarly, Humphrey's Virginia plantations were valued during their courtship at £300 per year while he remained in England, but after the marriage he is reported as "being under a Disappointment in his return" from those estates (131).

9. In particular, Moll's affinity for her half brother can be described in terms of what modern behavioral psychologists and anthropologists have dubbed the "aversion

experience." According to these scientists, adult individuals who are raised together as young children have an apparently innate resistance to any erotic attachment to one another. This pattern holds true even among children who have engaged in sexual play together when they were growing up. The "aversion experience" is the name given to the as-yet-unexplained mechanism by which this change is brought about (see Wilson 250–51, Nelson 135–38, McCabe 15–17). Although Nelson does not connect this idea directly to this novel, he does note that even in theory the aversion experience has nothing to do with blood relations; it operates only between individuals who are raised together and does not operate among family members who are raised apart (137). Thus a modern psychologist might conclude that Moll's fondness for her brother leads to incest primarily because the vagabond lives of the mother and both children have prevented the natural pattern of experimentation followed by aversion.

10. For a more detailed examination of the sibling relationships that have surfaced by the end of the novel, see Amy J. Pawl's essay "'And What Other Name May I Claim?'" (287–90).

11. In "The Plot of *Tom Jones*," Ronald S. Crane refers approvingly to the incest scare as a means of generating what he calls "the comic analogue of fear" (87). In the course of an essay that repeatedly praises Richardson at Fielding's expense, Frank Kermode condemns the incest scare in *Tom Jones* because this possibility turns out to have been illusory (109); Kermode believes that Fielding cannot be taken seriously as a moralist because Tom's errors do not finally have consequences.

12. A few recent critics have contended that the general tendency of *Tom Jones* is to lay the blame for Tom's problems at the feet of Fielding's female characters; see, for example, John Zomchick's "A Penetration which Nothing Can Deceive: Gender and Juridical Discourse in Some Eighteenth-Century Narratives," 539; and Christine Van Boheemen's *The Novel as Family Romance*, 78–91. According to this view, Jenny is a temptation Tom must learn to avoid so that he can reestablish his connections to Allworthy and Sophia. For an extended critique of this reading, see Jones DeRitter, *The Embodiment of Characters*, 118–45.

13. Sophia's muff is established as a symbol of her love for Tom in IV.xiv. When she discovers that Tom has been in bed with Jenny Waters, she abandons her muff on the bed, thereby prompting Tom's question (and an obscene double entendre as well).

WORKS CITED

Brown, Norman O. *Life Against Death*. Middletown: Wesleyan UP, 1959.
Bueler, Lois E. "The Structural Uses of Incest in English Renaissance Drama." *Renaissance Drama* 15 (1984): 115–45.
Burney, Frances. *Evelina*. New York: Norton, 1965.
Crane, Ronald S. "The Plot of *Tom Jones*." *Twentieth-Century Interpretations of Tom Jones*. Ed. Martin Battestin. Englewood Cliffs, N.J.: Prentice-Hall, 1968. 68–93.
Dalke, Anne. "Original Vice: The Political Implications of Incest in the Early American Novel." *Early American Literature* 23 (1988): 188–201.
Defoe, Daniel. *Moll Flanders*. Ed. David Blewett. New York: Penguin, 1978.
DeRitter, Jones. *The Embodiment of Characters*. Philadelphia: U of Pennsylvania P, 1994.

Doody, Margaret. *Frances Burney: The Life in the Works*. New Brunswick: Rutgers UP, 1988.

Fielding, Henry. *Joseph Andrews*. Ed. Martin C. Battestin. Middletown: Wesleyan UP, 1967.

———. *Tom Jones*. Ed. Martin C. Battestin and Fredson Bowers. Middletown: Wesleyan UP, 1975.

Fizer, Irene. "The Name of the Daughter: Identity and Incest in *Evelina*." *Refiguring the Father*. Ed. Patricia Yaeger and Beth Kowaleski-Wallace. Carbondale: Southern Illinois UP, 1989. 78–107.

Freud, Sigmund. *The Complete Introductory Lectures on Psychoanalysis*. Trans. and ed. James Strachey. New York: Norton, 1966.

Jones, Ernest. *Hamlet and Oedipus*. 1949. New York: Norton, 1976.

Kermode, Frank. "Richardson and Fielding." *Cambridge Journal* 4 (1950): 106–14.

Laslett, Peter. *The World We Have Lost*. New York: Scribner's, 1971.

McCabe, Richard A. *Incest, Drama, and Nature's Law: 1550–1700*. New York: Cambridge UP, 1993.

Nelson, T. G. A. "Incest in the Early Novel and Related Genres." *Eighteenth-Century Life* 16.1 (1992): 127–62.

Pawl, Amy J. "'And What Other Name May I Claim?': Names and Their Owners in Frances Burney's *Evelina*." *Eighteenth-Century Fiction* 3 (1991): 283–99.

Pollak, Ellen. "*Moll Flanders*, Incest, and the Structure of Exchange." *Eighteenth Century: Theory and Interpretation* 30 (1989): 3–21.

Poovey, Mary. "Fathers and Daughters: The Trauma of Growing Up Female." *Women in Literature* 2 (1982): 39–58.

Richardson, Alan. "The Dangers of Sympathy: Sibling Incest in English Romantic Poetry." *Studies in English Literature, 1500–1800* 25 (1985): 737–54.

Van Boheemen, Christine. *The Novel as Family Romance*. Ithaca: Cornell UP, 1987.

Wilson, W. Daniel. "Science, Natural Law, and Unwitting Sibling Incest in Eighteenth-Century Literature." *Studies in Eighteenth-Century Culture* 13 (1984): 249–70.

Zomchick, John P. "A Penetration which Nothing Can Deceive: Gender and Juridical Discourse in Some Eighteenth-Century Narratives." *SEL: Studies in English Literature* 29 (1989): 535–61.

Revolutionary Identity in Otway's *Venice Preserved*

Pat Gill

Down these mean streets a man must walk who is not himself mean
　—*Raymond Chandler,* The Simple Art of Murder

I am here, and thus, the shades of night around me, I look as if all Hell
were in my heart
　—*Jaffeir in* Venice Preserved

Critics generally find Otway's *Venice Preserved* confused and confusing in its depictions of heroes, villains, and politics. They concur, however, in believing it a Tory attack against contemporary Whig policy and strategies. Because the play's Venetian insurgents, the ostensible surrogates for Whigs, are heroic and often admirable, while the Venetian senators, the putative representatives of Tory sympathies, seem venal and depraved, both Tories and Whigs have on occasion found *Venice Preserved* too provocative.[1] In part because of these interestingly disorienting characterizations, the play has sustained critical attention throughout the centuries. Some writers attribute the perplexing portrayals to Otway's source material, an equally confounding "historical" account by Saint-Real. In his introduction to the play, Malcolm Kelsall observes: "Just as in Otway, so in Saint-Real, therefore, the reader is confused where to place his sympathies. The mixed motives of the conspiracy, the divided loyalties of Jaffeir, the inextricable inter-relation of personal emotion and political motive, even the uncertain well-being of the state itself, were clearly revealed in Saint-Real's narrative" (xvi). Kelsall concludes that Otway offers a very bleak view of life and politics. "In *Venice Preserved,*" he writes, "the lesson of history is that even the best men are wrong, all shall suffer, and there is nothing for our comfort" (xvii). While I do not wish to dispute this stunningly gloomy assessment, I want to elaborate on the contention that "there is nothing for our comfort." Otway provides a psychological displacement of the political onto the personal, a displacement that we now find very familiar and that may well be a defining feature of the modern gendered conception of self. Although earlier playwrights, especially the Jacobean dramatists to whom Otway has been most often compared, have compellingly presented contradictory characters and explored the conflicting calls of love and duty, Otway's overdetermined negotiations between public and private realms, his resolute refusal to let one be subordinated to or independent of the other, is a first in English drama and a hallmark of what has come to be known as bourgeois anxiety. The parasitic relation between public and private, with its attendant sexual resonances, quite overtly unmoors meaning and authority from a stable social reality. The loss of this stable social reality enables the male protagonists to form a sense, however tenuous and troubled, of personal integrity and moral validity.

In many ways, *Venice Preserved* shares the lachrymose temperament of certain contemporary dramas called pathetic tragedies, tragedies whose moral vision can be seen as the precursor of eighteenth-century sentimental fiction. For both Raymond Williams and Peter Brooks, sentimental fiction plays out and resolves social and political friction in terms of the (bourgeois) family. *Venice Preserved* and its pathetic siblings differ from their sentimental offspring in their refusal to disengage public from private while incurring conflict in both. They displace rather than substitute or reconcile. In the process of displacement, there is always a remainder or trace of the occulted element that prevents a simple binary distinction. *Venice Preserved* does not ground moral truth in either the family or the state. In this sense, the play is more like melodrama, a form that succeeded sentimental fiction in the nineteenth century when the family itself became a contestatory terrain and familial resolution lost some of its moral and social force. Like melodrama, a genre that champions the defenseless, *Venice Preserved* finds power to be evil and corrupting. And like melodrama, the play records the problematic nature of the family while alluding to a nostalgic vision of the past, a past when true worth was recognized and rewarded. Both sentimental fiction and melodrama tell of honest, just, but fraught individuals struggling against entrenched, unfair power structures—a plot that has come to be considered the bourgeois narrative *par excellence.*[2] Indeed, the interpretive confusion of *Venice Preserved* stems in large part from an incipiently melodramatic, bourgeois affect put in service of an appeal for the maintenance of aristocratic ideals.

Melodramatic passion colludes eerily with the somber account of life *Venice Preserved* unfolds. The play describes a murky, dangerous world. Corruption rots the social fabric. The senate, composed of inept, depraved men, governs haphazardly and cruelly. Traditional hierarchies have collapsed. Loyal veterans are censured, virtuous daughters forsaken, worthy men abused. Law and morality are at odds, and sex and gender roles uncertain. In this attenuated universe, only individual conviction can achieve moral validity. Once this conviction is put to the service of some formal cause, however, it immediately loses all integrity. This dark vision of moral decay presages another, much more recent set of narratives, those of film noir, made nearly three centuries later. At first glance, the overwrought and maudlin action of Otway's play would seem to have little to do with the stark, controlled emotional operation of film noirs.[3] But like noirs, *Venice Preserved* recounts a postwar world that has lost its connection to the established order, as well as its sense of a stable, univocal truth. J. P. Telotte suggests that "the *film noir* finds in our common stories and their received forms the context of its alterity. For this reason it often seems the flip or darker side of melodrama, but melodrama without the final restoration of social order, the sense of the world made right, that we expect from that form" (217). The noir protagonist finds comfort in neither the private (domestic) nor the public (social) realms—both seduce and betray him. He believes in and upholds a version of law and order, but this belief makes him an outsider, since those two concepts bear little if any relation to the flaccid and corrupt legal establishment and police departments of his present world. The noir landscape is generally shadowy, bleak, and urban, filled with menace and despair. Sexuality is always vexed: dangerous women and mysterious men suggest faintly (or garishly) illicit, degenerate gratifications, and the noir hero finds himself disgusted by but not always resistant to their offers. The noir protagonist is contaminated by his milieu: he has tasted or at least desired forbidden fruit, and although ruthlessly moral in some ways, he feels compromised and hollow. There is a kinship between the dramas of film noir and *Venice Preserved*, dramas implicitly or explicitly informed by a postwar alienation focusing on urban or state corruption, moral decay, social malaise, sexual perversions, and personal anguish.[4] Jaffeir and Pierre inhabit such a world, and like their cool, detached noir progeny, they adopt a tone of bitter cynicism to disguise their idealistic creed.

Film noir has been called the elaboration of a mood, "often one of foreboding; a peculiarly intense anxiety; obsession, usually sexual; and above all tension created by fear of violence and the inevitability of death" (Crowther 8). "These deeply unromantic films," explains Foster Hirsch, "shot through with visual and verbal ironies, take a sneaking delight in their display of passion gone wrong and of murderous calculation confounded" (5). "[M]oney and love," he writes, "as well as individual enterprise, lead not to fulfillment and the happy ending, but to crime and death—to defeats of nightmarish proportion" (11). "What results," J. P. Telotte explains in reference to Dashiell Hammett's Continental Op, "is a constant tension between the lure of the corrupt world and his character's stance—one that at times seems nearly pointless, given the pervasive criminality, and other times self-destructive, because of the dangers it involves. But that stance is finally crucial to the attraction of [Hammett's] tales, for the moral center it fashions reassures us that individually, man can cling to some human values, even as he is faced by corruption on all sides" (6). "These works depict *cultured* man," insists Telotte,

> the modern individual bound by the world he inhabits and the sense of self he has constructed for that world. In fact, the self-image that the *film noir* describes is of an individual perpetually bound by his own desires. What these films emphasize is how those desires seem to gain a new and forbidding force in the moment of their articulation, as they are translated into the common stock of discourse. Not only do our most threatening impulses thus reveal an origin in the self, but their patterns of operation show up as self-ordained too. (29)

Each author makes explicit his designation of film noir as a uniquely American cinematic development, one that reflects a postwar undercurrent of social disillusionment, institutional distrust, and personal uncertainty. The classification of a certain type of American crime drama made between 1941 and 1958 as film noir calls into question the designation of genre,[5] a form that repeats over time and, though always shaped by the particular historical moment in which it occurs, is recognizable from one period to another. The comparison between *Venice Preserved* and film noir is meant in part to corroborate the category of genre. Like the weepy "she-tragedies" of which it is near relation in its concern with sexual and social disorder and public and private elisions, *Venice Preserved* elaborates an identity that strikingly anticipates the modern one of the noirs. The cloying, claustrophobic urban setting populated with anxious, dissatisfied male characters afflicted by existential doubts makes the play seem uncannily recent. In its rendering of subjective insights that contest objective truths, *Venice Preserved* depicts with surprising acuity the personalization of moral predicaments characteristic of modern subjective experience.

Mulling over the fateful events and passions described in film noirs, Telotte writes that "these elements represent less an older, naturalistic sense of determinism than a very modern awareness of the various systems, including language itself, that construct our lives and often seem, on close scrutiny, bent on frustrating our hopes for order, certainty, or control" (218). For Telotte, film noir tells a story distinguished from and opposed to traditional fictions. He argues that classical narrative "appears to place viewers in a position of coherence, even omniscience, from which they view and judge the filmed world against a set of implicit norms. But *noir*'s typical subjects—sudden murders, illicit desires, official corruption—cut deeply into that coherence, questioning whether such a privileged and truthful position is possible, whether there are any such reliable norms" (221). While Otway's play does not seem to have as its primary purpose or intention the articulation of such questions, it nonetheless insistently poses them. As in the noirs, *Venice Preserved* offers local explanations but no general solutions. It is for this reason that its moral posture is so difficult to decipher. Very much like the modern accounts of the considerations Telotte enumerates, *Venice Preserved* employs sexuality as the ground on which to play out the tensions and support uncertain resolutions. In doing so, it tentatively posits an identity that is based on a recognition of a sense of the unbridgeable otherness of others and is determined by gender relations. The weird sexually charged alliances, the fanatic sacrifice of oneself and one's friends for a government that no longer upholds moral principles, and the radically personal sense of righteousness that secures neither social honors nor private recompense attest to forms of factious experience that make the play seem strangely current and afford an early glimpse of what will come to be known as a modern view of the world.

In *English Dramatic Form*, Laura Brown regards "she-tragedies" as the middle forms in the dramatic evolution from the Restoration to the eighteenth century. She charts a "smoothly continuous development from heroic to affective to bourgeois tragedy, and from satire to mixed to moral comedy" (147). I agree with Brown's account of the development, but I would argue that the smoothness is an end result rather than a precise description of the process. Pathetic or "she-tragedies," what Brown calls affective drama, reflect to a marked degree raw political and emotional agitation in sexual terms, and while the accession to bourgeois familial tragedy certainly smoothed the rougher edges, a troubling residue remained.[6] During their brief heyday, pathetic plays addressed concerns that would not be engaged or defined in such desolate, passionate, and excessive terms for nearly three hundred years. In the Restoration dramas, the inchoate bourgeois (pathetic) individual seems to experience an existential crisis before birth; in the film narratives, the well-established bourgeois (noir) individual seems to undergo similar pangs—perhaps throes of death before reincarnation as a postmodern, fragmented subject. The response to a familiar yet oddly and irrevocably altered postwar world, the recognition of the impossibility of true restoration, and the pervasive fear of corruption and conspiracy inform the affective tone of both narratives. This affective resonance suggests a historical curve to the dramatic working through of profound cultural disturbances, a working through enabled by a narrative displacement onto gender and sexual disturbances.

In the following pages, I look more closely at *Venice Preserved* and the worldview it shares with film noir. To reiterate briefly, this worldview is characterized by: the inept proceedings of government and law; the moral paucity of authority; the absence of both traditional standards of virtue and traditional practices of reward; the disintegration of gender and sexual boundaries; the erotic objectification and demonization of women; the emphasis on individual justifications and personal distress; and the ultimate ethical sanction of male loyalty. My reading is meant to offer both a fresh perspective on the play and a point of comparison with film noir.

Venice Preserved alludes broadly to the contemporary political turmoil (1678–1681) of the Popish Plot and the Exclusion Crisis. Chief among the newly formed Whigs, the earl of Shaftesbury effectively challenged Charles II's power by calling for the recognition of the popular duke of Monmouth, Charles's bastard son, as king and heir. Although Charles brilliantly defeated Whig attempts at policy control and managed to insure a peaceful succession, his victory instituted a permanent political division and made clear the cost and precariousness of peace. The civil war and its aftermath "bequeathed polemical styles and manners; the memory of the wars stalked the rest of the century, its culture as well as its politics."[7] Thought to be a "Tory Paean of Triumph" over the defeated Whig insurgents (Fink 145), *Venice Preserved* conveys not only the celebratory response to the failure of Whig opposition, but also the moral confusion of Restoration England.

The play's use of doubling, of characters and situations, suggests inherent, widespread disorder. The Shaftesbury proxy is both the power-mad, lecherous, rebel leader Renault and the childishly voluble, debased Senator Antonio. Correspondences abound and multiply; for example, the lascivious Renault also stands in for Priuli, the extraordinarily jealous father of Belvidera, and Jaffeir seems to imitate both his friend Pierre and his wife Belvidera by turns. As gender roles break down and the composition of authority breaks up, new ways of negotiating the social and moral terrain develop. In this chaotic world, abjection becomes a primary means to power. Vaska Tumir points out that the male characters in Rowe's *The Fair Penitent* and Otway's *The Orphan* have become infantalized and regressive, and that paternal authority takes on a far more oppressive, emasculating aspect than in Jacobean drama or heroic tragedy, an observation that holds true for the male characters in *Venice Preserved* as well. In all of these plays, young men respond to paternalistic authority in a manner that could be described as traditionally feminine—that is, they become dependent, helpless, and petulant—and they behave in markedly homoerotic ways toward men who share their feelings of frustration and powerlessness.

If, in *Venice Preserved*, men appear more effeminized in relation to power and sentiment, then women appear less so. Pierre's paramour Aquilina has sold her favors, an act that takes on special significance because the betrayal is not merely of a man but of a valued way of life. "Friend, to lose such beauty," Jaffeir laments to Pierre in commiseration, "The dearest purchase of thy noble labors; / She was thy right by conquest, as by love" (Otway I.i.165–67). In the better world of the idealized past, Aquilina would have remained a soldier's mistress rather than elect to be a senator's courtesan. Aquilina implicitly rejected Pierre's definition of her and himself, however, when she considered her body as her own to bestow. She challenged the old order, perhaps without meaning to, and she won.

Unlike Aquilina, Jaffeir's wife Belvidera does not pervert or distort the soft attributes of feminine compliance and tenderness; she is "[a]mazing brightness, purity, and truth, / Eternal joy, and everlasting love" (Otway I.i.340–41). Yet despite her sweet and virtuous disposition, she too betrays and destroys. Each woman's loving nature—what, in this play, is her essential self—is dissipating, distracting, and dangerous. The female characters in *Venice Preserved* may be depicted sympathetically, but the female *character* is not. As men acquire a fuller emotional register, an acqui-

sition that threatens to unsettle gender distinctions and moral categories, women move to passionate extremes, becoming the defining Other
through dangerous excess.[8] It is this passionate surplus that, even when
employed in noble causes, wreaks havoc.[9] It is not simply that Aquilina
and Belvidera always speak in highly personal and insistently seductive
terms, but also that they manifest as carnal: their sensuous presence punc-
tuates their persuasive rhetoric, giving it an erotic charge that both elec-
trifies and undercuts their moral contentions. As in film noir, it seems that
as men gain affective spirit, women become eroticized flesh.

In *Venice Preserved*, unbounded heterosexual desire is the disease that
infects men and corrupts morals. Although the conspirators feel that
money—the ability to buy what one has not earned—is the primary
source of contamination in Venice, it is the use to which money has been
put that causes the pollution they detest. Money can either purchase
or prevent sexual pleasure, and it is in this capacity that it is valuable.
Money serves solely as the means; the rebels would simply replace the
more civilized manner of barter with that of violent possession and leave
unchanged the depraved nature of the goal. Although the traitors feel
themselves to be different from the vicious world that spawned them, they
are inescapably products of it. Like unfavored sons, they come to claim
the "natural inheritance" denied them by the elderly, greedy fathers of
Venice.[10] It is not by accident that Pierre's concern for liberty began with
the loss of his mistress Aquilina to Senator Antonio. Censured by the senate for his attempts to oust his highborn rival, Pierre feels that just recompense for his years of loyal service has been denied him and that his bonds
to Venice are consequently dissolved. Willing to overthrow a government
because "a soldier's mistress . . . 's religion; / When that's profaned, all
other ties are broken" (Otway I.i.199–200), Pierre plots to overthrow the
state. Although his plan to reorganize Venice forcibly would restore Aquilina to him, it would hardly reestablish a virtuous social order.

Jaffeir's quarrel with the state is similar to that of Pierre and the other
conspirators. He, too, desires the property of a senator whose privilege allows him to retain it. Jaffeir feels that he has earned Belvidera by rescuing
her from a tragic early death, and he thinks her father, the senator Priuli,
unjust in his refusal to support them financially. Priuli, in turn, feels tricked
and abandoned. Sounding like a bereft lover, Priuli complains to Jaffeir:

> You stole her from me; like a thief you stole her,
> At dead of night; that cursed hour you chose
> To rifle me of all my heart held dear.

> May all your joys in her prove false like mine;
> A sterile fortune and a barren bed,
> Attend you both.
> (Otway I.i.49–54)

Priuli's angry claim that his daughter "forgot her duty to him" (I.i.69) barely masks his tenacious desire to have her solely to himself. Still unready after three years' absence to release his daughter to a life of her own, Priuli refuses to condone through provision a marriage that he considers a loathsome betrayal and a sexual violation, a refusal that resonates with startling sexual overtones.

Both Belvidera and Aquilina behave to men in a manner that seems designed to keep them in a constant state of sexual tension. Prototypes of the femme fatale, the women threaten the men who "own" them with separation and denial and tempt the men who desire them with possession. Belvidera sustains the tension in her relationship with Jaffeir through exorbitant, sexually charged descriptions of their marital bliss, passionate avowals of love, and fearful conjectures of forced separation. She never allows Jaffeir to attain a satiated state but always suspends him between past reminiscences of "the transporting hours of warmest love" and future encounters

> where I may throw my eager arms about thee,
> Give loose to love with kisses, kindling joy,
> And let off all the fire that's in my heart.
> (Otway I.i.353–54)

Paralyzed with desire, Jaffeir is unable to leave Belvidera even long enough to secure her financially. Belvidera uses the reverse tactic with her father. By comparing herself to her dead mother, she tempts Priuli with what he can never again possess:

> By all the joys she gave you,
> When in her blooming years she was your treasure,
> Look kindly on me; in my face behold
> The lineaments of hers y'have kissed so often.
> (V.v.42–45)

In the world of this play, then, women and sexuality are always and explicitly metonymically related.

Certainly few plays in the history of the English stage allude to conjugal activity more often and more rapturously than does this one. "Oh lead me to some desert wide and wild," Belvidera exclaims passionately upon meeting Jaffeir after an afternoon apart; "Oh I will love thee, even in madness love thee" (Otway I.i.347, 370). "Oh Pierre, wert thou but [Belvidera]," Jaffeir cries plaintively,

> How I could pull thee down into my heart,
> Gaze on thee till my eye-strings cracked with love,
> Fixed me upon the rack of ardent longing;
> Then swelling, sighing, raging to be blest,
> Come like a panting turtle to thy breast;
> On thy soft bosom hovering, bill and play,
> Confess the cause why last I fled away.
> (II.iii.228–36)

Jaffeir does not restrict these heated protestations of unrelenting love and desire to personal interchanges between Belvidera or his closest friend; he indulges in ecstatic public testimony as well. Standing before a group of enraged, homicidal rebels whom he met twenty minutes earlier, Jaffeir proclaims that he had for

> ... three whole happy years
> Lay in [Belvidera's] arms, and each kind night repeated
> The passionate vows of still increasing love.
> (II.iii.200–202)

While making this confession, Jaffeir hands over a dagger along with his wife, saying,

> To you, sirs, ... I bequeath her,
> And with her this [dagger], when I prove unworthy—
> You know the rest—Then strike it to her heart.
> (II.iii.198–99)

Clearly, women arouse more than an urge to protect in men. They do not merely trigger violence, they are wedded to it, always in an eroticized form, and, like their noir sisters and all properly functioning Others, they become both the cause of and scapegoat for inappropriate, excessive behavior.

I do not at all mean to suggest that the play blames women for the problems of the state or the failure of the rebellion. Rather, the play displaces the insoluble political dilemmas onto domestic trauma, specifically, onto gender disturbances. In working through and redefining the relation of (male) citizen to state, and (male) citizens to each other, *Venice Preserved* reevaluates the proper roles of women and the purpose of the private sphere, as well. Women acquire a certain provocatory nature that they are incapable of controlling but canny enough to use at times.[11] Once again: it is not that women are vile and untrustworthy, but that no matter how virtuous, women by nature provoke unwarranted and unreasonable responses in men. The old rebel leader Renault acts as if he were a newly wakened adolescent after one glimpse of Belvidera. He hazards reputation, position, and the success of the uprising for the chance to rape her at knifepoint. Senator Antonio gleefully debases himself whenever he sees Aquilina, enormously delighted when she threatens to beat or otherwise punish him. As a senator and a father, Priuli combines the sick, obsessive paternalism of home and state and illustrates perfectly how political corruption converts to domestic afflictions. Both the state and family are compromised, corrupting institutions that symbiotically feed on each other; destroying one would mean destroying the other. Following out a pattern familiar in the grim world of film noir, no one escapes this fateful contamination; as a consequence, there can be no restoration of past values, only of past structures. As structure, albeit adulterate, Venice must be preserved. Jaffeir and Pierre recognize their politically untenable position just soon enough to secure personal integrity for themselves by insisting on their difference from women.

While the rejection of what we would now call the feminine Other remasculinizes Jaffeir and allows the play to distinguish between virile mortification and unmanly abasement, gender issues are far from resolved. While wallowing, fawning, and begging are regarded as effeminate maneuvers, in Jaffeir they simultaneously become strangely ennobling masculine exercises. Indeed, *Venice Preserved* offers the most sustained delineation of male masochism in any publicly performed play before the twentieth century. The transcendently saccharine love of Jaffeir and Belvidera finds its obverse in the pet/master impersonations of Antonio and Aquilina. Senator Antonio personifies the exemplary figure of the fallen male, happily unmanned by feminine power, eager to beg or buy further humiliation and indignity. Antonio is not only the double of the lecherous rebel leader Renault, but also of the sexually vanquished Jaffeir. Solicitor and slave, beast and pet, Antonio cogently demonstrates the pathetic consequence of a doting attachment to a woman. "Ah, toad, toad, toad, toad! Spit in my face a little, Nacky—spit in my face, prithee, spit in my face never so little," Antonio alternately pleads and demands, "spit but a little bit—spit, spit, spit, spit when you are bid I say! Do prithee, spit—now, now, now, spit. What, you won't spit will you? Then I'll be a dog. . . . Do kick, kick on, now I am under the table, kick again—

kick harder—harder yet, bough waugh, waugh, waugh, bough" (Otway III.i.83–88 and 102–5). Antonio's comic masochism masks a serious moral: men who allow women to gain sexual power over them will lead a vile and contemptible life. Jaffeir only narrowly escapes this sorry end. In an ecstacy of submission, he tells his wife:

> Come, lead me forward now like a little tame lamb
> To sacrifice; thus in his fatal garlands,
> Decked fine, and pleased, the wanton skips and plays,
> Trots by the enticing, flattering priestess' side
> And much transported with his little pride,
> Forgets his dear companions of the plain
> Till by her, bound, he's on the altar lain;
> Yet then too hardly bleats, such pleasure's in the pain.
> (IV.i.87–94)

Sounding very much like the grotesque Antonio, Jaffeir capitulates one more time to Belvidera's demands, finding a certain exquisite anguish in his wretched condition as her minion and sacrifice.

It is only after his betrayal of Pierre that Jaffeir begins to feel true remorse for his behavior and to understand the debilitating power of women. His conduct had heretofore been a repetition of that enacted three years before the play begins. At that time, he betrayed the fatherly friendship and trust of Priuli by stealing away with Belvidera. In the course of the play, he betrays the friendship and trust of Pierre by (once again) stealing away with Belvidera. Pierre's disdainful reception of Jaffeir restores Jaffeir to his masculine senses and frees him from his ignominious dependence on his wife. Like a repentant lover, Jaffeir beseechingly implores Pierre's forgiveness:

> Use me reproachfully, and like a slave;
> Tread on me, buffet me, heap wrongs and wrongs
> On my poor head; I'll bear it all with patience
> Shall weary out thy most unfriendly cruelty,
> Lie at thy feet and kiss 'em though they spurn me,
> Till, wounded by my sufferings, thou relent,
> And raise me to thy arms with dear forgiveness.
> (Otway IV.ii.231–37)

Jaffeir's abjection before Pierre recalls his earlier abasement before Belvidera as well as Antonio's before Aquilina, but there is a vital difference: this time the entreaty is detached from both political consequences and the enervating effects of female sexual authority. Unlike his disconsolate submission to his wife, groveling humility before a brave and worthy soldier makes Jaffeir more of a man. In certainly one of the most extraordinary narrative turns in early modern English drama, homoerotic sadomasochism between men both politically and socially impotent reanimates masculine power and restores masculine integrity.

Although this affirmative process is good news for queer theorists interested in uncovering atypical sexual allusions and alliances in Restoration and eighteenth-century literature, as is often the case with the introduction of a new perspective, recognition exacts a cost. Not surprisingly, it is women who pay the price for this male bonding. Jaffeir's capitulation to the appeal of Belvidera directly brings about the capture of the conspirators, and she takes the blame for the men's fatal predicament. While the betrayal incited by Belvidera is heinous, infidelity to the rebel cause is commendable. The play had earlier linked the rebel plot to the desire for women and, by divorcing the men from both, the final act subtly detaches the men from their treasonous actions. Imprisoned and symbolically separated from their debased motive for rebellion, the men no longer seem a villainous crew of violent discontents. Powerless and literally separated from women, they reveal a brave and pure spirit of male camaraderie, enduring torture fearlessly and dying with honor. Jaffeir undergoes a similar purification process that allows him a comparable manly death. Using Pierre as a role model, Jaffeir finally treats Belvidera as an object to be exploited for the ends of his fellow men. Just as Pierre directs Aquilina to amuse her "old man" to prevent him from discovering Pierre's conspiracy, so Jaffeir commands Belvidera to seduce her father Priuli in an attempt to save Pierre. In fact, Jaffeir engages Belvidera as if she were Aquilina, speaking more like a pimp to his whore than a husband to his wife: "Melt the hard heart and wake dead nature in [Priuli], / Crush him in th'arms, and torture him with thy softness" (Otway IV.ii.427–28).

His manipulation of Belvidera affords Jaffeir the necessary emotional distance from her, it allows him to see Belvidera as an object for his pleasure rather than as a subject informing his decisions. Erotic desire is properly hierarchized but it is far from abolished. Like everyone else in the play, Jaffeir cannot imagine behaving on anything but sexual terms. He and Pierre die in an apotheosis of homoerotic triumph, using a dagger as a real as well as symbolic form of penetration. Their deaths seem poignant and admirable because they have rid themselves of the effeminate effects of women. Jaffeir and Pierre find honor and peace; Belvidera loses her mind. Her final, frantic madness underwrites by unequivocal contrast the moral superiority of male unions. Despite the moving nature of their deaths, it is the defensive gesture of gendered self-assertion that motivates the climactic actions of Jaffeir and Pierre. They die in a reaction against but not a transcendence of the desire for women.

Unlike plays that followed or preceded it, *Venice Preserved* captures a very modern, noir sense of the alienated man. Women, in both the play and film versions of this tortured state, seem not to suffer the exquisite vicissitudes of the divided self. Women may feel desperately torn between two alternatives, but they are not confused by the stakes of the choice. In both situations, women perform their now traditional function as elements rather than subjects of the problem. In *Venice Preserved*, they become the Other of politics and culture, and as a necessary consequence, the Other of (and for) men. The ways in which male alienation is played out is historically specific, and I do not claim that *Venice Preserved* in any way escapes its cultural context. I do claim, however, that a postwar malaise that has been thought to be a twentieth-century phenomenon, with its subsequent displacement of social anxieties onto sexual and private concerns and its insistent gendering of (im)proper feelings and behaviors, can be seen quite clearly in this seventeenth-century play.

Otway complicates the relatively stable Renaissance and Jacobean dramatic oppositions of personal morality or desires versus the claims of state or duty. His protagonists' polemical reasonings conform to no clear moral divisions but instead involve an adulterated dialectic of public and private that eventually synthesizes uneasily into the subjective. In this dialectic, the determination of right and wrong is not simply a matter of context or perspective; the moral opposites form an impossible amalgam. In sum, I contend that the similarities of *Venice Preserved* and certain other pathetic dramas to the dark mood of film noir are not coincidental occurrences but rather generic responses to the modern individual confronted with institutional corruption and uncertain personal boundaries. *Venice Preserved* employs the developing notion of sentiment to stretch the definition of the self, introducing a revolutionary conception of masculine self-evaluation to respond to a world that no longer provides reliable, cogent moral precepts. As modern subjects, we live out the gendered displacement in which Jaffeir and Pierre find themselves, a displacement that permits a contemptuous sanctioning of the status quo, that satisfies public indignation through private cruelty, and that makes a sense of alienation into a sign of moral worth.

NOTES

1. The finest account of the reception history of the play is still that of Aline Mackenzie Taylor.

2. My definition of bourgeois narrative derives from the classic study on this subject by Georg Lukac.

3. So termed because of their dark vision and the lighting used to reflect and enhance that cheerless perspective. I use the anglicized version of this term, but some of the critics I cite employ the French construction. Several of the films to which this description applies are: *Double Indemnity, The Postman Always Rings Twice, Murder, My Sweet, The Big Sleep,* and *Out of the Past.*

4. I would extend this claim to certain other plays of the era, although *Venice Preserved* is the most exemplary in its delineation of personal and social alienation. To varying degrees, however, pathetic drama such as Otway's *The Orphan,* Rowe's *The Fair Penitent* and *Jane Shore,* and Southerne's *Oroonoko* share the same bleak vision.

5. These dates reflect the majority consensus, but there is a healthy minority that would place the beginning date of these films firmly postwar, in 1945. For further discussion of this matter, as well as of the variations on the criteria of the category of film noir, see Hirsch, John S. Whitney 3–4, and Alain Silver and Elizabeth Ward, *Film Noir.*

6. Brown finds *The London Merchant* to be the ideological and formal culmination of this dramatic evolution, but even in this bourgeois masterpiece the provocative sexuality and unsettling emotional effect of the femme fatale, Marwood, argue against any claim of completely consistent moral action.

7. Kevin Sharpe and Steven Zwicker, 10. While I do not wish to deny the sense of stability and peace claimed by the generation of writers of the "Augustan Age," I want to qualify any assertion of its universal character. For discussions of the political and social uneasiness of this era, see D. R. Lacey; B. W. Hill; J. P. Kenyon; Howard Weinbrot; Christopher Hill; and Zwicker, *Lines of Authority.*

8. This reading is informed by the Lacanian notion of the "Other," which, in psycholinguistic terms, is the nonexistent lost object of desire—actually a version of oneself—that one seeks in imaginary relation to others. See Jacques Lacan's "the mirror stage as formative of the function of the I" (1–7) and "The Freudian thing" (114–45) in *Écrits.* For an excellent explanatory discussion of this and other related aspects of Lacan's theory, see Jacqueline Rose.

9. Since I argue here that *Venice Preserved* inaugurates the modern reworking of traditional gender roles, contemporary theories on the excessive, supplemental nature of the woman would be pertinent in a further exploration of the linguistic construction of the feminine Other. The theories of Jacques Lacan, especially as elaborated in "God and the *Jouissance* of The Woman," and of Jacques Derrida, particularly in *Of Grammatology* and *Spurs,* as well as the various critiques and revisions by feminist critics, would be especially useful.

10. The rebels' motives and plot bear a striking resemblance to Sigmund Freud's explanatory ur-myth of the establishment of patriarchal sexual and social relations in *Totem and Taboo.*

11. In his letters to Elizabeth Barry, who played the first Belvidera, Otway reveals a strong ambivalence about his amorous devotion. He both resents and revels in her

power over him, alternately soliciting her favors and accusing her of malicious designs. Evidently, Otway felt that Barry betrayed him when she declined his unsolicited offer of himself. His personal writings painfully demonstrate that he understands very little about women or mutual desire, and his play reifies his incomprehension into a drama that pits men against women in a battle for gendered self-assertion. See *Works*.

WORKS CITED

Brooks, Peter. *The Melodramatic Imagination: Balzac, Henry James, Melodrama, and the Mode of Excess*. New Haven: Yale UP, 1976.

Brown, Laura. *English Dramatic Form, 1660–1760*. New Haven: Yale UP, 1981.

Chandler, Raymond. *The Simple Art of Murder*. Boston: Houghton Mifflin, 1950.

Crowther, Bruce. *Film Noir: Reflections in a Dark Mirror*. London: Columbus, 1988.

Derrida, Jacques. *Of Grammatology*. Trans. Gayatri Chakravorty Spivak. Baltimore: Johns Hopkins UP, 1974.

———. *Spurs: Nietzsche's Styles*. Trans. Barbara Harlow. Chicago: U of Chicago P, 1979.

Fink, Zera. *The Classical Republicans*. Evanston, Ill.: Northwestern UP, 1945.

Freud, Sigmund. *Totem and Taboo*. Ed. and trans. A. A. Brill. New York: Vintage, 1946.

Hill, B. W. *The Growth of Parliamentary Parties 1689–1742*. London: Allen and Unwin, 1976.

Hill, Christopher. *Some Intellectual Consequences of the English Revolution*. Madison: U of Wisconsin P, 1980.

Hirsch, Foster. *The Dark Side of the Screen: Film Noir*. Jefferson, N. C.: McFarland, 1984.

Kenyon, J. P. *Revolution Principles: The Politics of Party 1689–1720*. Cambridge: Cambridge UP, 1977.

Lacan, Jacques. *Écrits: A Selection*. Trans. Alan Sheridan. New York: Norton, 1979.

———. "God and the *Jouissance* of The Woman." *Feminine Sexuality: Jacques Lacan and the ecole freudienne*. Ed. and trans. Juliet Mitchell and Jacqueline Rose. New York: Norton, 1982. 137–48.

Lacey, D. R. *Dissent and Parliamentary Politics in England, 1661–1689*. New Brunswick: Rutgers UP, 1969.

Lukac, Georg. *History and Class Consciousness*. London: Merlin, 1971.

Kelsall, Malcolm. Introduction. *Venice Preserved*. By Thomas Otway. Lincoln: U of Nebraska P, 1969. xi–xxii.

Mitchell, Juliet, and Jacqueline Rose, eds. and trans. *Feminine Sexuality: Jacques Lacan and the ecole freudienne*. New York: Norton, 1982.

Otway, Thomas. *Venice Preserved*. Ed. Malcolm Kelsall. Lincoln: U of Nebraska P, 1969.

———. *The Works of Thomas Otway: Plays, Poems, Love-Letters*. Ed. J. C. Ghosh. 2 vols. Oxford: Clarendon, 1968.

Rose, Jacqueline. "Introduction—II." *Feminine Sexuality: Jacques Lacan and the ecole freudienne*. Ed. and trans. Juliet Mitchell and Jacqueline Rose. New York: Norton, 1982. 27–57.

Sharpe, Kevin, and Steven Zwicker, eds. *The Politics of Discourse: The Literature and History of Seventeenth-Century England.* Berkeley and Los Angeles: U of California P, 1987.

Silver, Alain, and Elizabeth Ward, eds. *Film Noir: An Encyclopedia Reference to the American Style.* Woodstock, N.Y.: Overlook P, 1979.

Taylor, Aline Mackenzie. *Next to Shakespeare: Otway's* Venice Preserv'd *and* The Orphan *and Their History on the London Stage.* Durham: Duke UP, 1950.

Telotte, J. P. *Voices in the Dark: The Narrative Patterns of Film Noir.* Urbana: U of Illinois P, 1989.

Tumir, Vaska. "She-Tragedy and Its Men: Conflict and Form in *The Fair Penitent* and *The Orphan.*" *Studies in English Literature, 1500–1900* 50. 3 (summer 1990): 411–28.

Weinbrot, Howard. *Augustus Caesar in Augustan England: The Decline of the Classical Norm.* Princeton: Princeton UP, 1978.

Whitney, John S. "Filmography of *Film Noir.*" *Journal of Popular Film* 5 (1976): 321–71.

Williams, Raymond. *Modern Tragedy.* London: Chatto and Windus, 1966.

Zwicker, Steven. *Lines of Authority: Politics and English Literary Culture, 1649–1689.* Ithaca: Cornell UP, 1993.

The Rage of Caliban

Eighteenth-Century Molly Houses and the Twentieth-Century Search for Sexual Identity

Craig Patterson

Most recent work on the history of same-sex sexual activity assumes that "homosexuality" is in some sense a modern invention and that previous eras did not recognize a distinct category of persons but merely stigmatized a number of acts.[1] The most influential (and audacious) proponent of this view is Michel Foucault, who proclaims that the "homosexual" was "born" in 1870, that moment when he became a distinct "species" (43). Others, following the suggestion of Mary McIntosh, argue that a shift in the meaning of sodomitical activities occurred earlier, at the beginning of the eighteenth century, at the moment when distinct subcultures and places for sexual recreation (taverns, outdoor cruising grounds) were established in London and other large Western European cities. The most enthusiastic and prolific supporter of this position has been Randolph Trumbach, whose pioneering work on the sodomites (or mollies) of eighteenth-century London squarely places them in the historical and literary consciousness of the twentieth century.[2]

While it may be fruitless (and misleading) to search for what Eve Kosofsky Sedgwick wryly calls the "Great Paradigm Shift" (44), our understanding of the historical differences in the meaning of illicit sexual activities will obviously be greatly affected by our acknowledgment of the moment when these differences became crucial. Most scholars who have looked carefully at the eighteenth-century English sources have recognized such a marked shift in the organization and significance of sodomitical activity. Whereas the previous era associated sodomy with the licentious rake who strolled confidently with his catamite on one arm and his whore on the other, the early eighteenth century saw the emergence of a "new kind of sodomite who was identified principally by his effeminate manner" (Trumbach, "Birth" 135–36). The molly houses were places where they "enacted the rituals of their new identity" (137) and established themselves as a third gender position. Indeed, for Trumbach the stigmatized molly helped to smooth over the difficulties associated with the growing equality between the other two genders: "The majority of men who knew that men could not desire men, that only women did that, and that the molly was the outcast demonstration that this was so, such a majority, secure in at least one insurmountable difference between men and women, and a difference founded (so it was thought) in human biology and anatomy, could face with greater equanimity in other areas of life the growing equality between the two legitimate genders" ("Sodomy Transformed" 106). Here, then, is definitional coherence lent to what has been famously called "an utterly confused category" (Foucault 101): an important moment of generation, "the birth of the Queen" (Trumbach, "Birth" 129).

While it seems impossible to deny that a major shift in the figuration of the sodomite occurred during this period, it seems more difficult to accept that a new role or identity had been established. The accounts we have of the molly houses are confused and confusing texts, part of a discourse about crime and the city that provides shocking (and at the same time, titillating) evidence of human depravity in all its variety. While they read like a high camp romp through a world of gender inversion, they are vitriolic texts that condemn the mollies as monstrous aberrations. Rather than yielding secrets about the establishment of a new social identity, they encode the language of sexuality within a familiar trope of disorder: the world of gender turned upside down. Indeed, each of the four accounts we have of the molly houses is a shifting, unreliable text whose uncertainties render difficult any confident pronouncements about the existence of new identities.[3]

The first account we have of a molly house comes from Ned Ward's *Secret History of the Clubs* (1709), a work dedicated, appropriately, to "that Luciferous and Sublime Lunatick, the Emperor of the Moon" (Sig. A2r). It is a book that presents "the Madness of Mankind" and the "Lunacies of this World" (Sig. A5r), and Ward also includes accounts of the Farting Club, the Surly Club, the Lying Club, and the Club of Ugly Faces. These are, as he admits, "such amusing Denominations, that the most morose *Cynick* would be scarce able to hear their Titles without bursting into Laughter" (9).

The *Secret History of the Clubs* is, therefore, a work that enthusiastically signposts its own improbabilities. In the heavily determined world of eighteenth-century prefatory apologetics, it offers no claim of eyewitness veracity, no condemnation of those who would offer scandalous novels and romances under the guise of histories. Indeed it is itself a *secret* history rather than a history of *secret* clubs. We are dealing, in other words, in that strange narrative category of the remarkable and the prodigious, the world of the strange and therefore true.[4]

Indeed Ward is unable to sustain even the suggestion of firsthand knowledge of the mollies. He begins with a confident assertion that "At a certain Tavern in the City, whose Sign I shall not mention, because I am unwilling to fix an Odium upon the House," the mollies "have settl'd a constant Meeting every Evening of the Week" (1–2). He ends his account with what amounts to a disclaimer: the mollies "continu'd their odious Society for some Years," until they were "happily discover'd" through "cunning Management" of "the Under Agents to the *Reforming-Society . . .* by this means the Diabolical Society were forc'd to put a period to their scandalous Revels" (288). Present and past have thus become strangely confused: our brush with the illicit as a continuing phenomenon has been reduced to yesterday's news.

It is Ward's account that, in a number of ways, sets the tone for other molly house encounters, and it is frequently cited as the first evidence of a shift in meaning of same-sex sexual activity.[5] And yet it is a work mired in disavowal, a work that constantly (and openly) disclaims its veracity. In a narrative world vexed by the distinctions of *history* and *fiction*, it seems remarkably untroubled and unwilling to press any particular claim to authenticity.

The account itself presents a carnivalesque romp in a world of gender inversion. The mollies have "so far degenerated from masculine Deportment, or manly Exercises, that they rather fancy themselves Women, imitating all the little Vanities that Custom has reconcil'd to the Female Sex, affecting to Speak, Walk, Tattle, Cursy, Cry, Scold, and to mimick all Manner of Effeminacy, that ever has fallen within their several Observations" (284). They perform what have seemed to some scholars as their own rituals: a mock wedding and a parodic birth. They speak their own argot, calling each other "Sisters" and using "no other Dialect but what Gossips are wont to do upon such Loquatious Occasions" (286).

The molly house accounts have seemed to at least one modern observer like narratives "written by a jungle explorer who has just discovered an exotic new species, or by an anthropologist revealing a tribe with a new kinship system" (Greenberg 335). They are, it seems, benign (and largely factual?) narratives of strange acts by a previously undiscovered tribe. And yet this claim not only collapses historical distinctions but ignores the texts themselves.[6] (Not very far) beneath the surface froth of Ward's and other accounts lies an undiluted vitriol that figures the mollies as monstrous aberrations, threats to the proper hierarchies of gender.

Sodomy was, as the legal writers explained, "Contra ordinationem Creatoris, & naturae ordinem" (Coke 59), and it is the rhetoric of the unnatural that predominates in antisodomite diatribes. For Ward the mollies are a "Diabolical Society" (288) who commit "odious Beastialities" (288) and "praeternatural Pollutions" (284). In the piece of doggerel that ends his account, he presents them as the monstrous products of an unnatural coupling:

> Sure the curs'd Father of this Race,
> That does the Sexes thus disgrace
> Must be a Monster, Mad, or Drunk,
> Who, bedding some prepostrous Punk,
> Mistook the downy Seat of Love,
> And got them in the Sink above;
> So that, at first, a T——d and They
> Were born the very self same Way,
> From whence they draw this cursed Itch,
> Not to the Belly, but the Breech;
> Else who could Woman's Charms refuse,
> To such a beastly Practice use?
>
> .   .   .   .
>
> But *Sodomites* their Wives forsake,
> Unmanly Liberties to take,
> And fall in Love with one another,
> As if no Woman was their Mother.
> (288–89)

A note of caution need be sounded here, since the polemical strategies of a work such as Ward's are by no means straightforward. He has tantalized us with an intriguing picture of lunacy, a world of gender turned upside down, and is required, therefore, to expiate his voyeuristic guilt in an orgy of schoolboy scurrility.

And yet this focus on the monstrous and unnatural is a persistent feature of antisodomite diatribes. It figures prominently in the most famous piece of homophobic character assassination of the period, Pope's attack on Lord Hervey in "The Epistle to Dr. Arbuthnot":

> In Puns, or Politicks, or Tales, or Lyes,
> Or Spite, or Smut, or Rymes, or Blasphemies.
> His Wit all see-saw between *that* and *this*,
> Now high, now low, now Master up, now Miss,
> And he himself one vile Antithesis.
> Amphibious Thing! that acting either Part,
> The trifling Head, or the corrupted Heart!
> Fop at the Toilet, Flatt'rer at the Board,
> Now trips a Lady, and now struts a Lord.
> (321–29)

Hervey is here transformed into a seething mass of irreconcilable contraries, a "vile Antithesis" whose disordering potential is inscribed within the poem as its stately, measured couplets are perverted into the sibilant triple rhyme: "this . . . Miss . . . Antithesis." Here, as in Pope's *Dunciad*, the corruption of art is symptomatic of a generalized social disorder. Hervey is also depicted as a satanic corrupter of the state, who squats toadlike at the ear of that most unlikely of Eves, Queen Caroline. Indeed, the poet's own inability to describe his victim adequately becomes yet another index of Hervey's variability. He is not only a demonical toad and a sodomite but also an annoying insect and a fawning spaniel. His place on the chain of being is thus unfixable and he makes, therefore, a mockery of nature's hierarchy. Order is, for Pope, a cherished concept, and in the words of the "Essay on Man," "who but wishes to invert the laws / Of ORDER, sins against th'Eternal Cause" (1: 129–30). Hervey's personal disorder, and his animus toward Pope, are emblematic of the social, poetic, and political turbulence that have spurred the poet to take up his pen against his enemies.[7]

Pope was, of course, by no means the only writer who appealed to Nature to uphold the social and political, and these ready-made associations meant that the trope of sodomy as contradiction provided a useful weapon for the clever political satirist. That staunch bulwark of Protestantism William III was, for example, lampooned in a verse that played both on the conventional association of sodomy as "the Italian vice" and on the King's Dutch origins (and pro-Dutch foreign policy):

> But ye loss of our auncient and laudable Fasshion
> Has lost our good King one halfe of ye Nation
> Letts pray for ye good of our State & his soule
> That He'd putt his Roger into ye the right Hole,
>   For the Case is such,
>   The People think much,
> That yor love is Italian, & Government Dutch.
> Ah who wou'd have thought that a low Country Stallion,
> And a Protestant Prince shou'd prove an Italian.
> ("Ladys complaint" 37–44)[8]

The comic thrust of the passage relies on the yoking together of irreconcilable political, national, religious, and sexual contraries. The language of inversion renders William a comic contradiction, a political, religious, and sexual absurdity. He too is an unstable "Amphibious thing" who "makes love like Italians, as He rules like a Turk" (4).

Indeed, inversion has infected the entire court and even threatens the procreative duties of the royal couple:

> The Q[u]een too (God bless her) as 'tis said by some,
> Matrimonyall service receives at her bum,
> And that is ye reason ye doctors all tell yee,
> She has a great A—— instead of great belly
>   But ye matters not much
>   For shou'd it prove Dutch,
> Her fruitfullness we shou'd have reason to grutch.
> ("Lady's complaint" 19–22)

Once again we have the suggestion of a monstrous birth emerging from an unnatural coupling, although here the concern is national rather than sexual.

The language of sexual contradiction thus provided a vehicle for any number of complaints, a way of signaling disorder that might be easily employed by the poetic satirist. But while poets (of whatever stature) might use the trope to parade their brittle wits, it was also part of the language of denunciation in popular accounts of the mollies. As the street robber James Dalton explained, a molly was "neither a Man's Man, nor a Woman's Man, neither a Whore's Friend, nor a Rogue's Confident, but a

Persecutor of the Party he falls in with, and a Traytor to both Sexes" (35). Or, as another famous criminal, Jonathan Wild, noted, the mollies acted "as if they were a mixture of wanton Males and Females" (39).[9] While Dalton and Wild have not cloaked their attacks in the fancy dress of a Horatian verse epistle, they too present a profusion of, to use Pope's phrase, vile antitheses.

"The existence of monsters," as Georges Canguilhem reminds us, "throws doubt on life's ability to teach us order" (27). It is precisely this disordering quality of undifferentiated gender mixtures that is featured prominently in the accounts we have of the molly houses. When Samuel Stevens testified at the trial of Margaret Clap in 1726, he drew attention to the unnatural, monstrous quality of the mollies' behavior: "Sometimes they would sit in one anothers Laps, kissing in a lewd Manner, and using their Hand [sic] indecently. Then they would get up, Dance and make Curtsies, and mimick the Voices of Women. O, Fie, Sir!—Pray Sir—Dear Sir.— Lord, how can you serve me so?—I swear I'll cry out—You're a wicked Devil,—and you're a bold Face—Eh ye little Toad! Com, bus!" (*Select Trials* 2: 209). Stevens may, in fact, present a reliable eyewitness account of molly repartee, but there are shadows that cast doubt on his credibility. In the first place, he seems to have been an informer for one of the reforming societies and thus hardly qualifies as an unbiased observer.[10] His account comes not from an official record but rather from a commercial publication, a collection of trial reports, Sessions papers, and accounts by the ordinaries of Newgate.[11] Like most compendiums of criminal narrative, *Select Trials* is a miscellaneous compilation, and as its editor promises, "with the serious, we shall intermix the Pleasant, to Divert, as well as Instruct" (1: 1).

Stevens's testimony also conveys what had already been established as proper molly behavior. Mollies were supposed to disport themselves with an exaggerated effeminacy. Stevens could rely, at this point, on the testimony of another unreliable witness, the archcriminal Jonathan Wild who, in 1718, provided a "Diverting Scene of a Sodomitish Academy" in a pamphlet entitled *An Answer to a Late Insolent Libel*.[12] The libel in question was another pamphlet, by Charles Hitchen, the city undermarshal, with whom Wild was vying for control of the London criminal underworld.[13] Wild's account is, predictably, an exercise in character assassination in which Hitchen is cast as the sexually corrupt insider, while Wild plays the ingenue, an unlikely role for a man who would later be accused of sacrificing more than 120 men to the gallows for the sake of the forty-pound reward (Defoe 257).[14] Indeed, Wild affects complete confusion when Hitchen first proposes visiting a "Company of *He-Whores*" (38): "The Man [i.e. Wild] not apprehending his meaning, ask'd if they were Hermaphrodites: No ye Fool, said the M——l, they are Sodomites, such as deal with their own Sex instead of Females. This being a Curiosity the M——l's Man had not hitherto met with, he willingly accompanied his Master to the House" (38). While Wild remains a naive and curious outsider, Hitchen is, however, well apprised of the customs of the place and "Dallied with the young Sparks with a great deal of Pleasure" (39).[15]

Wild's molly house is thus remarkably similar to Ward's. Hitchen is "Complemented by the Company with the Titles of Madam, and Ladyship . . . a familiar Language peculiar to that House" (38). He also tells Wild of a house in Holborn where "these sorts of Persons us'd to Repair, and Dress themselves in Woman's Apparel for the Entertainment of Others of the same Inclinations" (39). Here, then, is the persistence of subcultural social practices: a new social role based on transvestism and effeminacy.

And yet Wild, no less than Ward, is a highly dubious narrator. He ends his molly adventures, for example, with a final salvo at Hitchen: "Any Gentleman who wants to be Acquainted with the Sodomitish Academy may be inform'd where it is, and be graciously Introduc'd by the accomplish'd Mr. H——n" (41). While Wild's attempts at irony never quite get off the ground, the pamphlet is a relatively witty response to Hitchen's own rather heavy-handed denunciation of Wild as "King amongst the Thieves, and Lying Master General of *England*, Captain General of the Army of Plunderers, and Embassador Extraordinary from the Prince of the Air" (Hitchen 5). We are, in other words, in the midst of yet another feud, with none of the verbal finesse, but all of the viciousness, of the better-known dispute between Pope and Hervey. Nor can we be certain that the similarities between Wild's and other accounts indicate the persistence of sodomite practices. The world of eighteenth-century pamphlet publishing was rife with what sometimes appears to be outright plagiarism but is perhaps better characterized as the circulation of texts within a network of cultural exchange. Taking Wild's life as an example, we can note numerous times when passages or indeed entire biographies were reprinted directly or borrowed and recast.[16]

The conjunction of sodomy and more common criminality also occurs in the molly house account given by the notorious street robber James Dalton.[17] Dalton also situates his narrative within a larger framework of, as the title page puts it, "very pleasant and remarkable Adventures." Once again we are in the strange but true world of "an Adventure of a quite different Nature from any Thing we have hitherto taken Notice of" included for "the further Entertainment of the Reader" (31). For Dalton the mollies are "Beasts in the Shape of Men" (35) who perpetrate an act "in Comparison of which, he accounted all the wicked Actions of his Life but as so many Virtues" (34).

Like Ward's mollies, Dalton's perform a mock lying-in, a monstrous parody of an unnatural birth. "To make themselves as ridiculous as Extravagance and Effeminacy can render them, they sometimes have a Lying-in, when one of them is plac'd in a Chair, and the others attending with Napkins, a Bason of Water, &c. *Susan Guzzle*, a Gentleman's Servant, is the Midwife, and with a great Deal of Ceremony, a jointed Baby is brought from under the Chair he sits on" (40). The jointed baby was also a part of Ward's molly ritual and its reappearance here may suggest a continuity (after twenty-one years) of a subcultural ritual. But it may also merely represent what by now had become a convention of popular literature, a mockery of gender that is a mockery of nature.

It seems clear that the early eighteenth century witnessed a shift in the figuration of the sodomite, a move that is accompanied by our knowledge of the establishment of places of resort (taverns and outdoor cruising grounds) frequented by those who might pursue this "wicked sport" (Smith, *Complete History* 579).[18] But our knowledge is limited to hostile accounts by unreliable narrators. The mollies are a kind of sideshow in the great urban circus of depravity, an amusing but ultimately disgusting renegotiation of gender.

And their effeminacy, in any case, was also figured as a kind of archmisogyny, a relation that needs to be further explored. For Ward, for example, the mollies imitate the "little Effeminate Weaknesses which Women are subject to when Gossiping . . . on purpose to extinguish that Natural Affection which is due the Fair Sex" (288). The sodomite's rejection of women can be found in a range of seventeenth- and eighteenth-century texts. It is present, for example, in the libertine musings of the "Song," attributed to Rochester, "Love a woman? You're an ass" when the "insipid passion" (2) of his mistress is rejected in favor of his "sweet, soft page" who "Does the trick worth forty wenches" (Rochester 15–16). The poem "The Woman-Hater's Lamentation" celebrates the capture and suicide of some early eighteenth-century sodomites, the poem's very title providing the raison d'être for their perverse behavior. "I hate Woman and their Lunacies" proclaims "Caiphas" to his lover "Ganymede," "no sooner we have Commerce with that foul unclean libidinous Creature Woman, than she surfeits and disgorges this ambrosial Morsel—but Man never returns, he retains the Gift and is grateful" (*Address* 14). Indeed, the brutal behavior of women toward sodomites in the pillory suggests that the sodomite as misogynist was a widely embraced commonplace.[19]

To suggest, however, that we have an inauguration of a new social role, a shift in sodomitical practices, on the basis of the molly house accounts, is to slice through a Gordian knot of uncertainties and render lucid texts that are as shadowy as the underworld they describe. While we can point to a shift in antisodomite rhetoric, it is much harder to accept that we can somehow sift through these diatribes and establish the existence of a new identity. Nor, in a sense, should we expect to.

Any enquiry into the history of illicit sexual activity is necessarily constrained, not only by the availability of sources but also by the representational potential of the texts themselves. Questions of identity are not easily solved by combing (however sedulously) through satirical attacks or criminal pamphlets. If our search is for evidence of what Foucault defined as a "kind of interior androgyny, a hermaphrodism of the soul" (43), then we can hardly expect to find it in works that look at the mollies and their rituals from the position of hostile outsiders. By the same token, we would doubtless find no evidence of David Halperin's "highest expression" of "homosexuality," the "straight-acting and -appearing male" (9), were we to go hunting through the speeches of fundamentalist homophobes or the pages of scandalous tabloids.

And as Sedgwick reminds us, even today homosexuality is "a space of overlapping, contradictory and conflictual definitional forces" rather than a "coherent definitional field" (45). Sodomites are still demonized from pulpits, and church and state refuse to recognize the distinction of sodomitical acts and homosexual persons. Our search for a single moment of generation is a part of our understanding of the eighteenth century as an era of important social, literary, and political beginnings: to quote from the titles of three well-known studies, the period witnessed the rise of the egalitarian family, the origins of the novel, and the growth of political stability. Here, then, are the roots of modernity, the foundation of a world that is recognizably ours. And yet the attempt to rewrite history to include the marginalized is fraught with the danger of pressing too hard in order that we may find ourselves too readily.

NOTES

1. Most, but not all. For an argument that challenges "new inventionism" see Cady, who also provides a useful summary of the major arguments for and against the eighteenth and nineteenth centuries as the moment when sodomites were "born."

2. Trumbach has modified his position somewhat from its first expression in "London's Sodomites." For a summary of his modified position see his "Birth" 129–30, "Sodomitical Assaults" 407–9, and "Sodomitical Subcultures." His supposition has been widely debated, especially by those who challenge the notion of sexuality as a historical construct. For a summary of this debate see Rousseau, "Introduction," 80–81 n. 2.

3. For modern accounts of the molly houses see, for example, Bray 81–114; Trumbach, "London's Sodomites"; Greenberg 333–35; Norton 54–66.

4. For the epistemological uncertainties of eighteenth-century fiction see, for example, McKeon; Davis; and Hunter. For the *chronique scandeleuse* see, for example, Richetti 119–67.

5. For Ward's prominence see Trumbach, "Birth" 138; and Norton 55.

6. While Greenberg acknowledges that these accounts may be "exaggerated for rhetorical purposes," he concludes that "the descriptions are too consistent to be dismissed as fictitious." (333). His anthropological metaphor is paralleled in Trumbach's situating the mollies within worldwide patterns of sexual behavior. For an account of these see "Birth" 129–30, and "Gender" 149–54.

7. For the feud between Pope and Hervey see Mack 644–48 and Halsband 175–78.

8. The word "Roger" (40) has been amended to "finger." In an earlier line (7), "f——ing his pages" has been changed to "loving." The entire manuscript shows signs of similar editorial liberties, including entire poems (maddeningly) that have been scribbled over into illegibility. For a brief discussion of this poem and its relation to other contemporary satires see O'Neill.

9. The copy I examined (Bodleian Pamph. 346) is both mispaginated (1–32; 25–32; 41–44) and missigned (F2 is signed F3). Since all of these irregularities occur within signature F, the same signature in which the molly episode takes place, this may suggest that alterations were made in the process of printing. (I have not, however, examined other copies.) This and subsequent references are to the "actual" rather than printed page number.

10. Stevens, along with Thomas Newton, testified at a number of molly trials after what has been characterized as a "raid" (Bray 82) on Margaret Clap's establishment. As he testified at the trial of Gabriel Lawrence, he had been at Clap's "several Times in order to detect those that frequented it" (*Select Trials* 2: 193). For the work of the reforming societies see, for example, Bristow.

11. For the circulation of criminal trials see Harris. For the Sessions papers see Langbein. For the accounts by Newgate's official chaplain, the ordinary, see Linebaugh.

12. The full title of the work is *An Answer to a late Insolent Libel entitled A Discovery of the Conduct of Receivers and Thief-takers, in and about the City of London. Set forth in several Entertaining Stories, Comical Intrigues, merry Adventures, particularly of the M——l and his Man the Buckle Maker. With a Diverting Scene of a Sodomitish Academy.*

13. Wild was first attacked by *A True Discovery of the Conduct of Receivers and Thief-Takers* (1718). Wild responded in the same year with *An Answer to A late Insolent Libel* (1718), and Hitchen, in turn, produced *The Regulator: Or, A Discovery of the Conduct of Thieves and Thief-Takers* (1718). On the feud between the two, see Howson 112. Howson suggests that Wild's response was ghostwritten, although he offers no

source other than to note that "everybody knew that Wild had either written it or had dictated the substance of it to a hack-writer" (103). Howson, however, offers no evidence to substantiate this claim.

14. Wild, himself, claimed a more modest seventy-five. For his list, see Howson 306–11.

15. In 1727 Hitchen would be convicted of attempted sodomy. For his trial see *Select Trials* 2: 243–44.

16. Howson's bibliography suggests some of the relation between these texts. One might add that the preface to Captain Alexander Smith's *The Memoirs of the Life and Times of the famous Jonathan Wild* (1725) is an almost verbatim reprint of Bernard Mandeville's *Enquiry into the Causes of the Frequent Executions at Tyburn* (1725). For criminal narratives more generally, see Faller and Bell.

17. For other examples of sodomy used to spice up a criminal's biography see, for example, *A Compleat and Genuine Account*, and Smith's life of Stephen Margrove and others (574–81). Another life of Dalton (*The Life and Actions of James Dalton*) was published in 1730. It makes no mention of sodomites and, predictably, complains of "false and spurious" biographies and claims to present "the true and exact Account" (Sig. A2r).

18. For a discussion of these developments see Trumbach, "London's Sodomites"; Norton 51–83.

19. The pillory was used to punish those convicted of attempted buggery. Buggery, a capital offense, required the proof of both penetration and emission. See Coke 59–60. For accounts of the behavior of crowds toward pilloried sodomites, see Crompton 21, 22, 163–66, 251–52. See also the behavior of a group of whores toward a sodomite in Fielding 25.

WORKS CITED

An Address from the Ladies of the Provinces of Munster and Leinster . . . to which are added, some LOVE-LETTERS which passed between Caiphas and his Favorite Ganymede C—— m——. London, 1754.

Bell, Ian A. *Literature and Crime in Augustan England*. London: Routledge, 1991.

Bray, Alan. *Homosexuality in Renaissance England*. London: Gay Men's P, 1982.

Bristow, Edward J. *Vice and Vigilance: Purity Movements in Britain since 1700*. London: Gill and Macmillan, 1977.

Cady, Joseph. "'Masculine Love,' Renaissance Writing, and the 'New Invention' of Homosexuality." *Homosexuality in Renaissance and Enlightenment England: Literary Representations in Historical Context*. Ed. Claude J. Summers. New York: Harrington Park P, 1992. 9–40.

Canguilhem, Georges. "Monstrosity and the Monstrous." *Diogenes* 40 (1962): 27–42.

Coke, Edward. *The Third Part of the Institutes of the Laws of England*. London, 1648.

A Compleat and Genuine Account of the Life and Actions of Joseph Powis. London, 1732.

Crompton, Louis. *Byron and Greek Love: Homophobia in Nineteenth-Century England*. London: Faber, 1985.

Dalton, James. *A Genuine Narrative of All the Street Robberies Committed since October Last, by James Dalton, and His Accomplices*. London, 1728.

Davis, Lennard J. *Factual Fictions: The Origins of the English Novel.* New York: Columbia UP, 1983.

Defoe, Daniel. *The True and Genuine Account of the Life and Actions of the Late Jonathan Wild* (1725) in Henry Fielding's *Jonathan Wild.* Ed. David Nokes. Harmondsworth: Penguin, 1982.

Faller, Lincoln. *Turned to Account: The Forms and Functions of Criminal Biography in Late Seventeenth- and Early Eighteenth-Century England.* Cambridge: Cambridge UP, 1987.

Fielding, Henry. *Amelia.* Ed. David Blewett. Harmondsworth: Penguin, 1987.

Foucault, Michel. *The History of Sexuality. Volume 1: An Introduction.* Trans. Robert Hurley. New York: Vintage, 1990.

Greenberg, David F. *The Construction of Homosexuality.* Chicago: U of Chicago P, 1988.

Halperin, David. *One Hundred Years of Homosexuality.* New York: Routledge, 1989.

Halsband, Robert. *Lord Hervey: Eighteenth-Century Courtier.* Oxford: Clarendon, 1973.

Harris, Michael. "Trials and Criminal Biographies: A Case Study in Distribution." *Sale and Distribution of Books from 1700.* Ed. Robin Myers and Michael Harris. Oxford: Oxford Polytechnic P, 1982. 1–36.

Hitchen, Charles. *The Regulator: Or, A Discovery of the Conduct of Thieves and Thief-Takers.* London, 1718.

———. *A True Discovery of the Conduct of Receivers and Thief-Takers, In and About the City of London.* London, 1718.

Howson, Gerald. *Thieftaker General: The Rise and Fall of Jonathan Wild.* London: Hutchinson, 1970.

Hunter, J. Paul. *Before Novels: The Cultural Contexts of Eighteenth Century English Fiction.* New York: Norton, 1990.

"The Ladys complaint." Additional ms. 29,497. Fol. 101r-v. British Library, London.

Langbein, John H. "The Criminal Trial Before the Lawyers." *University of Chicago Law Review* 45 (1978): 263–316.

The Life and Actions of James Dalton. London, 1730.

Linebaugh, Peter. "The Ordinary of Newgate and His Account." *Crime in England 1550–1800.* Ed. J. S. Cockburn. London: Methuen, 1977. 246–69.

Mack, Maynard. *Alexander Pope: A Life.* New York: Norton, 1985.

Mandeville, Bernard. *Enquiry into the Causes of the Frequent Executions at Tyburn.* London, 1725.

McIntosh, Mary. "The Homosexual Role." *Social Problems* 16 (1968): 182–92.

McKeon, Michael. *The Origins of the English Novel 1600–1740.* Baltimore: Johns Hopkins UP, 1987.

Norton, Rictor. *Mother Clap's Molly House: The Gay Subculture in England 1700–1830.* London: Gay Men's P, 1992.

O'Neill, John H. "Sexuality, Deviance, and Moral Character in the Personal Satire of the Restoration." *Eighteenth-Century Life* 2.1 (1975): 16–19.

Pope, Alexander. *The Poems of Alexander Pope.* Ed. John Butt. London: Methuen, 1963.

Richetti, John. *Popular Fiction Before Richardson: Narrative Patterns, 1700–1739.* Oxford: Clarendon, 1969.

Rochester, earl of. "Song" ["Love a Woman, You're an ass!"]. *The Complete Poems of John Wilmot, Earl of Rochester*. Ed. David M. Vieth. New Haven: Yale UP, 1968.

Rousseau, G. S. "An Introduction to the *Love-Letters:* Circumstances of Publication, Context, and Cultural Commentary." *Love Letters Between a Certain Late Nobleman and the Famous Mr. Wilson*. Ed. Michael S. Kimmel. New York: Harrington Park P, 1990. 47–92.

———. "The Pursuit of Homosexuality in the Eighteenth Century: 'Utterly Confused Category' and/or Rich Repository?" *Eighteenth-Century Life* 9.3 (1985): 133–68.

Sedgwick, Eve Kosofsky. *Epistemology of the Closet*. Berkeley and Los Angeles: U of California P, 1990.

Smith, Captain Alexander. *A Complete History of the Lives and Robberies of the Most Notorious Highwaymen*. Ed. Arthur L. Hayward. London: Routledge, 1933.

———. *The Memoirs of the Life and Times of the famous Jonathan Wild*. London, 1725.

Trumbach, Randolph. "The Birth of the Queen: Sodomy and the Emergence of Gender Equality in Modern Culture, 1660–1750." *Hidden from History: Reclaiming the Gay and Lesbian Past*. Ed. Martin Bauml Duberman, Martha Vicinus, and George Chauncey Jr. New York: New American Library, 1989. 129–40.

———. "Gender and the Homosexual Role in Modern Western Culture: The Eighteenth and Nineteenth Centuries Compared." *Homosexuality, which Homosexuality*. Ed. Dennis Altman et al. London: Gay Men's P, 1989. 149–70.

———. "London's Sodomites: Homosexual Behaviour and Western Culture in the Eighteenth Century." *Journal of Social History* 2 (1977): 1–33.

———. "Sodomitical Assaults, Gender Role, and Sexual Development in Eighteenth-Century London." *The Pursuit of Sodomy: Male Homosexuality in Renaissance and Enlightenment Europe*. Ed. Kent Gerard and Gert Hekma. New York: Harrington Park P, 1989. 407–32.

———. "Sodomitical Subcultures, Sodomitical Roles, and the Gender Revolution of the Eighteenth Century." *'Tis Nature's Fault': Unauthorized Sexuality During the Enlightenment*. Ed. Robert Purks Maccubbin. Cambridge: Cambridge UP, 1987. 109–21.

———. "Sodomy Transformed: Aristocratic Libertinage, Public Reputation and the Gender Revolution of the Eighteenth Century." *Love Letters Between a Certain Late Nobleman and the Famous Mr. Wilson*. Ed. Michael S. Kimmel. New York: Harrington Park P, 1990. 105–24.

———. ed. *Select Trials at the Sessions House in the Old Bailey*. 2 vols. New York: Garland, 1985.

[Ward, Edward]. *The Secret History of Clubs*. London, 1709.

Wild, Jonathan. *An Answer to a Late Insolent Libel*. London, 1718.

The Woman-Hater's Lamentation. Rpt. in *Sodomy Trials, Seven Documents*. Ed. Randolph Trumbach. New York: Garland, 1986.

Contributors

Robert Bataille is professor of English at Iowa State University. He has recently completed a study of Hugh Kelly and has published articles and notes on various aspects of eighteenth-century British journalism.

Catherine Craft-Fairchild, associate professor of English at the University of St. Thomas in Minnesota, is the author of *Masquerade and Gender: Disguise and Female Identity in Eighteenth-Century Fictions by Women.* She has published in *Modern Language Review* and *Restoration and Eighteenth-Century Theatre Research.* At this time she is working on a book about cross-dressing and the early novel.

Jones DeRitter is an associate professor of English at the University of Scranton. He is the author of *The Embodiment of Characters: The Representation of Physical Experience on Stage and In Print, 1728–1749,* as well as of essays in *Genders, Comparative Drama,* and *Restoration.*

Thomas DiPiero, associate professor of French and of Visual and Cultural Studies at the University of Rochester, is the author of *Dangerous Truths and Criminal Passions: The Evolution of the French Novel, 1569–1791.* He has published essays on eighteenth-century literature, as well as on film and psychoanalysis. He is currently completing a book on the genealogy of white masculinity in Europe and the United States.

William F. Edmiston is professor of French and chair of the department at the University of South Carolina. He is the author of *Diderot and the Family* and *Hindsight and Insight: Focalization in Four Eighteenth-Century French Novels.* He has published articles on Diderot, Sade, Restif de la Bretonne, and other French writers of the eighteenth century.

David R. Evans, assistant professor of English at Cornell College, has published essays on heroic drama, Restoration panegyric, travel literature, and performance art. He is currently at work on a study of the Grand Tour in the late seventeenth and early eighteenth centuries.

Irene Fizer is completing a dissertation at the University of Pennsylvania entitled *Natural Daughters: Gender and Illegitimacy in the Eighteenth-Century English Novel.* She has published essays on *The Coquette* in *Eighteenth Century: Theory and Interpretation* and on *Evelina* in *Refiguring the Father: New Feminist Readings of Patriarchy* and has been awarded two paper prizes from the American Society for Eighteenth-Century Studies.

Pat Gill, associate professor of English at Western Michigan University, has written essays on Restoration and eighteenth-century drama, ideology, incest, filth, and fun. She is the author of *Interpreting Ladies: Women, Wit, and Morality in the Restoration Comedy of Manners.*

George E. Haggerty, an associate professor of English at the University of California-Riverside, is the author of *Gothic Fiction/Gothic Form* and co-editor of *Professions of Desire: Lesbian and Gay Studies in Literature* for MLA. He has published a wide variety of essays on later eighteenth-century literature.

Nancy Johnson is a graduate student of English at McGill University. She has published on law and literature and is currently working on the Clarissa project. Her work-in-progress concerns law and the Jacobin novel.

Craig Patterson teaches Communications at Humber College. He has written essays on crime and sexuality in the eighteenth and twentieth centuries.

Rajani Sudan is an assistant professor of English at the University of Texas at Arlington. She has published articles on De Quincey, Johnson, and Wollstonecraft, as well as on film and popular culture. She is currently completing a book entitled *Fair Exotics: Xenophobia in the Age of Romanticism.*

Kathryn Temple, assistant professor of English at Georgetown University, has published in the *Yale Journal of Law & the Humanities* and in *Law and Literature.* Currently she is completing a book entitled *The Author in Public: Literary Scandals, Legal Regulation, and National Identity in Eighteenth-Century Britain.* Her essay on Radcliffe in this volume is part of a larger project on women, space, and the law in the later part of the eighteenth century.